Solutions

Elementary Teacher's Book

Marta Umińska, Caroline Krantz
Tim Falla, Paul A Davies

OXFORD
UNIVERSITY PRESS

OXFORD

UNIVERSITY PRESS

Great Clarendon Street, Oxford OX2 6DP

Oxford University Press is a department of the University of Oxford.
It furthers the University's objective of excellence in research, scholarship,
and education by publishing worldwide in

Oxford New York

Auckland Cape Town Dar es Salaam Hong Kong Karachi
Kuala Lumpur Madrid Melbourne Mexico City Nairobi
New Delhi Shanghai Taipei Toronto

With offices in

Argentina Austria Brazil Chile Czech Republic France Greece
Guatemala Hungary Italy Japan Poland Portugal Singapore
South Korea Switzerland Thailand Turkey Ukraine Vietnam

OXFORD and OXFORD ENGLISH are registered trade marks of
Oxford University Press in the UK and in certain other countries

ISBN: 978 0 19 4551625

Printed in China

ACKNOWLEDGEMENTS

*The publisher and authors are grateful to the many teachers and students who read
and piloted the manuscript, and provided invaluable feedback. With special thanks
to the following for their contribution to the development of the Solutions series:*
Zinta Andzane, Latvia; Irena Budreikiene, Lithuania; Kati Elekes, Hungary;
Danica Gondová, Slovakia; Ferenc Kelemen, Hungary; Natasha Koltko,
Ukraine; Mario Maleta, Croatia; Juraj Marcek, Slovakia; Dace Miška, Latvia;
Anna Morris, Ukraine; Hana Musílková, Czech Republic; Zsuzsanna Nyirő,
Hungary; Eva Paulerová, Czech Republic; Zoltán Rézmüves, Hungary;
Rita Rudiatiene, Lithuania; Ela Rudniak, Poland; Dagmar Škorpíková,
Czech Republic

The publisher and authors would like to extend their special thanks to Emma Watkins
for the part she played in developing the material.

The publisher and the authors would like to thank the author of Dyslexia: a guide for
teachers: Katarzyna Bogdanowicz

The publisher would like to thank the following for their permission to use photographs:
Fotolia p123 (all but Steve, Jenny, Joshua); Getty Images pp125 (Wayne
Rooney/John Peters); Istock p123.

Illustrations by: Claude Bordeleau/Agent 002 p133; Dylan Gibson p127; David
Oakley/Arnos Design Ltd pp124,126, 134

CONTENTS

A note from the authors

Our work on *Solutions* began in the spring of 2005 with a research trip. We travelled from city to city with colleagues from Oxford University Press, visiting schools, watching lessons and talking to teachers and students. The information we gathered on that trip, and many subsequent trips across Central and Eastern Europe, gave us valuable insights into what secondary students and teachers want from a new book. These became our guiding principles while writing *Solutions*. Most people we spoke to asked for:

- a clear focus on exam topics and tasks
- easy-to-follow lessons which always have a clear outcome
- plenty of support for speaking and writing
- plenty of extra practice material

In response, we designed a book which has a crystal-clear structure: one lesson in the book = one lesson in the classroom. We included twenty pages of extra vocabulary and grammar practice within the Student's Book itself to provide more flexibility. We included ten specific lessons to prepare students for the school-leaving exam, and ensured that the book as a whole corresponds to the syllabus topics required in this exam. And we recognised the difficulties that students naturally have with speaking and writing, and therefore ensured that these activities are always well prepared and well supported. Achievable activities are essential for motivation!

Our research trips also taught us that no two schools or classes are identical. That is why *Solutions* is designed to be flexible. There are five levels (Elementary, Pre-intermediate, Intermediate, Upper-intermediate, Advanced) so that you can choose the one which best fits your students' needs.

Solutions has benefited from collaboration with teachers with extensive experience of teaching 14–19 year olds and of preparing students for their school-leaving exam. We would like to thank Marta Umińska for sharing her expertise in writing the procedural notes in the Teacher's Book. Cultural and language notes as well as the photocopiable supplements in the Teacher's Book were provided by Caroline Krantz.

We are confident that *Solutions* will be easy to use, both for students and for teachers. We hope it will also be interesting, engaging and stimulating!

Tim Falla and Paul A Davies

The components of the course

The Student's Book

The Student's Book contains:

- an Introduction unit to revise the basics
- 10 topic-based units, each covering 7 lessons
- 5 *Language Review/Skills Round-up* sections, providing a language test of the previous two units and a cumulative skills-based review
- 10 *Get ready for your exam* lessons providing typical tasks and preparation for the students' final exam
- 10 *Vocabulary Builders* with practice and extension options
- 10 *Grammar Builders* containing grammar reference and further exercises
- tip boxes throughout giving advice on specific skills and how best to approach different task types in all four main skills

You will find more details on pages 5–7 in the section 'A tour of the Student's Book'.

Three class audio CDs

The three audio CDs contain all the listening material from the Student's Book.

The Workbook

The Workbook mirrors and reinforces the content of the Student's Book. It offers:

- further practice, lesson-by-lesson of the material taught in class
- additional exam tasks with support for students and teachers
- *Challenge!* exercises to stretch stronger students
- writing guides to provide a clear structural framework for writing tasks
- regular *Self-checks* with *Can do* statements to promote conscious learner development
- cumulative reviews to develop students' awareness of their progress
- a *Functions Bank* for reference
- an irregular verbs list
- a *Wordlist* which contains the vocabulary activated in the Student's Book units

Procedural notes, transcripts and keys for the Workbook can be easily found on the *Solutions* Teacher's Website at www.oup.com/elt/teacher/solutions.

The MultiROM

The MultiROM is an interactive self-study tool that has been designed to give guidance, practice, support and consolidation of the language and skills taught in the Student's Book. The MultiROM is divided into units and lessons corresponding with those of the Student's Book.

- every grammar lesson in the book is extensively practised and is accompanied by a simple explanation
- all target vocabulary is consolidated with crossword, word search, and gap-fill activities
- one exam-type listening activity per unit is included so that students are able to practise listening at their own pace
- speaking and writing sections help students improve these skills outside of the classroom
- an audio CD element is included, with all the exam listening tasks from the Workbook, which can be played on a CD player

The Teacher's Book

The Teacher's Book gives full procedural notes for the whole course, including ideas for tackling mixed-ability teaching. In addition, it offers:

- optional activities throughout for greater flexibility
- structured speaking tasks to get students talking confidently
- useful tips and strategies to improve students' exam technique
- a teacher's guide to dyslexia in the classroom
- 20 photocopiable pages to recycle and activate the language of each unit in a fun, communicative context

Test Bank MultiROM

A separate resource MultiROM contains:

- unit tests
- mid-year and end-of-year progress tests
- short tests

Solutions and the exam

Solutions Elementary is intended to introduce students to the task types and format of the basic level of the school-leaving exam. The emphasis is on preparation and familiarisation, helping students to build good study habits and exam strategies. Typical exam requirements are reflected throughout the course in the choice of topics, task-types, texts and grammar structures. In addition to this, *Solutions* offers a comprehensive range of exam support:

Student's Book

The Student's Book includes ten exam-specific lessons designed to familiarise students with the task-types and requirements of their final exam. The lessons provide strategies and exam techniques as well as the language needed for students to be able to tackle exam tasks with confidence.

Workbook

The Workbook provides further practice for both the oral and the written exam. Work in class can be followed up with Workbook tasks done as homework.

The listening material for the Workbook listening tasks is available on the MultiROM.

Teacher's Book

The exam lessons in the Student's Book are accompanied by full procedural notes with advice and tips for exam preparation.

A tour of the Student's Book

There are ten main units in the Student's Book. Each unit has seven lessons (A–G). Each lesson provides material for one classroom lesson of approximately 45 minutes.

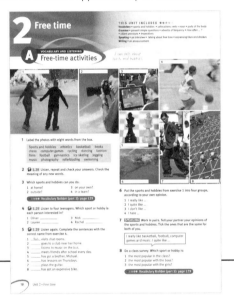

Lesson A – Vocabulary and listening

- The unit menu states the main language and skills to be taught.
- Every lesson has an explicit learning objective, beginning 'I can ...'.
- Lesson A introduces the topic of the unit, presents the main vocabulary set, and practises it through listening and other activities.
- This lesson links to the *Vocabulary Builder* at the back of the book, which provides extra practice and extension.

Lesson B – Grammar

- Lesson B presents and practises the first main grammar point of the unit.
- The new language is presented in a short text or other meaningful context.
- There are clear grammar tables.
- *Look out!* boxes appear wherever necessary and help students to avoid common errors.
- This lesson links to the *Grammar Builder* at the back of the book which provides extra practice and grammar reference.

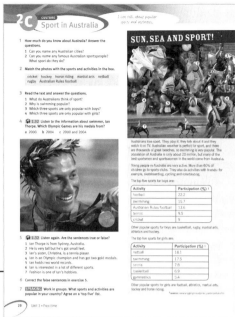

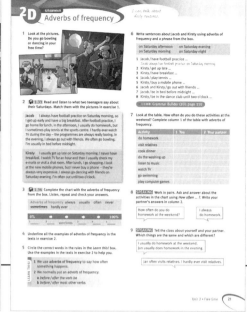

Lesson C – Culture

- Lesson C has a reading text which provides cultural information about Britain, the USA or other English-speaking countries.
- Students are encouraged to make cultural comparisons.
- New vocabulary is clearly presented in boxes wherever it is needed.

Lesson D – Grammar

- Lesson D presents and practises the second main grammar point of the unit.
- The grammar presentation is interactive: students often have to complete tables and rules, helping them focus on the structures.
- *Learn this!* boxes present key information in a clear and concise form.
- This lesson links to the *Grammar Builder* at the back of the book which provides extra practice and grammar reference notes.
- A final speaking activity allows students to personalise the new language.

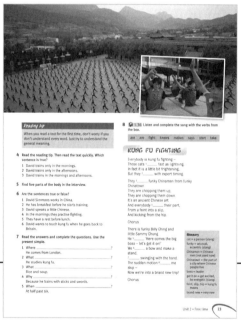

Lesson E – Reading

- Lesson E contains the main reading text of the unit.
- It occupies two pages though it is still designed for one lesson in class.
- The text is always interesting and relevant to the students, and links with the topic of the unit.
- The text recycles the main grammar points from lessons B and D.
- Important new vocabulary is highlighted in the text and practised in a follow-up activity and in the Workbook.

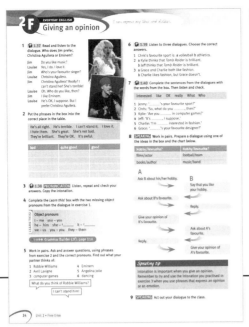

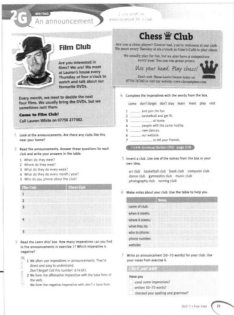

Lesson F – Everyday English

- Lesson F presents a functional dialogue.
- The lesson always includes listening practice.
- Extra vocabulary is presented, if necessary.
- Students follow a clear guide when they produce their own dialogue.
- Useful functional phrases are taught and practised.
- The step-by-step approach of 'presentation, practice and production' is suitable for mixed-ability classes and offers achievable goals.

Lesson G – Writing

- Lesson G focuses on writing and normally involves one of the text types required for the students' final exam.
- The lesson always begins by looking at a model text or texts and studying the structure and format.
- Students learn and practise useful phrases.
- There is a clear writing guide for the students to produce their own text.
- This supported approach to writing increases students' linguistic confidence.

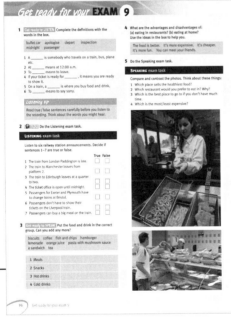

Get ready for your exam

- There are ten *Get ready for your exam* lessons (two after units 1, 3, 5, 7 and 9) which focus on exam skills and preparation.
- The lessons include exam tasks for reading, speaking and listening.
- Each lesson includes activities to prepare students for the exam tasks and provide them with the language and skills they need to do them successfully.
- These lessons also recycle the language from the previous two units and link with the topics.

Language Review/Skills Round-up

- There are five two-page reviews (after units 2, 4, 6, 8 and 10).
- The first lesson of each review is a *Language Review* of the preceding two units.
- There are exercises focusing on vocabulary, grammar and functions.
- The marks always total 50, so it is easy to monitor progress through the book.
- The second lesson of each review is a *Skills Round-up* which covers all the preceding units of the book.
- The lesson includes practice of all four skills: listening, reading, writing and speaking.
- The material is centred around a Hungarian boy called Márton, who is living and working in Britain.

Tips and ideas

Teaching vocabulary

Vocabulary notebooks

Encourage your students to record new words in a notebook. They can group words according to the topic or by part of speech. Tell them to write a translation and an example sentence that shows the word in context.

Vocabulary doesn't just appear on Vocabulary pages. You can ask students to make a list of all the verbs that appear in a Grammar section, or to choose five useful words from a reading text and learn them.

Learning phrases

We often learn words in isolation, but a vocabulary item can be more than one word, e.g. *surf the Internet, have a shower.* Make students aware of this and encourage them to record phrases as well as individual words.

Revision

Regularly revise previously learned sets of vocabulary. Here are two games you could try in class:
- **Odd one out.** Give four words, either orally or written on the board. Students say which is the odd one out. You can choose three words from one vocabulary set and one word from a different set (a relatively easy task) or four words from the same set, e.g. *kind, confident, rude, friendly*, where *rude* is the odd one out as it's the only word with negative connotations.
- **Word tennis.** This game can be played to revise word sets. Call out words in the set, and nominate a student to answer. The student must respond with another word in the set. Continue around the class.
  Students must not repeat any previous words. For example, with clothes:
  T: T-shirt
  S1:   jeans
  T: sweatshirt
  S2:   top

Teaching grammar

Concept checking

The concept is important. Do not rush from the presentation to the practice before the students have fully absorbed the meaning of the new language. You can check that they truly understand a new structure by:
- asking them to translate examples into their own language.
- talking about the practice activities as you do them, asking students to explain their answers.
- looking beyond incorrect answers: they may be careless errors or they may be the result of a misunderstanding.
- contrasting new structures with forms that they already know in English and in their own language.

Practice

Practice makes perfect. Learning a new structure is not easy, and students need plenty of practice. Use the extra activities in the *Grammar Builders* and on the MultiROM.

Progression

Mechanical practice should come before personalised practice. This allows students to master the basic form and use first, without having to think about what they are trying to express at the same time.

Teaching reading

Predicting content

Before reading the text, ask students to look at the picture and tell you what they can see or what is happening. You can also discuss the title and topic with them.

Dealing with difficult vocabulary

Here are some ideas:
- Pre-teach vocabulary. Anticipate which words students will have difficulty with. Put them on the board before you read the text with the class and pre-teach them. You can combine this with a prediction activity by putting a list of words on the board and asking students to guess which ones will not appear in the text. For example, for the text about kung fu on page 22 of the Student's Book, list these words:
  training   practise   kicking   blonde   fight   grandmother   dangerous
  Ask students to look at the pictures and tell you which two words they are not going to find in the text (*grandmother* and *blonde*). At the same time, check that they understand the other five words.
- Having read through the text once, tell students to write down three or four words from the text that they don't understand. Then ask them to call out the words. You can then explain or translate them.
- Rather than immediately explaining difficult vocabulary, ask students to identify the part of speech of the word they don't know. Knowing the part of speech sometimes helps them to guess the meaning.
- After working on a text, ask students to choose four or five new words from the text that they would like to learn and to write these in their vocabulary notebooks.

Teaching listening

Pre-listening

This is an important stage. Listening to something 'cold' is not easy, so prepare the students well. Focus on teaching rather than on testing. Here are some things you can do:
- Tell the students in broad terms what they are going to hear (e.g. a boy and girl making arrangements to go out).
- Predict the content. If there's a picture, ask students to look at the picture and tell you what they can see or what is happening.
- Pre-teach vocabulary. Put new vocabulary on the board and pre-teach it. Translating the words is perfectly acceptable.
- Read through the exercise carefully and slowly before the students listen. Ensure that the students understand both the task and all the vocabulary in the exercise. (You can check that they understand the task by asking a student to explain it in their own language.)

Familiar procedure

It isn't easy to listen, read the exercise and write the answers all at the same time. Take some pressure off the students by telling them you'll play the recording a number of times, and that they shouldn't worry if they don't get the answers immediately. Tell students not to write anything the first time they listen.

Monitor

While the students are listening, stand at the back of the class and check that they can all hear.

Teaching writing

Use a model

Ensure that the students understand that the text in Lesson G serves as a model for their own writing.

Preparation

Encourage your students to brainstorm ideas and make notes, either alone or in pairs, before they attempt to write a composition.

Draft

Tell them to prepare a rough draft of the composition before they write out the final version.

Checking

Encourage them to read through their composition carefully and check it for spelling mistakes and grammatical errors.

Correction

Establish a set of marks that you use to correct students' written work. For example:

sp	indicates a spelling mistake
w	indicates a missing word
gr	indicates a grammatical error
v	indicates a lexical error
wo	indicates incorrect word order

Self correction

Consider indicating but not correcting mistakes, and asking students to try to correct them.

Teaching speaking

Confidence building

Be aware that speaking is a challenge for most students. Build their confidence and they will speak more; undermine it and they will be silent. This means:

- encourage and praise your students when they speak.
- do not over-correct or interrupt.
- ask other students to be quiet and attentive while a classmate speaks.
- listen and react when a student speaks, with phrases like 'Really?' or 'That's interesting'.

Preparation

Allow students time to prepare their ideas before asking them to speak. This means they will not have to search for ideas at the same time as trying to express them.

Support

Help students to prepare their ideas: make suggestions and provide useful words. Allow them to work in pairs, if appropriate.

Choral drilling

Listen and repeat activities, which the class does together, can help to build confidence because the students feel less exposed. They are also a good chance to practise word stress and intonation.

Teaching mixed ability classes

Teaching mixed ability classes is demanding and can be very frustrating. There are no easy solutions, but here are some ideas that may help.

Preparation

Try to anticipate problems and prepare in advance. Draw up a list of the five strongest students in the class and the five weakest. Think about how they will cope in the next lesson. Which group is likely to pose more of a problem – the stronger students because they'll finish quickly and get bored, or the slower students because they won't be able to keep up? Think how you will attempt to deal with this. The Teacher's Book includes ideas and suggestions for activities and fillers for different abilities.

Independent learning

There is the temptation in class to give most of your attention to the higher-level students as they are more responsive and they keep the lesson moving. But which of your students can best work on their own or in pairs? It's often the stronger ones, so consider spending more time in class with the weaker ones, and finding things to keep the fast-finishers occupied while the others catch up.

Peer support

If you are doing pairwork, consider pairing stronger students with weaker students.

Project work

Provide on-going work for stronger students. You can give your stronger students extended tasks that they do alone in spare moments. For example, you could give them readers, ask them to keep a diary in English or work on a project. They can turn to these whenever they are waiting for the rest of the class to finish an activity.

Correcting mistakes

How much we correct should depend on the purpose of the activity. The key question is: is the activity designed to improve accuracy or fluency?

Accuracy

With controlled grammar and vocabulary activities, where the emphasis is on the accurate production of a particular language point, it's best to correct all mistakes, and to do so immediately you hear them. You want your students to master the forms now and not repeat the mistake in later work.

Fluency

With activities such as role-play or freer grammar exercises it may be better not to interrupt and correct every mistake you hear. The important mistakes to correct in these cases are those that cause a breakdown in communication. We shouldn't show interest only in the language; we should also be asking ourselves, 'How well did the students communicate?'. During the activity, you can make a note of any serious grammatical and lexical errors and put them on the board at the end of the activity. You can then go through them with the whole class.

Self correction

Give students a chance to correct themselves before you supply the correct version.

Modelling

When you correct an individual student always ask him or her to repeat the answer after you correctly.

Peer correction

You can involve the rest of the class in the process of correction. Ask: *Is that answer correct?* You can do this when the student has given a correct answer as well as when the answer is incorrect.

Introduction

THIS UNIT INCLUDES ● ● ○ ○
Vocabulary • alphabet • numbers • describing people
• time, days, months and seasons
Grammar • *be* • possessive adjectives • demonstrative pronouns • *have got*
Speaking • introducing yourself
Writing • a description of a friend or family member
WORKBOOK pages 4–7

A EVERYDAY ENGLISH
Saying hello

LESSON SUMMARY ● ● ● ○ ○
Functional English: introducing yourself
Listening: short dialogues
Vocabulary: letters and numbers
Speaking: introducing yourself
Topic: people

SHORTCUT *To do the lesson in 30 minutes, have only a few pairs act out their dialogues in exercise 12.*

➜ Lead-in 4–5 minutes
• If this is your first lesson with this class, ask everyone to take a piece of paper and write down as many English words as they can remember in one minute. If some students seem at a loss, point out that they might, for example, know titles of songs in English. Share ideas as a class, asking each student to read out a word from their list. They must not repeat a word that has already been said.

Exercise 1 page 4
• Draw students' attention to the photo. Ask the question in the book and help with comprehension if necessary, by saying for example: *How old is he / she? Fifteen, sixteen, seventeen, eighteen?* You could write the numbers on the board as you speak. Students guess the ages of the people in the photo.

Exercise 2 page 4 🎧 1.01
• After playing the dialogue ask: *So, how old is Ben? How old is Francesca?* You can ask a few students: *How old are you?*

Exercise 3 page 4 🎧 1.02
• Play the alphabet for students to listen to, then model it for them to repeat in groups of 2–4 letters. Students repeat chorally and individually.
• Point out the easily confused *G* and *J*, and suggest some abbreviations which the students may know and which may be used as mnemonics: for example, *DJ* or *GPS*.

Exercise 4 page 4 🎧 1.03
• Play the recording twice, pausing after each name. If students haven't written all the names, play the recording as many times as they need. Finally, write the names on the board, saying each letter aloud as you write it.

Transcript 1.03

Russell Crowe	Catherine Zeta Jones
Whitney Houston	Roger Federer

Exercise 5 page 4
• Students think of the names of up to three famous people. They can write them down if they wish. (Spelling out without seeing the word is extremely difficult for visual learners!) As they spell the names out, circulate and monitor. If someone cannot guess a name, their partner has to spell it again, loudly, clearly and slowly. The other person can write if it helps them.

Exercise 6 page 4 🎧 1.04
• Play the numbers for students to listen to, then model the pronunciation for them to repeat in groups of 3–4 numbers (e.g. 1,2,3 – 4,5,6, etc.). With a **weaker class**, display the numbers written as words on the board, OHP or a poster and have students practise in pairs.

Transcript 1.04

1, 2, 3, 4, 5, 6, 7, 8, 9, 10, 11, 12, 13, 14, 15, 16, 17, 18, 19, 20, 21, 22, 23, 30, 40, 50

Exercise 7 page 4
• Again, in a **weaker class** students may need to see the numbers in order to repeat them. With a **stronger class**, see how quickly they can do it (you may wish to repeat the activity a few times, faster each time). You can also decide that anyone who makes a mistake has to pay a forfeit, for example, say the name of an English song, say the name of three countries where English is spoken, etc.

Exercise 8 page 4 🎧 1.05
• Play the recording twice, then ask students if they need to listen again. Play it again if required. Finally play the recording to check, pausing after every name has been spelled and writing it on the board.

KEY

1	**Name:** Siobhan		**Name:** Dafydd	
	Age: 15		**Age:** 15	
2	**Name:** Abdullah		**Name:** Katharine	
	Age: 17		**Age:** 16	

Transcript 1.05

1
Siobhan Hello. My name's Siobhan. What's your name?
Dafydd Dafydd. Nice to meet you.
Siobhan Nice to meet you too.
Dafydd How do you spell your name, Siobhan?
Siobhan S-I-O-B-H-A-N. How do you spell your name?
Dafydd D-A-F-Y-D-D. How old are you, Siobhan?
Siobhan I'm 15. How old are you?
Dafydd I'm 15 too.

2
Abdullah Hello. My name's Abdullah. Nice to meet you.
Katharine Hi Abdullah. Nice to meet you too. I'm Katharine. That's K-A-T-H-A-R-I-N-E. How do you spell your name?
Abdullah A-B-D-U-L-L-A-H.
Katharine How old are you, Abdullah?
Abdullah I'm 17. How old are you?
Katharine I'm 16.

Exercise 9 page 4
• Students do the task individually and compare answers in pairs. Check as a class.

KEY

1 b   2 d   3 a   4 c

Exercise 10 page 4 🎧 1.06

- Work on the pronunciation of the questions. Play each one several times and ask students to repeat chorally and individually, paying attention to the following features:
- Each question is one tone unit, which means it should be pronounced 'like one word', without stopping: '*Howoldareyou?*' (it is not necessary to teach students the term 'tone unit').
- In each question there is a stressed word – the one that carries the key meaning: *What's your **name**? How **old** are you?* Practise the question intonation.
- You may also point out that the sentence stress in *How old are you?* changes when the second person asks the question: *How **old** are you? I'm 16. How old are **you**?*

Exercise 11 page 4

- Students work on their dialogues. In a **stronger class** encourage them to try without writing the dialogues out in full. Help them practise the phrases, but don't insist if they find it hard to do everything orally.

Exercise 12 page 4

- Depending on time and on students' patience, have 3–5 pairs act out their dialogues in front of the class. Choose pairs who speak fairly loudly and clearly. Give feedback: praise good performances and correct a few mistakes (especially concerning pronunciation or the language from this lesson).

OPTIONAL ACTIVITY

Ask students to say the alphabet around the class. If it proves too easy and nobody makes any mistakes, ask them to say the alphabet backwards. Whoever makes a mistake (gives the wrong letter or pronounces it incorrectly) must pay a forfeit. The real activity is doing the forfeits, so make sure there are quite a few. Here are some ideas for what students have to do for forfeits:

1 Say three English names used by men/women.
2 Say the name of a country in English.
3 Say the names of two cities in Britain.
4 Say two titles of songs in English.
5 Say the title of a film in English.

➡ Lesson outcome

Ask students: *What have we talked about today?*
Elicit: *introductions* or *saying hello* or *saying how old you are.*
Ask students to repeat the alphabet and count from 1 to 20. Draw students' attention to the lesson statement: *I can introduce myself.*

I B GRAMMAR
be, possessives and pronouns

LESSON SUMMARY ● ● ○ ○ ○

Grammar: *be*, possessives, pronouns
Reading: a short personal profile
Speaking: asking and answering about personal information

SHORTCUT *To do the lesson in 30 minutes, do exercises 2 and 6 as a class. If you are short of time, you could split the questions in exercise 5, so that each student in a pair answers half of the questions.*

➡ Lead-in 2 minutes

- Ask a few students the question: *How old are you?* This is revision of the previous lesson, but it will also lead in into this lesson. After a few students have told you their age, name a few students and say: *So, you are 16. And he is 15. She is also 15. They are 15.* Explain that today's lesson will be on the conjugation of the verb *to be*.

Exercise 1 page 5

- Draw students' attention to the photo. Say something like: *See – this is Ben from lesson A.* Students read the text and answer the questions. Check answers with the whole class.

KEY

1 T   2 F   3 F

Exercise 2 page 5

- Remind students that *be* is the infinitive. Ask them to do the tasks. When checking, ask for equivalents of the forms in the students' own language. Point out the short answers and emphasise that they are used a lot.

KEY

1 'm / am	3 're / are	5 isn't / is not
2 's / is	4 'm not / am not	6 aren't / are not

LANGUAGE NOTE – USAGE

Contractions (short forms) of the verb *to be* are presented here and used throughout *Solutions*. Point out to students that contractions are almost always preferred in fluent speech and informal writing and that the use of the full form sounds unnatural.

Exercise 3 page 5

- Make sure students understand what they have to do: complete the sentences so that they are true about them. Help with any language that needs explaining (for example: *bag, yellow, cold, hungry*).
- Go over answers with the whole class. Where two different answers are possible, try to find students with different answers and ask them both to read their sentences.

KEY

1 am / am not	4 is / isn't	7 am / am not
2 are / aren't	5 aren't	8 is / isn't
3 are	6 is / isn't	

Exercise 4 page 5

- Explain *thirsty* and any other unknown vocabulary. In a **stronger class**, refer students to the table in exercise 2, and ask them to look at how questions are formed. In a **weaker class**, talk through the structure together, and do the first one or two questions as a class. Students do the task individually and compare answers in pairs. Check answers with the whole class.

KEY

1 Are you 15 years old?
2 Is Ronaldinho your favourite footballer?
3 Is our teacher in the classroom?
4 Are we from Hungary?
5 Is Julia Roberts your favourite actress?
6 Are you thirsty?
7 Are your friends at home?

Exercise 5 page 5

- Do the first two or three questions in open pairs (two students ask and answer and the rest of the group listens) to make sure they are getting it right. Insist on answers in the form *Yes, I am / No, I'm not* + the correct information as opposed to just *yes* and *no*. Students continue in closed pairs. Circulate and monitor.

Exercise 6 page 5

- Explain what possessive adjectives are. You can ask a few students questions like: *Is this your pen? No it isn't? Oh, is it his?* (with gestures to indicate your meaning). Students look back at the text in exercise 1 and fill in the table individually. Check with the whole class.

KEY

1 my	2 her	3 our

Exercise 7 page 5

- Demonstrate the meaning of demonstrative pronouns using objects in the classroom, for example: *This is my bag. These are markers. That's a map of Britain. Those are posters.*
- Students read the *Learn this!* box. Check understanding by eliciting some examples from the class. Ask students why they have used *this*, *that*, *these*, or *those – Is the object close or further away? Is there one object or more than one?*
- Students look at the pictures and write questions. Check with the whole class.
- Practise the pronunciation of /ð/ – show how the sound can be produced by putting the tip of the tongue against or even between the teeth.

KEY

2 Are those your books?
3 Are these your trainers?
4 Is that your bike?
5 Is this your CD?
6 Are these your pencils?

➡ Lesson outcome

Ask students: *What have we talked about today?* Try to elicit: *to be; my, your, his, her, this, that* or *possessives* and *demonstrative pronouns*, but accept any answer that refers to the content of the lesson. Briefly revise the conjugation of *to be*. Draw students' attention to the lesson statement: *I can ask and answer questions.*

LESSON SUMMARY ● ● ● ○ ○ ○

Grammar: *have got*
Vocabulary: personal appearance
Listening: short dialogue
Speaking: talking about what people have got and what people look like
Writing: a short description of a family member
Topic: people

SHORTCUT *To do the lesson in 30 minutes, set exercise 7 and possibly exercise 3 as homework*

➡ Lead-in 4–5 minutes

- If you've got a sister or brother, show the class his/her photo and say: *This is my sister.* Ask students around the class: *Have you got a sister? Have you got a brother?* Report the students' answers to the class. If you haven't got any siblings, you can start by talking about your dog, cat, bike, etc. Finally, write on the board: *have got* and say this is the topic of the lesson.

Exercise 1 page 6 🎧 1.07

- Tell students they are going to hear a conversation between Ben and Francesca. Focus students' attention on the photo and ask them to read the task. Play the recording once. Allow a moment for everyone to finish answering and then check as a class.

KEY

1 hasn't	2 has	3 haven't

Exercise 2 page 6

- Students read the instructions and complete the table. In a **weaker class**, go through the dialogue together first, and underline the examples as a class.
- To check, either have students write the answers on the board, or display the completed chart on an OHP.
- Explain that *'ve* and *'s* are short forms of *have* and *has*. Point out that nearly all the forms are the same, just one is different. Which one? When students answer (*he/she/it has*), you may choose to tell them that they will later find that a lot, but not all, of third person singular forms end in –s.

KEY

Dialogue: They've got a lovely house, Have you got brothers or sisters? I haven't got a sister, but I've got a brother. He's got blue eyes, but he hasn't got fair hair. Have they got children?
Table:

1 has	3 Have	5 hasn't
2 have	4 haven't	6 haven't

Exercise 3 page 6

- Read the example and do the first two sentences with the whole class as a model. With a **strong class**, you can do the exercise orally. With a **weaker class**, check any unknown vocabulary first and do a few examples together.

KEY

1 He's got a bike.	6 He's got a watch.
2 He hasn't got a computer.	7 He's got a mobile phone.
3 He's got a pet.	8 He hasn't got a DVD
4 He hasn't got an MP3 player.	player.
5 He's got a skateboard.	

Exercise 4 page 6

- You may wish to ask students to work with partners they don't know very well (otherwise they are likely to know the answers to all the questions they ask), but this needs to be handled sensitively. Some of the questions are about quite expensive possessions, and it is important that nobody should feel embarrassed by having to make statements about their material status. If you think this is likely to be a problem, tell students that they don't have to tell the truth, they should focus on practising the language.

Exercise 5 page 6

- Ask students around the class for the meaning of the adjectives in the table. Accept translations.
- The order of adjectives before *hair* needs to be pointed out. Put these examples on the board:
  He's got long, black hair. She's got short, curly hair. He's got straight, fair hair. Now ask students to put these three adjectives in the right order before the word *hair*: She's got *wavy / dark / long* hair. (Answer: *She's got long, wavy, dark hair.*)
- When the words have been studied and their pronunciation and order practised, students can go on to describe the first photo. Then let students talk about the remaining ones in pairs. Circulate and monitor, help with sentence-building and pronunciation. Finally, ask a few students to describe the photos to the whole class. Give feedback: praise good sentences, correct errors in target language (*has got* and the appearance words).

Exercise 6 page 6

- You may wish to specify the number of questions each pair should ask, for example, one about each person in the room, or one with each word, or a total of 10.

Exercise 7 page 6

- Remind students of the language they can use in writing the description:
  He is /She is x years old. (Lesson B)
  He's got/She's got... (the features listed in exercise 5).
- Tell students it is also possible to say: *Her eyes are blue. His hair is long and dark.* (Point out that *hair* is not plural – in English it is seen as one substance, one mass of something.)
- If the writing is set as homework, you may encourage students to include a photo with the description.

➡ Lesson outcome

Ask students: *What have we talked about today?* Elicit: *have got* and *appearance.* Ask everyone to say one word they learned from the lesson. Draw students' attention to the lesson statement: *I can describe people.*

D VOCABULARY
Time, days, months and seasons

LESSON SUMMARY ● ● ● ● ● ●
Vocabulary: time, days, months, seasons
Functional English: asking for and telling the time
Speaking: talking about time, days, months and seasons

SHORTCUT *To do the lesson in 30 minutes, set exercise 10 as a written exercise for homework.*

➡ Lead-in 2 minutes

- Write the date on the board, first as numbers, then as words, e.g.: *15/09/2009 (Wed) – Today is Wednesday, the fifteenth of September two thousand and nine.*
- Read aloud what you have written.
- Write the time, first as numbers, then as words, e.g.: 10.10 – *It is ten past ten.*

- Inform the class of the lesson topic. It would be good to have a calendar with the names of the days and months in English on the wall in your classroom.

Exercise 1 page 7 1.08

- Ask students to open their books and look at the clocks (you may wish to teach *clock*). Play the recording once for students to listen, and then again, pausing after each time for them to repeat.

Exercise 2 page 7 🎧 1.09

- Make sure everyone understands what they have to do. Play the recording through once, then again, pausing after each time. Ask a student to write each time on the board in numbers: 4.00, 7.45, etc. (If you are short of time, write them yourself.)

KEY

1	4
2	5
3	6

Transcript 1.09

four o'clock	half past six
quarter to eight	twenty to eleven
five past ten	quarter past three

Exercise 3 page 7 🎧 1.10

- Allow a moment for students to read the instructions, the dialogue and the words in the box. Make sure everyone understands what they have to do. Check answers by getting a pair of confident students to read out the dialogue.

KEY

1 Excuse	3 to	5 welcome
2 time	4 very	

LANGUAGE NOTE – SAYING THE TIME

To say a time when the minutes are not a multiple of five, the word *minutes* must be added, e.g. *It's two minutes past ten* not *It's two past ten.*

Exercise 4 page 7

- First practise reading the dialogue from exercise 3 in open pairs several times (two students sitting in different places read, the rest of the class listens). Work on intonation. You may play the recording again. When you feel students have had sufficient pronunciation practice, ask them to talk about the times in this exercise. Circulate and monitor.

Exercise 5 page 7

- Ask students to look at the task and read the instructions. Ask them to pick out a few words which are days of the week and a few which are months.
- Students work on the exercise in pairs. If you have a calendar with those words in English, encourage them to walk up to it and use it as a resource. You may want to introduce a certain condition: they can walk up to the calendar, but they must not take their notebooks with them. Instead, they must remember as much as they can and then go back to their desks and write it down.

Exercise 6 page 7 🎧 1.11

- When everyone has finished exercise 5, play the part of the recording with the days of the week. Play it through for students to check their answers, and then again, pausing after each item for them to repeat. Point out the silent letters in *Wednesday* and practise the pronunciation of *Thursday*.
- Repeat the same procedure with the names of the months. Point out especially the pronunciation of the *Au* in *August* – not /aʊ/ but /ɔː/.

Transcript 1.11

Days

1	Sunday	5	Thursday
2	Monday	6	Friday
3	Tuesday	7	Saturday
4	Wednesday		

Months

1	January	7	July
2	February	8	August
3	March	9	September
4	April	10	October
5	May	11	November
6	June	12	December

Exercise 7 page 7

- Give students a minute or two to look at the pictures. Then ask them to match the pictures with the seasons.

KEY

1 spring   2 summer   3 autumn   4 winter

Exercise 8 page 7 🎧 1.12

- Play the recording and check students' answers to exercise 7. Then students repeat the seasons chorally and individually. Pay special attention to the pronunciation of the *Au* in *autumn* – not /aʊ/ but /ɔː/, just as in *August*.

Exercise 9 page 7

- Students discuss the months and seasons in pairs. Check with the whole class.

OPTIONAL ACTIVITY – MONTHS AND SEASONS

You may bring four big photos showing the four seasons (cut out of calendars) and attach them to the board with magnets. After exercise 8, ask four students to come and write the names of the seasons on the board under the photos. After exercise 9, ask 12 students (in turns – four at a time) to come to the board and write the names of the months under the names of the seasons. The students then return to their seats. Discuss the answers on the board with the class – are they accurate?

Exercise 10 page 7

- Students may ask and answer the questions with the classmates they are sitting with, or you may ask them to stand up and ask each question of a different person.

➡ Lesson outcome

Ask students: *What have we talked about today?* Elicit: *time* or *days of the week, months and seasons.* Ask seven students to say the days of the week in order, then twelve to say the months in order. Draw students' attention to the lesson statement: *I can ask the time and talk about the months of the year.*

1 My network

A VOCABULARY AND LISTENING
Family and friends

THIS UNIT INCLUDES ● ● ○ ○
Vocabulary • family • possessive *'s* • plural noun forms • everyday activities • sports and hobbies • dates
Grammar • present simple affirmative and negative
Speaking • talking about family and friends • introducing friends • talking about everyday activities
Writing • an informal letter
WORKBOOK pages 8–14

LESSON SUMMARY ● ● ● ○ ○
Vocabulary: family members
Listening: description of a social network
Grammar: possessive *'s* singular and plural
Speaking: talking about family and friends
Topic: family life and relationships

SHORTCUT *To do the lesson in 30 minutes, set Vocabulary Builder (part 1) exercise 4 as homework. Limit the number of questions in exercise 6 to 2–3 and set exercise 8 as homework too (exercise 9 will then provide a method of checking that piece of homework in the next lesson).*

➡ Lead-in 2 minutes
- With books closed, inform the class of the lesson objectives by saying: *Today's topic is family.* Write *family* on the board. Ask: *Do you know any words for members of the family/ people in the family?* If students don't understand, prompt them: *For example, 'mother' or ...?* Write any words the students say on the board around the word *family*.

Exercise 1 page 8
- Students fill in the chart individually or in pairs. If possible, dictionaries should be available.
- Elicit the fact that the word *cousin* is the same for boys and girls.

KEY
A: aunt, cousin, daughter, granddaughter, grandmother, mother, niece, sister, wife
B: brother, cousin, father, grandfather, grandson, husband, nephew, son, uncle
cousin is in both groups

Exercise 2 page 8 🎧 1.13
- Play the recording once, pausing after each item for students to repeat chorally and individually. Point out that the final *-r* in *mother, father, sister,* etc. is completely silent, at least in British English. (Students are likely to have some experience of American English pronunciation from films, etc.).
- If students' pronunciation needs correcting, repeat the words yourself as many times as is necessary, so that they have a model to imitate.

Exercise 3 page 8 🎧 1.14
- Play the words for students to hear. You can also model the pronunciation yourself. Ask a few students to repeat.

KEY
grandmother   husband   son   uncle   brother   grandson

Exercise 4 page 8 🎧 1.15
- Play the recording once for students to check their answers; then play it again and have them repeat the words individually. Pay attention to the pronunciation of /ʌ/.

Exercise 5 page 8
- Write on the board: *my uncle's wife.* Ask: *Who's my uncle's wife?* hoping to elicit: *Your aunt* or *Aunt.*
- Allow a minute for students to study the *Learn this!* box. With a **weaker class**, write on the board: *my dad's car* and *my parents' car*, point to the apostrophe in the different positions, and say: *singular – plural.*
- Students complete the puzzles. Check with the whole class.

KEY
1	uncle	4	mother (or aunt)
2	uncle	5	niece
3	cousin	6	brother

LANGUAGE NOTE – POSSESSIVE *'S*
If a name ends in *s*, it is possible to add *'s* or just an apostrophe, e.g. *Charles' sister* or *Charles's sister*. In both cases the pronunciation is /ɪz/.

Exercise 6 page 8
- With a **weaker class** specify: *Write 2 or 3 more questions.*
- With a **stronger class**, you can provide a model like this: *Who is my father's granddaughter's mother?* (answer: *you* – for a girl; or *your wife* – for a boy; or *your sister*, or *your brother's wife*) or: *Who is my son's brother's mother?* (answer: *you* – for a girl; or *your wife* – for a boy)
- You may start with the whole class – two or three students ask a question each, the whole class answers. After that, students ask and answer in pairs.

For more practice of family vocabulary and possessive 's, go to:

Vocabulary Builder (part 1): Student's Book page 128

KEY
1
1	brother	4	husband	7	nephew
2	grandmother	5	aunt	8	cousins
3	niece	6	grandson		

2–3 Open answers

4 3 That's Jane's skateboard.
   4 John is at his cousins' house.
   5 Have you got Mark's MP3 player?
   6 The dog's ball is under the tree.
   7 What's Maria's phone number?
   8 Where are the students' books?
   9 These are Peter's pens.
   10 That's my grandparents' house.

Exercise 7 page 8 🎧 1.16
- Draw students attention to Laura's network. The 'ME' in the middle is Laura; she has classified the people in her life into three different categories: school, family, free time.
- When students have identified the categories in the picture, you may wish to ask them: *Would your categories be the same or different?* Help students to put their ideas into words. Play the recording.

KEY

volleyball team: Hannah	**friends:** Pete; Amy's cousin, Jake
music group: Molly	**family:** Mark and Lucy; Sam
favourite teachers: Mr Baker	

Transcript 1.16

Hi! I'm Laura. I've got one brother, and his name is Sam. I haven't got a sister, but I've got two cousins – Mark and Lucy. Our house is near the centre of town. I'm a student at Whiteside Secondary School. It's OK. My favourite teachers are Mr Baker and Miss Blair, and my best friends are Tina, Pete and Amy. Amy has got a cousin – Jake. He's really nice! My hobbies are volleyball and music. I'm in a volleyball team. Our two best players are Janice and Hannah. I'm also in a music group with two friends, Bob and Molly.

Exercise 8 page 8

- If the class are artistic, you may wish to provide them with large size paper, allow more time and possibly display the results on the walls. If time's short, this exercise can be done at home.

Exercise 9 page 8

- Provide a model first. Put 3–4 names of real people from your own network on the board and encourage students to ask: *Who's...?* Write the names your family and friends use normally, to show students that there's no need for artificial English names just because you're speaking English.
- Whenever students do an activity in which they scribble a few words which are only important to this one exercise, try to provide scrap paper, and train them not to put such irrelevant notes in their notebooks. The notebook should be a resource and contain information of lasting value.

For work on plural forms of nouns, go to:

> **Vocabulary Builder (part 2):** Student's Book page 128

KEY

5 1 noses   2 watches   3 boxes   4 videos   5 tomatoes
   6 stories   7 leaves

6 foot – feet   child – children   man – men
   tooth – teeth   person – people   woman – women

7 2 These <u>potatoes</u> and <u>tomatoes</u> are delicious. potato, tomato
   3 Where are those <u>men</u> and <u>women</u> from? man, woman
   4 She's got big <u>eyes</u>, and beautiful, white <u>teeth</u>. eye, tooth
   5 The <u>children</u>'s <u>dictionaries</u> are in the classroom. child, dictionary
   6 Have you got <u>nephews</u> and <u>nieces</u>? nephew, niece
   7 The <u>glasses</u> are on the <u>shelves</u> in the kitchen. glass, shelf

8 1 babies   4 keys   7 children
   2 feet   5 sandwiches
   3 watches   6 knives

➡ Lesson outcome

Ask students: *What have we talked about today?* Elicit: *family.* Ask: *Can you give me some words for family members?* Praise the students who come up with the more sophisticated ones, such as *cousin, niece, grandfather*, etc. Draw attention to the lesson statement: *I can talk about people I meet regularly.*

Notes for Photocopiable activity 1.1

Who's who?

Pairwork
Language: possessive *'s*, family vocabulary, numbers

Materials: One copy of the worksheet per pair of students (Teacher's Book page 123)

- If necessary, briefly revise family vocabulary by drawing a family tree on the board and eliciting the words to describe the relationship between the family members.
- Divide students into pairs and hand out the worksheets. Ask them to sit so that they can't see their partner's worksheet. Students fill in the missing names and ages in the family tree by asking and answering questions in pairs.
- Demonstrate the activity by taking the part of Student B and asking e.g. *Who's Tony's father?* Student A: *He's Peter.* Student B: *How old is he?* Student A: *He's 74.*
- Tell students to ask all their questions in relation to Tony. When they have finished they can look at their partner's worksheet to check their answers.
- Next ask students to draw their own family tree and then talk their partner through it giving extra information, for example, *Adam's my brother. He's 19. He studies at university.*

1B GRAMMAR
Present simple: affirmative

LESSON SUMMARY

Grammar: present simple: affirmative
Speaking: making statements about yourself and your family

SHORTCUT *To do the lesson in 30 minutes, read the text in exercise 1 aloud with students following it in their books, do exercise 4 as a class, and set the Grammar Builder as homework.*

➡ Lead-in 2-3 minutes

- Write on the board: *present, past, future.* Ask if students know what these words mean. (Accept answers in the students' own language.)
- Write the sentence *I live in* (insert the name of your town/city/village). Ask: *Is this present, past or future?* After eliciting *present*, erase *past* and *future* from the board, so that what's left is: *present – I live in (town).* Add the word *simple* after *present* and say: *Today, we're going to learn a tense called the present simple.*

Exercise 1 page 9

- Draw students' attention to the picture of The Simpsons. Elicit some names of his family members.

KEY

His dad's name is Homer. His mum's name is Marge. He's got two sisters called Lisa and Maggie.

Exercise 2 page 9

- As students read, monitor to see whether they're coping well with the text. Does everyone understand *lazy, classmates, power station*, and *studies hard?* If some students do not know these words, maybe others do and can explain/translate them. With a **weaker class**, be prepared to explain the vocabulary yourself (e.g. *If you don't like work, you're lazy. Daniel, Marta, Eva and so on are your classmates – people in the same class*). With a **stronger class**, ask students to use their dictionaries.

Exercise 3 page 9

• Draw students' attention to the table. You may wish to mention that English verbs are quite easy in one way, as many forms are the same: *I work, you work, we work.* Ask students to look for the third person singular in the text and see whether it is the same too.

• After checking this part of the exercise, read the box that outlines the use of the present simple. Quote sentences from the text as examples: *Eleven million Americans watch it every week.* (something that happens regularly); *The Simpsons live in Springfield* (something that is always true).

KEY

works

Exercise 4 page 9

• Students work individually. **Fast finishers** write one more sentence said by a member of the Simpson family. They can read their sentences aloud and the whole class guesses the person who says the sentence. Check answers as a class.

KEY

1 work – Homer	3 studies – Bart	5 like – Bart
2 go – Lisa	4 stays – Homer	6 live – Marge

For further practice of the present simple (affirmative), go to:

Grammar Builder 1B: Student's Book page 108

KEY

1 2 watches 5 does 8 plays
   3 goes 6 likes
   4 flies 7 finishes

2 1 watches 4 goes 7 likes
   2 does 5 studies 8 flies
   3 finishes 6 plays

3 2 My brother loves pizza.
   3 We go to school by bike.
   4 My classmates like me.
   5 His grandmother speaks French.
   6 My cousins and I play football.
   7 My friend's aunt lives in New York.

4 1 reads 4 work 7 cooks
   2 speak 5 drive 8 get up
   3 live 6 teaches

Exercise 5 page 9 🎧 1.17

• Students repeat the third person forms individually. Make sure they differentiate between /s/ in e.g. *likes* and /z/ in e.g. *plays*. Explain that the syllable /ɪz/ is added after /s/, /z/, /ʃ/, /tʃ/ after which /s/ would be difficult to either pronounce or hear.

Exercise 6 page 9 🎧 1.18

• Play the recording 2–3 times, depending on students' response.

• The table requires them to differentiate between just two categories: /s/ or /z/ and /ɪz/. However, when they have listened, you may want to ask them to repeat the verb forms. Insist on correct pronunciation of the final consonant /s/ and /z/ or the final syllable /ɪz/.

KEY

/s/ or /z/: does, drives, hates, listens, looks, loves, speaks, stays, tells
/ɪz/ dances, teaches, washes

Exercise 7 page 9

• Point out to students that some of the forms used will be the third person singular, e.g. (elicit:) *lives*, and others will be other forms, e.g. (elicit:) *we go*.

• As students do the exercise, monitor and make sure they understand *next door* and *get up*. Be prepared to explain.

• Ask two students in turn to read the text aloud. Help with pronunciation, especially of the present simple third person forms: *lives, goes*, etc.

KEY

1	lives	5	gets up	9	hates
2	go	6	finish	10	thinks
3	walk	7	listen	11	loves
4	goes	8	like		

Exercise 8 page 9

• Model the activity. Have one true and one false sentence about yourself or a member of your family prepared. Read your sentences to the whole class and ask: *Is this true?* Students then work on their own sentences.

• **Fast finishers** write more sentences.

Exercise 9 page 9

• Students talk in pairs. Circulate and monitor.

➡ Lesson outcome

Ask students (in their own language if necessary): *What tense have we looked at today?* to elicit: *The present simple tense.* Conduct a brief drill, using verbs from the lesson. Draw students' attention to the lesson statement: *I can talk about my family and friends.*

1C CULTURE
The Royal Family

LESSON SUMMARY

Reading: a text about Queen Elizabeth II
Listening: interviews
Speaking: talking about the British Royal Family
Topic: culture

SHORTCUT *To do the lesson in 30 minutes, ask students to read the text for the first time and do exercise 2 at home.*

➡ Lead-in 2 minutes

• Before students open their books, ask them if they know any names of British kings or queens from history. Then ask for names of contemporary members of the Royal Family and anything students know about them.

Exercise 1 page 10

• Students look at the photos and do the task. If they find it interesting, you can ask them to draw a family tree of the three generations of the Royal Family shown in the pictures.

CULTURE NOTE – THE ROYAL FAMILY

Camilla Parker-Bowles had a relationship with Prince Charles for many years before marrying him in April 2005. The majority of the British public supported the marriage, despite Princess Diana's great popularity.

Prince **Charles,** the Prince of Wales, is the first son of Queen Elizabeth II. He is expected to become the next British king. He is well known for his interest in architecture and his concern for the environment.

Diana, Princess of Wales, was the first wife of Prince Charles. She was the most popular member of the royal family and was often referred to as Di. She died in a car accident in Paris while trying to escape photographers.

Prince **Harry** is the younger son of Charles and Diana. He is in the British army.

Prince **Philip**, Duke of Edinburgh, is the Queen's husband. He is well-known in Britain for making jokes during public visits that can sometimes cause offence.

Prince **William** is the first child of Charles and Diana. He is the second in line to the British throne. He studied Art History at university and then changed to Geography. He joined his younger brother in the army in 2006.

Exercise 2 page 10

- This may be the first time some of the students have seen a task of this type, so explain it to them, pointing out especially that there is one extra heading, which does not fit anywhere. Allow students to compare answers in pairs, then go over them with the whole class. If there are any wrong answers, discuss why, for example, *Why is D 'The Queen's job' and not 'The Queen's travels'?* – Because only one sentence is about travels, and the whole paragraph is about various types of work.

KEY

A	Introduction	D	The Queen's job
B	The Queen's home	E	The Queen's free time
C	The Queen's family		

Exercise 3 page 10

- Students read the text more carefully now and answer the questions. Do the first one as a class. The word *charity* may need explaining.

KEY

1 T
2 T
3 F Prince Philip is the Queen's husband.
4 F Camilla is Charles's wife.
5 F The Queen meets the Prime Minister every week / Tuesday.
6 F She goes to the horse races in May and June.

Exercise 4 page 10

- Students go through the text again. Let them compare answers in pairs, then check with the whole class. When checking, pay attention to the pronunciation of *century* (weak vowel) and *monarch* (final /k/). You can reinforce the words by asking questions about the students' own country like: *Can you give me the name of a famous **monarch**? Do you remember which **century** he/she lived in?*

KEY

1	at the moment	3	castle, palace	5	monarch
2	prince	4	century	6	discuss

Exercise 5 page 10   1.19

- Before playing the recording, check understanding of the statements and the task. With a **weaker class,** read the opinions with the whole class. *Expensive* and *modern* may need explaining.
- Play the recording through once. Then play Speaker 1 only and ask how many of the opinions listed in the task she expresses. If more than a few students are not sure, play Speaker 1 again. Ask a student which opinions the old lady expressed. Follow the same procedure for Speakers 2 and 3.

KEY

They're a bit boring. 3		They work hard. 3
They're very expensive. 1		They aren't modern. 1
I like reading about them. 2		They have interesting lives. 2

Transcript 1.19

1 Int. Do you think the royal family is important?
 Woman Important? No! They're very expensive.
 Int. Really?
 Woman Yes. We spend millions of pounds on them. And they aren't modern. They're old-fashioned! I want a republic!
2 Int. What do you think of the royal family?
 Man I love them. I like reading about them in newspapers and magazines.
 Int. So you think they're important?
 Man Oh, yes, very important. They have really interesting lives.
3 Int. What do you think of the royal family?
 Man They're OK, I suppose.
 Int. So you don't really like them.
 Man Well, I don't mind them. They're a bit boring, but they work hard.

Exercise 6 page 10

- If a student says a sentence that's true but incorrect, help them correct it. If a student says a sentence that's correct but false, ask the class: *Is that true?* and let them try to correct it. If a student says a sentence which is not a statement of fact, but an opinion (such as, *They have interesting lives.*) accept it, but point out that it is opinion.

➡ Lesson outcome

Ask students: *What have we talked about today?* Elicit: *the Royal Family* or *the Queen* or *kings and queens*. Draw students' attention to the lesson statement: *I can understand information and opinions on the Royal Family.*

1D GRAMMAR
Present simple: negative

LESSON SUMMARY

Grammar: present simple negative
Listening: listening for specific information (true/false)
Speaking: speaking about your habits

SHORTCUT *To do the lesson in 30 minutes, don't ask students to write all 12 sentences in exercise 5 (2–3 affirmative and 2–3 negative should be enough.) Set the Grammar Builder for homework.*

➡ Lead-in 2 minutes

- Recall something one of the students said about themselves in exercise 10 in lesson 1B. Start this lesson by saying something contrary to what he/she said, e.g. if Paul said: *I get up at seven*, say: *Paul, you get up at five, is that true?* When the student replies *no*, write on the board and say: *I don't get up at five o'clock.* Tell students that today they're going to study the negative form of the present simple tense.

Exercise 1 page 11

- Draw students' attention to the photos. Students read and match the names to the photos. Explain *athletic*: someone who is fit and good at sports, but not necessarily massively muscular. Check answers.

KEY

1 Ben   2 Josh

Exercise 2 page 11

- Find the first example with the whole class. After that students continue on their own. Circulate and look over their shoulders to see if they're getting it right. With a **weaker class**, you may want to copy the table onto a transparency or write it on the board for students to see and check.
- Point out or elicit that the only different form is the third person singular with *–es*, which is the same as the *–s* in affirmative sentences.

KEY

1 don't   2 doesn't   3 don't   4 don't

Exercise 3 page 11

- Do the first three sentences as a class. Students do the rest individually.
- Check as a class. Pay attention to the pronunciation of these words: *science* – there is *no* /tʃ/; ice hockey – the final sound is /i/ not /eɪ/; com**pu**ter – the stress on the second syllable. *Computer games* is a tone unit, stressed on the first word.

KEY

1 I don't live in England.
2 We don't come from London.
3 Sarah doesn't study science.
4 Mick doesn't play ice hockey.

5 My parents don't work in an office.
6 You don't like computer games.
7 Tom and I don't walk to school.
8 Katharine doesn't get up at five o'clock.

For further practice of the present simple, go to:

Grammar Builder 1D: Student's Book page 108

KEY

5	1 doesn't	5 don't	8 don't
	2 don't	6 doesn't	9 doesn't
	3 doesn't	7 don't	10 don't
	4 don't		

6	1 don't know	4 stay	7 doesn't work
	2 walk	5 hates	8 doesn't listen
	3 doesn't like	6 love	

7 2 He doesn't walk to school. He goes to school by bike.
   3 She doesn't listen to music in her bedroom. She watches TV in her bedroom.
   4 He doesn't get up early on Sundays. He stays in bed on Sundays.
   5 She teaches maths. She doesn't teach English.

Exercise 4 page 11   1.20

- Point to the photos. Say: *This is Mark. This is Sally. They're students.* Draw students' attention to the table. Explain that you are going to play the recording straight through once, then play it again stopping to check the answers.

KEY

	1	2	3	4	5	6
Mark:	F	T	F	F	T	T
Sally:	F	F	T	T	F	T

Transcript 1.20

Mark	My name's Mark. I come from London, but I live in Liverpool. I'm a student. I study French at Liverpool University. My hobbies are basketball and playing the guitar. I play in a band at university. I study hard during the week. At the weekends I work in a restaurant.
Sally	Hi, I'm Sally. I'm a student at Cardiff University, but I'm not from Cardiff. My family comes from London. I study medicine. I want to be a doctor. What are my hobbies? Well, I love shopping. I go shopping every Saturday morning. I also like sport – I play tennis. I sometimes work in a shop on Saturdays.

Exercise 5 page 11

- Read the examples and do one or two sentences with the whole class. After that students can continue individually.
- **Fast finishers** can also write sentences containing corrected information, *Mark doesn't study maths. He studies French.*
- With a **stronger class** you may not require all students to write all 10 sentences. Half of the class could do Mark and the other half Sally, or you can just do 2–3 affirmative sentences and the same number of negative ones.

KEY

He doesn't study maths.	She doesn't live in London.
He doesn't enjoy playing the piano	She studies medicine.
He plays basketball.	She enjoys shopping.
He works in a restaurant.	She doesn't play volleyball.
Sally doesn't come from Cardiff.	She works in a shop.

Exercise 6 page 11

- Remind students that the present simple is used to speak about regular activities and things that are true all the time. With a **stronger class**, ask students to produce at least three sentences each based on their own ideas.

Exercise 7 page 11

- First students work in pairs. You may wish to put them in pairs with classmates they don't normally sit with, so that they learn something new about them.
- Then students report back to the class. If your group is big, this stage may take a long time and students might stop paying attention. You may wish to ask students to tell the class only the 3–4 most interesting things about their partner.

→ Lesson outcome

Ask students: *What have we talked about today?* Try to elicit: *the present simple negative,* but accept all answers relevant to the content of the lesson. Briefly practise the grammar by saying a few sentences in the present simple and asking students for the negative forms. Draw students' attention to the lesson statement: *I can say what someone does and doesn't do.*

Notes for Photcopiable activity 1.2

Two cousins: Sonia and Suzy
Pairwork
Language: present simple affirmative and negative
Materials: One copy of worksheet 1.2 cut in half per pair of students (Teacher's Book page 124)

- Divide students into pairs. Give Students A worksheet A, and Students B worksheet B. Tell students not to show each other their worksheets. Demonstrate the activity by eliciting one sentence about Sonia from worksheet A and one about Suzy from worksheet B, e.g. *Sonia goes to Springtown School in Oxford. Suzy goes to Manchester High School.*
- In pairs students take it in turns to make a sentence about the cousins using their pictures. Tell students to write down anything that they have in common. (They don't smoke, they play the guitar, they play tennis.)
- Share answers as a class. Ask students to tell you the sentences they made about each cousin.

1E READING Family life

LESSON SUMMARY

Reading: a text about an unusual family; reading for gist and for specific information
Speaking: speaking about home life and household duties
Vocabulary: everyday family activities
Topic: family life and relationships

SHORTCUT *To do the lesson in 30 minutes, either ask students to read the text for the first time at home, or keep exercises 1 and 7 short, and let students work in pairs for exercises 3 and 4.*

→ Lead-in 2 minutes

- Tell the class: *I've got ___ brother(s) and ___ sister(s).* Ask one or two students: *How many brothers and sisters*

have you got? (If you know something about the students' families, it's best to choose two whose situations are very different – an only child and one of four, for example.) Ask: *Is that a good number of brothers and sisters?* Then announce the topic: *Today we're going to talk about family life.* At this point, show the big photo on page 12.

Exercise 1 page 13

- Draw students' attention to the photo. Students answer the questions in pairs. Discuss question 1 as a class.

Exercise 2 page 13

- Ask students to look at the photo on page 12 and tell them they are going to read about this family. Ask them to read the text quickly first and answer the three questions in exercise 2. Ask them to underline the sentences where they found the information so they can justify their answers with lines from the text. Check with the whole class, asking for justification.

KEY
1 F (She's a mother with 15 children.)
2 F (Her husband goes to work.)
3 T ('I love my big family. ... I want more children!')

> **CULTURE NOTE – UK FAMILIES**
> The Povey family is obviously exceptionally large. The average family in the UK has 1.3 children. This is much smaller than in most European countries.

Exercise 3 page 13

- Ask students to read the Exam tip first and check if they have understood by asking: *So what should you read first? When should you read the options?* Students read the text a second time and do the task. With a **weaker class**, you may ask them to underline the relevant lines in the text. Check answers with the whole class.

KEY
1 b	2 b	3 c	4 a	5 b

Exercise 4 page 13

- This is a very important exercise, as it can make students aware of the existence and importance of collocations.
- Students look for the collocations in the text and note them down in the table. When they've finished, read each collocation aloud, taking care to pronounce it as one tone unit, and ask a different student to repeat each one. Ask the students some questions, for example, *Do you clean the house? Do you clean your room? What time do you come home from school? Who cooks dinner in your house? Do you do the washing? Does your mother or father drive you to school? What time do you get up? Does your mum go to work? Do you go to the supermarket with your mother or father? Do you iron your clothes? Does your mum make breakfast for you?*

KEY
clean the house	get up
come home	go to work
cook dinner	go to the supermarket
do the washing	iron clothes
drive the children to school	make breakfast

Exercise 5 page 13

- Ask students to write out the sentences in their notebooks. Circulate and monitor. **Fast finishers** can write two or three more sentences.

Exercise 6 page 13

- Students write their sentences. Circulate and monitor. Correct selected errors: missing third person singular –s, and errors in the production of the collocations which are the focus of the exercise. When correcting, always wait for a student to finish the sentence, point out the error and ask them to repeat the whole sentence.

Exercise 7 page 13

- The game can be played as a class or, if the class is very large, in several groups. The student who remembers the longest chain of activities is the winner.
- If there are persistent errors of pronunciation or in the use of the collocations, make a note of them and correct them as a class when the game is over.

ADDITIONAL SPEAKING ACTIVITY

Preparation: Before the lesson, cut out a photograph of two students (aged 20-something), or two separate photographs of students, from a youth magazine. Mount them on pieces of card.

- Hold up the photos and introduce the characters: *This is Richard. How old do you think he is?* (Accept any sensible answers.) *What does he do?* (He's a student.) *What does he study?* (Accept any ideas.) *This is Michael. How old is he?* etc. *Richard and Michael share a flat. They live together in the same apartment.*
- Introduce the task by saying: *What time do you think Richard gets up? What time does Michael get up? Who do you think cleans the flat? Who makes breakfast?*
- Put students in pairs and tell them it is now their task to imagine and describe Richard and Michael's habits and the division of housework in their household. Point out they can use the text, the chart in exercise 4 and the sentences in exercise 5 as a resource.
- Students prepare their ideas in writing (this can be in note form) e.g. : *Richard: gets up early, makes breakfast, does the washing; Michael: … etc.*
- Pairs present their ideas to the whole class.

➡ Lesson outcome

Ask students: *What have we talked about today?* Try to elicit: *home* or *family life* or *things we do at home*, but accept all answers relevant to the content of the lesson. Ask: *Which words or phrases from today do you think will be useful to you?* Accept any lexical items that appeared in the lesson, but encourage students to recall collocations rather than single words. Draw students' attention to the lesson statement: *I can understand an article and talk about everyday activities.*

1 F EVERYDAY ENGLISH
Introducing people

LESSON SUMMARY

Functional English: introducing people
Listening: a dialogue; completing sentences
Speaking: introducing people
Topic: family life and relationships

SHORTCUT *To do the lesson in 30 minutes, do exercises 3 and 7 as a class, and have fewer pairs perform their dialogues in exercise 10.*

➡ Lead-in 2 minutes

- Ask students to look at the photo at the top of page 14. Say: *These are Rachel, Mark and Susan. Who are they?* (Students.) *Where are they?* (At school.) *What do you think they're saying?* (Accept any answers.) Explain: *In fact, Susan* (point to one of the girls in the photo) *is a new student.* Tell students they are going to hear a conversation between the students in the photo and to learn about introducing people. (Either explain 'introduce' or ask: *What's 'introduce/introducing?'* – accept a translation.)

Exercise 1 page 14

- Ask students to read the dialogue and the words in the box and see if they can fill in the gaps.

KEY

1	How	4	from	7	doesn't
2	this	5	got	8	you
3	too	6	old		

Exercise 2 page 14 🎧 1.21

- Play the recording twice – once without stopping, then stopping after each gap to check. With a **weaker class**, play the dialogue as many times as the students need.

Exercise 3 page 14

- Before students read the dialogue in groups, practise the pronunciation of key phrases. Model each phrase yourself, taking care to pronounce it slowly but very fluently, as one tone unit. Ask a few students to repeat individually, then the whole class chorally:

How are you?	*Have you got any brothers or sisters?*
This is Susan.	*How old are they?*
Nice to meet you.	*See you.*
Where are you from?	

Exercise 4 page 14

- In a **stronger class**, encourage students to do the exercise without looking back at the dialogue first and then check. Check answers with the whole class.

KEY

1	London	3	18	5	14
2	one, one	4	university	6	12C

Exercise 5 page 14 🎧 1.22

- Tell students they are going to hear two more dialogues. Allow a minute to read the instructions and the statements.
- Say they will hear the recordings twice. Introduce the first dialogue by saying: *Dialogue 1: Jenny, Alfie and Sam.* Play the first dialogue through, then play it a second time pausing after each answer to check answers to questions 1–3. Follow the same procedure with the second dialogue.
- Make sure everyone understands *neighbour*. Point out *the same* (in *the same street, the same dance class*). You may draw attention to the phrase *dance class* and relate it to students' experience by asking: *Who goes to a dance class? Does anyone go to a music class? a drama class?* etc.

KEY

1 T		2 T		3 F		4 T		5 F		6 T

Transcript 1.22

1

Jenny	Hello, Alfie! Nice to see you!
Alfie	Hi, Jenny. Nice to see you too.
Jenny	Alfie, this is Sam.
Alfie	Hello, Sam.
Sam	Hi, Alfie.
Jenny	Alfie is my new neighbour. He lives in our street. He goes to Elston Secondary School.
Sam	Oh, really. My cousin goes there. It's a good school.
Jenny	Alfie's got a sister.
Sam	Oh, really. What's her name?
Alfie	Sarah.
Sam	Is she at the same school?
Alfie	No. She's 20. She doesn't go to school. She works in a shop.

2

Ella	Hi, Rosie!
Rosie	Hello, Ella. How are you?
Ella	Fine, thanks. Rosie, this is my friend, Jane.
Rosie	Hi, Jane.
Jane	Hello, Rosie.
Ella	Jane goes to the same dance class as me.
Rosie	Really?
Jane	Yes, but I go to a different school – Walton Manor.
Rosie	Really? My mum works at that school!
Jane	Is she a teacher?
Rosie	Yes, she is. She teaches Italian.
Jane	Oh, right. I don't study Italian.
Ella	There's our bus! See you at school tomorrow, Rosie!
Rosie	Yes, see you at school, Ella. Bye for now.
Jane	Bye. Nice to meet you, Rosie.
Rosie	Nice to meet you, too. Bye, Jane.

Exercise 6 page 14 🎧 1.22

- Students complete the sentences. In a **weaker class,** play the recording while they're doing it, stopping after each relevant sentence. Check answers with the whole class.

KEY

1 new	3 doesn't, works	5 goes, same
2 goes, School	4 this, friend	6 works, teaches

Exercise 7 page 14

- Read the instructions. Explain *reply* if necessary. Ask a strong student to do the first sentence as an example. Students match the remaining sentences. To check, ask various students to read the two-line dialogues in open pairs.

KEY

1 e	2 a	3 c	4 g	5 b	6 f	7 d

Exercise 8 page 14

- Explain to students that in the next exercise they are going to act out a conversation, but first they have to prepare some information about the characters. Students complete the sentences in the exercise. **Fast finishers** can write additional sentences, for example: *You live in the same street as … . You go to the same drama class as … .*

Exercise 9 page 14

- Students work on their conversations. Circulate and monitor, correcting errors and doing little bits of pronunciation practice if needed. Students need to read their dialogues together at least once before they present them in front of the class. Ask stronger students if they could say their dialogues without reading, maybe from a few notes or prompts.

Exercise 10 page 14

- Before students perform, read the speaking tip as a class. Depending on time and on students' patience, have 3–6 groups act out their dialogues in front of the class. Pick students who speak loudly and clearly and/or whose dialogues have something interesting or funny about them.

➡ Lesson outcome

Ask students: *What did you learn to do today?* Elicit: *To introduce people.* Ask students to say some phrases they learned in the lesson. Draw students' attention to the lesson statement: *I can introduce people.*

1G WRITING
An informal letter

LESSON SUMMARY

Writing: an informal letter
Reading: an informal letter
Topic: family life and relationships

SHORTCUT *To do the lesson in 30 minutes, do exercise 2 quickly as a class and set the writing as homework.*

➡ Lead-in 2 minutes

- Inform the class of the lesson topic. Ask: *Do you ever write letters? How often? Who to? Have you ever had a penfriend?* (If you get very little response to the questions about letters ask: *Do you write e-mails? How often? Who to? Do you have an e-mail friend?*) If you find that your students hardly ever write letters, you can make the topic relevant to them by saying that you would write an e-mail to a friend in a similar way to the letter presented in the unit.

Exercise 1 page 15

- Ask students to look at the letter and the photo. What do they expect the letter to be about? Ask them to read through the letter quickly. Were their predictions right? What kind of information is included in the letter?
- Now ask students to do the task. After checking the answers with the whole class, discuss the structure of a letter and emphasise the importance of writing in paragraphs. Point out that each paragraph in Robbie's letter is about something specific, and explain that the general idea of a paragraph is that it contains one point or one topic.

KEY

1 A	2 C	3 A	4 B	5 A	6 C

Exercise 2 page 15

- Read and answer the questions as a class. This may be a good opportunity to elicit answers from the weakest students and boost their confidence.

KEY

1 16
2 Manchester
3 Karen
4 11
5 He takes the dog for a walk and does his homework.
6 Karen and Robbie

Exercise 3 page 15

- Emphasise that students must learn this writing tip! Firstly, letters (or e-mails) are something that most people do write in real life. Secondly, in many exams, candidates are asked to write letters, and one of the first things an examiner will look at is: Does it have an appropriate opening and ending? With a **stronger class**, teach a few more openings and endings: *Hi, All the best, Yours*, etc.

KEY

Dear   Best wishes

Exercise 4 page 15 🎧 1.23

- Ask students to look at the numbers in the box. Explain or elicit that ordinal numbers are used for dates.
- Play the recording for students to listen and then again for students to repeat. Practise the pronunciation until students are comfortable with it. You may want to drill the ordinals, by writing a cardinal number on the board, and asking students to say the ordinal number.

Exercise 5 page 15

- Students can work in pairs, or work individually and then compare answers in pairs. Check as a class by having individual students write the numbers on the board.

KEY

eighteenth – 18th	twenty-first – 21st
fourteenth – 14th	fifth – 5th
seventeenth – 17th	first – 1st
third – 3rd	second – 2nd
thirty-first – 31st	tenth – 10th
twenty-second – 22nd	thirtieth – 30th
eighth – 8th	twentieth – 20th
fifteenth – 15th	ninth – 9th
twelfth – 12th	sixth – 6th

LANGUAGE NOTE – THE 21ST CENTURY

In British English 2001 is pronounced *two thousand and one*. 2002 is pronounced *two thousand and two*, etc. In American English the word *and* is not used e.g. *two thousand one*. It is predicted that from 2010 the years will be pronounced: *twenty ten, twenty eleven*, etc (since this follows the same format as *nineteen eighty, eighteen twenty*, etc), although nobody knows exactly what will happen.

Exercise 6 page 15 🎧 1.24

- Read the *Learn this!* box with the class. Play the recording for students to listen and write the dates.

KEY

1 3rd March 2006	4 8th May 1972
2 19th July 2000	5 31st October 2007
3 1st August 2020	6 4th September 1995

Transcript 1.24

1 the third of March, two thousand and six
2 the nineteenth of July, two thousand
3 the first of August, twenty twenty
4 The eighth of May, nineteen seventy-two
5 The thirty-first of October, two thousand and seven
6 The fourth of September, nineteen ninety-five

Exercise 7 page 15 🎧 1.25

- Look back at the *Learn this!* box and the answers in exercise 5. Do the first one as an example for the class, then ask students to try saying the dates.
- Play the recording for the students to check, then play it again, pausing after each date for students to repeat individually and chorally.

Transcript 1.25

1 the twenty-first of January, two thousand and seven
2 the eighth of October, nineteen ninety-five
3 the fifth of May, two thousand and ten
4 the twenty-ninth of March, nineteen hundred
5 the twenty-second of September, two thousand and eight
6 the fourth of December, twenty twenty

Exercise 8 page 15

- Model the first question for the students by giving your date of birth (or one of your family's if you prefer to keep your own private).
- Students ask and answer about the different dates. Circulate and monitor to make sure they are saying the dates properly.
- Share a few answers as a class by asking the questions in open pairs across the classroom.

Exercise 9 page 15

- Allow about two minutes for students to read through the instructions and guidelines. Make sure they understand what they are asked to write. Go through the topics under each paragraph. If the writing is done in class, circulate and monitor. If you notice common errors, write them on the board and ask the class to correct them. Ask students to proofread each other's first drafts. Has all the information been included? Are there any errors? After peer correction students write a second draft and hand it in.

ALTERNATIVE WRITING TASK

Students choose a celebrity that they know something about. If the writing task is being done for homework, you could ask them to do some research. If they are doing it in class, they could work in pairs or make up the details.

They write back to Robbie's letter as the celebrity.

- Begin with: *Thank you for your letter and for the photo.*
- In your answer mention the things Robbie writes about, for example: *I've also got ... but I haven't got ... After work I ...*
- Ask Robbie a question about himself.

➡ Lesson outcome

Ask students: *What have we talked about today?* Elicit: *informal letters, a typical way to start and finish an informal letter, how to say dates*, etc. Draw students' attention to the lesson statement: *I can write an informal letter to a penfriend.*

➡ Lead-in 2–5 minutes

- Explain to students that these pages help them practise some exam tasks, so that they become familiar with the types of exercises in school-leaving exams.
- Ask students to briefly summarise what they have covered in this unit. Elicit *introducing people, saying how old people are, talking about family and friends*.

Exercise 1 page 16

- Ask students to look at the photo of the boy. Ask: *How old do you think he is?*

Exercise 2 page 16

E Use of English: text gapfill

- Students work on the task individually and compare answers in pairs. Ask one or two students to read the completed text aloud. Help with intonation and pausing. The text is meant as a model for speaking, so students should be encouraged not to read in flat, wooden voices!

KEY

1	got	4	the	7	studies
2	old	5	in	8	an
3	my	6	is	9	at

Exercise 3 page 16

- Tell students they are now going to talk in the same way about their families, but first they need to prepare some notes. A lot of help may be needed with parents' jobs – you might choose to have a big dictionary around in case some of them are really unusual!
- Students go on to complete the sentences. Circulate and monitor. Encourage them to use short forms, e.g. *My mum's a nurse,* to create more natural prompts for spoken language. In pairs, students read their sentences to each other. Finally, have a few students read their sentences to the whole class.

Exercise 4 page 16 🎧 1.26

- Ask students to read the Speaking exam task in exercise 6 and the questions in exercise 4. Make sure everybody understands that they are going to hear a candidate attempting the exam task in exercise 6. Play the recording through once, then play it again, stopping after each answer.

KEY

1 A sister and a brother
2 At home
3 Her dad works in an office and her mum in a supermarket

Transcript 1.26

Examiner Hello, Anna.
Student Hello, Mrs Wilson.
Examiner Can you tell me about your family? Have you got any brothers and sisters?
Anna Yes, I have. I got a sister and a brother.
Examiner I'm sorry, I can't hear you very well. Can you speak up?
Anna Yes, sorry. I got a sister and a brother. Um, my sister is 13, my brother he is 19.

Examiner And is your sister at the same school as you?
Anna Yes she is, but, she isn't in the same class.
Examiner Tell me something about your brother.
Anna He is very intelligent. He's at university.
Examiner Does he live at home, with you?
Anna Yes, he do.
Examiner Uh, huh. And do your parents work?
Anna Yes. My dad work in an office in Prague. And my mum works in supermarket.
Examiner OK, thank you Anna.

Exercise 5 page 16

- Students correct the errors in pairs. Check with the whole class.
- Discuss Anna's task with the class. Did she speak loudly and clearly, did she give enough information? Pick out or elicit good points, like when she gives more information than was in the question (ages of brothers and sisters) which is good as long as it's relevant.

KEY

1	I**'ve** got	4	My dad work**s**
2	My brother h̶e̶ is 19	5	in **a** supermarket
3	Yes, he do**es**.		

Exercise 6 page 16

E Speaking: an interview

- Read the speaking tip together before students do the task.
- One of the students will have to be the examiner and ask the questions. You may play the recording again for students to write down the three questions asked by the examiner. With a **stronger class,** ask students to try to recall the questions before listening, then play the recording to check. With a **weaker class**, you might simply supply the questions by writing them on the board.
- Students do the Speaking exam task in pairs. They can then switch roles and do the same task again, or switch roles to do the optional task.

OPTIONAL ACTIVITY

Speaking: an interview

You and your friend are visiting your friend in New York.

- Introduce your friend.
- Say a few words about his / her family.
- Say what you are planning to do in New York.

(The student starts the conversation.)

Exercise 7 page 16

- Read the listening tip with students. Then look at the sentences in the Listening exam task in exercise 8. Allow a minute or two for students to read the sentences, then check understanding by asking for ideas about the kind of information that might be missing.

KEY – Suggested answers

2 workplaces
3 morning/afternoon
4 places
5 hobbies, leisure activities
6 transport: bus, train, car
7 time
8 housing: flat, apartment etc.

Exercise 8 page 16 🎧 1.27

E Listening: completing statements

- Play the recording straight through. Then ask if students heard anything that matched their predictions.
- Play the recording again. Students listen and complete the sentences.
- Check the answers with the class.

Transcript 1.27

My name is Annabelle Green. I live in Watford, a town near London. I'm a nurse, and I work in the hospital in the town centre. My daily routine is quite unusual, because I work at night. I get up at four o'clock in the afternoon, and have breakfast. Then, I usually go to town. Sometimes I go to the supermarket. After that I go home, and I watch television or listen to music. I go to work at ten o'clock in the evening. I don't drive, I take the bus. I start work at ten thirty, and I finish at six o'clock in the morning. I come home at about seven o'clock, and I cook dinner. After dinner, I usually clean the flat, and do some washing. Then I listen to the news on the radio, and go to bed.

KEY

1	nurse	5	watches television
2	hospital (in the town centre)	6	bus
3	in the afternoon	7	ten thirty
4	supermarket	8	flat

➡ Lesson outcome

Ask students: *What did we talk about today?* Elicit: *about an exam speaking task / giving information about yourself* or any other relevant answers.

Get ready for your EXAM 2

TOPIC ●●●●○

Family life and relationships

➡ Lead-in 2–3 minutes

- Introduce the topic by asking students: *Have you got Internet friends? How many? Where do they live? How often do you chat with them? How often do you e-mail them? What do you chat and e-mail about? Do you meet your Internet friends in real life? Do you want to meet them?*

Exercise 1 page 17

- Draw students' attention to the text. Ask them to read the task. Point out that they only need to read the text quickly and not very carefully to do the task.
- Students read individually and compare answers in pairs. Check with the whole class.

KEY

1 – 2	2 – 4	3 – 1

Exercise 2 page 17

E Reading: matching headings with paragraphs

- Ask students to read the rubric and the six headings. Help with any language problems (e.g. *seem, How do 'friends' websites work, best advice*). With a **weaker class**, you might read the headings aloud with the whole class.
- Make sure everyone understands that there is one extra heading. For example, you might ask: *How many headings are there? How many paragraphs has the text got?*

- Ask students to read the first paragraph and discuss which is the right heading for it. Do not give the answer at this point.
- Ask students to read the second paragraph and discuss which is the right heading for it. Repeat the procedure with paragraphs 3, 4 and 5. Ask them to underline the parts of the text that are relevant to the answers.
- Ask students to read the heading that is left and check that it really is the odd one out.
- Finally, ask them to read the whole text with headings to see if it feels right.
- Allow up to 10 minutes for the task.
- Check as a class. Ask students to answer the questions posed in the headings, e.g. *Why do 'friends' websites seem dangerous? – Because it's impossible to know that the information on a homepage is true. Perhaps the 16-year old girl you talk to online is really a 40-year-old man.*

KEY

1 D	2 B	3 F	4 A	5 C

Exercise 3 page 17

- Ask students to turn back to the photos on page 6, and to read the adjectives in the box. Ask students what these adjectives describe (*appearance*).
- Ask for ideas about which words could be used to describe the photos below and on page 16. Elicit *long hair, dark hair, curly hair, glasses, blue / brown eyes.*

Exercise 4 page 17

- Read the list of adjectives aloud so that students know how they are pronounced. Students work with dictionaries to find out the meanings. Check understanding either simply by eliciting translations or by asking questions such as: *Gerald gives money to poor people. Gerald is …?* or *Millie smiles a lot* (mime) *and always seems happy. Millie is …?* Then ask everyone individually to choose the three qualities they consider to be most important in a friend. Students compare their choices in small groups.

Exercise 5 page 17

E Speaking: topic-based discussion

- Students do the Speaking exam task in pairs. If possible, put students with someone they don't usually sit with, so they can describe a person who their partner does not know. Students take turns to describe a person and to listen to the description.
- Circulate and monitor. Check that students are correctly using adjectives to describe appearance and personality.

OPTIONAL ACTIVITY

Imagine you are interviewing a famous person for your school magazine.

- Work in pairs. Choose a celebrity and make notes about three things you would like to find out about them.
- Write your interview with a partner.

You could ask three or four pairs to perform their interviews to the class.

➡ Lesson outcome

Ask students: *What have we done today?* Elicit: *a reading task with headings* or equivalent and: *speaking about a friend* or equivalent. Elicit some information about the tasks, e.g. how many headings there are in a reading task (one more than the number of paragraphs), or what you have to do when describing a person.

THIS UNIT INCLUDES ● ● ○ ○
Vocabulary • sports and hobbies • collocations: verb + noun • parts of the body
Grammar • present simple questions • adverbs of frequency • *How often ... ?*
• object pronouns • imperatives
Speaking • an interview • talking about free time • expressing likes and dislikes
Writing • an announcement
WORKBOOK pages 16–22

A VOCABULARY AND LISTENING
Free-time activities

LESSON SUMMARY ● ● ● ○ ○
Vocabulary: free-time activities
Listening: short monologues; listening for specific information
Speaking: talking about likes and dislikes
Topic: sport and leisure activities

SHORTCUT *To do the lesson in 30 minutes, set Vocabulary Builder (part 1) exercises 1 and 2 as homework and keep exercises 7 and 8 brief.*

➡ Lead-in 2 minutes
• Write *free time* on the board. Say one true sentence about your free-time activities, e.g. *I read a lot in my free time.* or, *In my free time I watch films on DVD.* Write the name of the activity on the board: *reading* or *films*, or whatever you said. Ask: *Who else likes reading/films/... ?* Add two or three more simple names of popular activities which you think some of your students may like : *football, walking, dancing, drawing.* For each of them ask: *Who likes ... ?* Then add the word *activities* (and the hyphen in free-time) to the board to complete the title of the lesson: *free-time time activities.* Say: *Today we're going to talk about free-time activities.*

Exercise 1 page 18
• Students open their books and match words to photos. Encourage them to compare answers in pairs before checking as a class.

KEY
See Transcript 1.28

Exercise 2 page 18 🎧 1.28
• Play the recording once for students to listen and check their answers, then a second time, pausing after each item and asking students to repeat. Students look up any unknown words in their dictionaries. Pay attention especially to the pronunciation of *computer games* (stress on *pu* and the whole phrase pronounced as one word), *fashion* (reduced vowel in final syllable) and *photography* (stress on *to* and two reduced vowels, in first and penultimate syllable).

Transcript 1.28
1	ice skating	4	basketball	7	rollerblading
2	photography	5	chess	8	athletics
3	computer games	6	swimming		

Not illustrated: books cycling dancing fashion films
football gymnastics jogging music

Exercise 3 page 18
• Students categorise the vocabulary. Point out that the same word can go into more than one category. If some students come up with unexpected answers (e.g. you can play football at home or alone), rather than dismissing those choices as wrong, exploit it as an opportunity for more talking: *Why? / Why do you say that? Do you play football at home? Where? Who with? Do you use a normal football?* etc.

KEY – Sample answers
1 **at home**: books, chess, computer games, dancing, fashion, films, music, photography
2 **outside**: athletics, basketball, books, chess, cycling, dancing, football, ice skating, jogging, music, photography, rollerblading, swimming
3 **on your own**: athletics, books, computer games, cycling, films, gymnastics, ice skating, jogging, music, photography, rollerblading, swimming
4 **in a team**: basketball, football, (students may wish to include sports such as swimming, which can be individual sports, but may also be seen as a team sport in an event like the Olympic Games.)

For further practice of free-time activities, go to:

Vocabulary Builder (part 1): Student's Book page 129

KEY
1	1 jogging		3 fashion		5 gymnastics	
	2 cycling		4 football		6 dancing	
2	1 swimming		4 basketball		7 rollerblading	
	2 music		5 photography		8 chess	
	3 films		6 books			

3–4 Open answers

Exercise 4 page 18 🎧 1.29
• Tell students they are going to hear four teenagers talking about their interests and favourite free-time activities. Play the recording once without stopping and check whether most students have got the answers. If not, play it again. If everyone has got answers 1, 2, and 3, but some people are missing 4, play just that section a second time. Check answers.

KEY
1	Oliver – music	3	Nick – computer games
2	Lauren – cycling	4	Rachel – gymnastics

Transcript 1.29
1 Oliver I love all kinds: rock, jazz, hip-hop, rap. I listen to songs on the bus every morning – I've got an MP3 player with 2000 songs on it. My favourite band at the moment is Kaiser Chiefs. I play the guitar, but I'm not in a band. I just play at home – in my bedroom!

2 Lauren I don't go to school by bike – I go by bus, with my friends. But every weekend, I go cycling with my brother, Michael. We've both got expensive bikes. I ride a Spanish bike. I love it. It's silver and black.

3 Nick I've got a computer in my room, and I use it a lot. I visit chat rooms and chat about new games. It's really interesting. My friends and I meet after school every day and play computer games for two or three hours.

4 Rachel We don't do it at school, but I go to a club near my home. I go on Thursdays, and I have lessons there. It's a difficult sport, but I really like it. My best friend goes to the same gymnastics club, so we have a good time together.

Exercise 5 page 18 🎧 1.29

* Allow a minute or two for students to read the exercise and see how many answers they can recall without listening again. Then play the recording once without stopping and check whether most students have got all the answers. With a **weaker class**, play it one more time, pausing after each bit of information relevant to the task.

KEY

1 Nick	4 Nick	7 Oliver
2 Rachel	5 Lauren	8 Lauren
3 Oliver	6 Rachel	

Exercise 6 page 18

* Students categorise the sports and hobbies according to their likes and dislikes. In a **stronger class**, ask them to add one more activity to each group. Help with vocabulary.

Exercise 7 page 18

* For this speaking activity, put students in pairs or groups of three with other classmates than those they usually work with – not their best friends – so that they find out about the likes and dislikes of someone they don't know very well. With a **stronger class,** teach the phrase *in common.* Write on the board: *What have you got in common?* Ask pairs to decide if they could spend an afternoon together!

Exercise 8 page 18

* Set up the activity carefully, so that students know exactly what they need to do. Students list all the activities from exercise 1 in a column, then make four extra columns for *I really like, I quite like, I don't like, I hate.*
* Explain they are going to stand up and interview everyone in the class to find out how much they like those activities. Elicit the question that they will need to ask: *Do you like...?* (With a **weaker class**, put the question on the board.) You may also model the responses: *Yes, I really like it. / Yes, I quite like it. / No, I don't like it. / No, I hate it!*
* Explain they have to mark the number of responses in the appropriate columns so that they can later count them. When you're confident everyone has understood what they're supposed to do, give the signal for everyone to stand up and begin. Monitor the activity.
* When the survey is completed, students return to their seats to write it up. Allow any in-depth analysis if it seems to generate some discussion or writing in English. Help students with the language they need to express their results in English.

For work on verb + noun collocations, go to:

Vocabulary Builder (part 2): Student's Book page 129

KEY

5 **play:** basketball, football, tennis
go: cycling, rollerblading, swimming
do: athletics, gymnastics, karate

6 Open answers

7
1 read	4 a film	7 watch
2 a photo	5 go for	8 chess
3 play	6 music	

8
1 plays	4 listens	7 go
2 goes	5 does	8 play
3 goes	6 plays	9 watch

9 Open answers

➡ Lesson outcome

Ask students: *What have we talked about today?* Elicit: *free time (activities)* or equivalent. Ask: *What useful words have you learned?* Accept any relevant answers. Draw the students' attention to the lesson statement: *I can talk about sports and hobbies.*

2B GRAMMAR
Present simple: questions

LESSON SUMMARY ● ● ● ● ●

Grammar: present simple questions
Listening: an interview; matching
Speaking: asking and answering questions

SHORTCUT *To do the lesson in 30 minutes, skip exercise 12 and set the Grammar Builder as homework.*

➡ Lead-in 2 minutes

* Write on the board: *What? Who? When? Where? How? Why?* and ask: *What do you think today's lesson will be about?* The expected answer is: *questions* (accept an answer in the students' own language) then you can inform students that the exact topic is: *Questions in the present simple tense.* Ask the class for equivalents of the question words on the board. Explain that present simple questions can begin with a question word or *Do / Does*, and that they will see both forms in this lesson.

Exercise 1 page 19

* Elicit the name of the sport in the photo.

KEY

snowboarding

Exercise 2 page 19 🎧 1.30

* Ask students to close their books. Explain that they are going to listen to an interview with a teenage snowboarding star.
* Pre-teach *competition.* Ask students to listen carefully to (*not* write down) the four questions that the interviewer asks. Play the recording once. Now students open their books and do exercise 2. Play the recording again to check.

KEY

1 c	2 a	3 d	4 b

Exercise 3 page 19

* Allow a minute or two for students to look at the *Learn this!* box and try to complete it, then read it as a class.

KEY

1 Do	3 don't	5 does
2 do	4 Does	6 doesn't

Exercise 4 page 19

- Read the example aloud. Do sentence 2 as a class (with a **weaker class**, do 2 and 3) then students continue individually. Check with the whole class. If there are errors, explain one more time:
- The basic form of a question in English is:
  auxiliary verb ('little grammatical verb') + subject (the person) + 'the rest of the verb'
  Or, to make it simpler, just for present simple tense:
  Do / Does + subject (the person) + infinitive
- *Do,* like all other verbs, has –s on the end of the 3rd person singular in the present simple tense: *he, she, it does.* When you use this form in a question, for example (write on the board): *Does he play chess?* you don't need another –s on the end of the main verb (point to where there is no –s after *play*) because you already have the one in *does.*

KEY

1 Do you go snowboarding?
2 Do your friends like computer games?
3 Does Wayne Rooney play football?
4 Do you watch a lot of films?
5 Does your best friend do athletics?
6 Do you like dancing?

LANGUAGE NOTE – SHORT ANSWERS

Short answers (*Yes, I do* and *No, I don't*) are difficult for students because the auxiliaries *do* and *does* are unfamiliar. However, it is important that they don't omit them since this will make them sound abrupt and impolite.

Exercise 5 page 19

- As students ask and answer the questions from exercise 4, circulate and monitor. Chat to **fast finishers**, asking additional questions or making comments.

Exercise 6 page 19

- Read the *Learn this!* box as a class. Elicit translations of the question words. Make sure students write them down unless they clearly know them.

Exercise 7 page 19

- Tell students they are going to hear the second part of the interview with Jed Bright in a moment. Ask them to read the instructions. Students work individually.

KEY

1 Where	3 How	5 When
2 Who	4 What	

Exercise 8 🎧 1.31

- Play the recording through once, then play it again stopping after each sentence with a gap in it. Ask students to repeat the questions as single tone units with the right intonation. Use the recording or yourself as a model. Point out the preposition at the end of a question in *Who do you live with?*

OPTIONAL ACTIVITY

In pairs, ask students to ask the five questions from exercise 7, but give true answers about themselves. Model the activity by asking a student with good pronunciation to ask you the four questions.

For further practice of present simple questions, go to:

Grammar Builder 2B: Student's Book page 110

KEY

1
2 Does, does	5 Does, doesn't	7 Do, do
3 Do, don't	6 Does, does	8 Do, don't
4 Do, do		

2
1 Do you like dancing?
2 Does your mum work?
3 Does your best friend play chess?
4 Do you speak Russian?
5 Do you and your friends go to the cinema?
6 Do you play computer games?

3 Open answers

4
1 How	3 When	5 Where
2 Who	4 What	

5
1 Where	3 When	5 What
2 Who	4 How	

6 Open answers

Exercise 9 page 19

- Students do the matching task in pairs. Check answers with the whole class, paying attention to pronunciation. Then let students ask and answer the questions.

KEY

1 c   2 e   3 a   4 b   5 d   6 f

Exercise 10 page 19

- Make sure students work with different partners than in the previous pairwork exercises, so they don't end up asking the same people the same questions. Both partners write questions (five each) on loose sheets of paper.

Exercise 11 page 19

- Partners swap sheets and answer each other's questions. Then they prepare to read the interviews aloud. They may decide which of the two sets of answers they find better/ more interesting/ funnier and choose to present those to the class. As students prepare the interviews, monitor their work so that you can choose the best ones to be presented to the whole class: those that are linguistically the best – especially where pronunciation is really clear – and the ones with the funniest ideas.

Exercise 12 page 19

- As pairs act out their interviews, take notes of errors and provide feedback. If a pair make a lot of errors, don't comment on them all; focus on the target language of the lesson.

➡ Lesson outcome

Ask students: *What did we do today?* Try to elicit: *questions,* but accept any response that shows a student learned something, even single new words. Briefly go over question words. Draw students' attention to the lesson statement: *I can ask about people's hobbies and interests.*

Notes for Photocopiable activity 2.1

Wayne Rooney Fact File
Pairwork
Language: present simple questions, question words
Materials: one copy of the worksheet per pair of students
(Teacher's Book page 125)
- Ask the class what they know about Wayne Rooney.
- Divide the class into two groups, A and B. Give out a copy of Worksheet A to the students in group A and Worksheet B to the students in group B. Students work in pairs with another student from the same group to write the questions that they will need to ask students in the other group in order to complete their fact files. Go round and check that the questions are correctly formed.
- Ask students to form new pairs so that each student with worksheet A is working with a student with Worksheet B. They mustn't look at each other's worksheets. Students take it in turns to ask the questions they have prepared. They write the answers in the spaces in their worksheets.
- When they have finished they can look at their partner's worksheet to check the answers.

2C CULTURE
Sport in Australia

LESSON SUMMARY ● ● ● ● ● ●
Reading: a text about sports in Australia
Listening: a profile of Ian Thorpe, Australian swimmer; true or false
Speaking: talking about sports and sportspeople
Topic: sport and culture

SHORTCUT *To do the lesson in 30 minutes, do exercise 6 quickly as a class, combining it with exercise 5. You may also ask students to read the text for the first time at home.*

➡ Lead-in 2 minutes
- With books closed, ask students: *When you think 'Australia', what do you think about?* You may find you have to explain in the students' own language that you mean first associations. As students produce their associations, help them with language. Finally, say: *Today we are going to talk about sport in Australia.*

Exercise 1 page 20
- It would be good to have a map of Australia on the wall for this lesson.
- The question about Australia, which first came up in the lead-in, is now narrowed down to cities and sportspeople.

KEY – Sample answers
Cities: Sydney, Melbourne, Perth, Brisbane, Adelaide
Sportspeople: Ian Thorpe (swimming), Lleyton Hewitt, Mark Philippousis (tennis), Shane Warne (cricket), Cathy Freeman (track athletics), Mike Doohan, Troy Bayliss (motorcycle racing)

Exercise 2 page 20
- Draw students' attention to the photos. Ask if they know the sports. When checking, ask: *Does anyone play rugby? Does anyone do any martial arts? Does anyone go horse riding?*

KEY

1 martial arts	4 cricket	7 horse riding
2 netball	5 rugby	
3 Australian Rules football	6 hockey	

CULTURE NOTE – SPORTS
Australian Rules Football is the national sport of Australia. It is a cross between football and rugby.

Cricket originated in England, but is very popular in Australia, and they often beat the English at it. *The Ashes* is a very important cricket competition in which the two nations play against each other.

Hockey is field hockey, which is played by boys and girls at school.

Netball is a game that is similar to basketball, but it is often played by girls and women. The rules are different, you are not allowed to run with the ball as you do in basketball, it has to be passed as soon as it is caught. Netball is a non-contact sport.

Exercise 3 page 20
- Students read the text. When going over the answers, you can ask: *Is it the same in your country (or different)?*

KEY
1 They love sport.
2 Because the weather is perfect and there are thousands of beaches.
3 Australian Rules football, rugby and cricket
4 netball, gymnastics and horse riding

Exercise 4 page 20 🎧 1.32
- Ask students if they have heard of Ian Thorpe. Tell them they are going to hear some information about him. Introduce the task and make sure students know they only need to listen for one piece of information at this point.

KEY
c

Transcript 1.32
Ian Thorpe is a famous swimmer. He's from Sydney, in Australia. He doesn't swim in competitions now but he's still very popular in Australia. And he's also popular with millions of people in other countries. He is very tall – nearly two metres – and he's got very big feet.

Sport is very popular in Ian's family. His father, Ken, plays cricket and his sister, Christina, is also a swimmer.

Ian Thorpe is an Olympic champion. He's got five gold medals from the Olympic games in 2000 and 2004. He also holds two world records.

But Ian Thorpe is not a typical Australian sportsman. He isn't really interested in other sports, like football or cricket. His hobby is fashion. He wears expensive clothes and has a company that makes jewellery.

Exercise 5 page 20 🎧 1.32
- Play the recording as many times as students need to listen. Check with the whole class.

KEY

1 T	2 F	3 F	4 F	5 T	6 F	7 T

Exercise 6 page 20

- This exercise can be done together with exercise 5 – when checking the answers to 5, ask *why* the false ones are false.

KEY

2 He's got big feet.
3 She's also a swimmer.
4 He's got five gold medals.
6 He isn't interested in other sports.

Exercise 7 page 20

- Students agree on 'top five' lists of popular sports in groups of 3–5. Then have a class discussion and see if agreement is possible.

OPTIONAL ACTIVITY

Put students in pairs or groups of three. Make sure there is someone who's interested in sport in every group. In groups, ask students to think of a European sportsperson. What do they know about him/her? Write sentences on the board or display them on the OHP, for example:

X is a … (swimmer/ footballer/…) from … (*city/ country?*)
He/She is … years old.
He/She is … (tall/short/thin/…)
He/She has got … (*how many?*) medals.
He/She is also interested in …

Ask the teams to write as much information as they can about their sportsperson, using some of the structures on the board. Allow 3–4 minutes. Circulate and help with language. All groups read out their profiles.

➡ Lesson outcome

Ask students: *What have we talked about today?* Elicit: *Australia/ sport/ sport in Australia.* Elicit some facts students have learned in the lesson. Draw students' attention to the lesson statement: *I can talk about popular sports and activities*.

2D GRAMMAR Adverbs of frequency

LESSON SUMMARY ● ● ● ● ○ ○
Grammar/Vocabulary: adverbs of frequency
Listening: short monologues
Speaking: talking about how often we do things

SHORTCUT *To do the lesson in 30 minutes, do exercise 6 as a class and skip exercise 9 or set the Grammar Builder as homework*

➡ Lead-in 2 minutes

- Ask students to look at the title of the lesson in the book: *Adverbs of frequency*. Write it on the board. Ask if anyone knows the equivalent of *frequency*. Ask if anyone knows *adverbs* – they probably won't, so tell them the equivalent, and make sure they understand the meaning. Elicit either some examples in the students' own language or a general explanation. Once you're reasonably confident students understand what *adverbs of frequency* are, proceed with the lesson.

Exercise 1 page 21

- Draw students' attention to the pictures and ask a few students: *Do you go bowling in your free time? Do you go dancing? How often do you go? Who do you go with?*

Exercise 2 page 21 🎧 1.33

- Play the recording once. Check answers.
- With a **stronger class**, ask: *What else does Jacob do on Saturdays? What else does Kirsty do?* and elicit: *He has football practice, does homework, plays tennis, goes out with friends. She watches TV, checks e-mails, visits a chat room, and goes shopping.* If someone says that Jacob watches TV, point out that he says: *I hardly ever watch TV – the programmes are always boring* and ask: *So what do you think 'hardly ever' means?* Accept any answer that's close in meaning, e.g. *not much, not often, almost never, almost not*, then explain: *'hardly ever' means 'almost never'* (write on the board: *hardly ever = almost never*).

KEY

bowling: Jacob   **dancing:** Kirsty

Exercise 3 page 21 🎧 1.34

- Draw students' attention to the chart and make sure everyone understands it is supposed to show adverbs in order of increasing frequency. With a **weaker class**, you may want to do one or two adverbs (e.g. *first* and *last*) with the whole class. Play the recording once for students to listen and check. Then play it again and ask students to repeat first individually, then chorally. Say that these words are the *adverbs of frequency* that are the subject of today's lesson.

KEY

1 never   3 often   5 always
2 hardly ever 4 usually

Exercise 4 page 21

- In a **stronger class**, there's no need to check this exercise by reading aloud; just look over students' shoulders as they're doing it.

KEY

Jacob: I always have football practice on Saturday morning. I usually do homework. I sometimes play tennis. I hardly ever watch TV. The programmes are always really boring. I always go out with friends. We often go bowling. I'm usually in bed before midnight.
Kirsty: I usually get up late. I never have breakfast. I usually check my e-mails. I never buy a phone. They're always very expensive. I always go dancing. I'm often out until two o'clock.

Exercise 5 page 21

- Ask students to look back at the sentences they underlined in exercise 4 and try to complete the rules. Allow 1–2 minutes, then write these examples on the board:
  I sometimes play tennis at the sports centre.
  I always go out with friends.
  I'm usually in bed before midnight.
  Write or underline the adverbs in one colour and the verbs in another, so that their relative position is clearly visible. Discuss the position of adverbs of frequency – after *be*, but before most other verbs – using the examples and pointing to the words.

KEY

a after
b before

Exercise 6 page 21

- Read the example and do sentences 2 and 3 as a class. Students do the rest individually, then check as a class.

KEY

2 Kirsty usually gets up late on Saturday morning.
3 Kirsty never has breakfast on Saturday morning.
4 Jacob sometimes plays tennis on Saturday afternoon.
5 Kirsty never buys a mobile phone on Saturday afternoon.
6 Jacob and Kirsty always go out with friends on Saturday evening.
7 Jacob is usually in bed before midnight on Saturday night.
8 Kirsty is often in the dance club until two o'clock on Saturday night.

For further practice of adverbs of frequency, go to:

Grammar Builder 2D: Student's Book page 110

KEY

7 1 I'm never late for school.
2 I always speak English in English class.
3 I often do my homework before dinner.
4 I hardly ever read a book in English.
5 I sometimes help my friends with their homework.
6 I'm usually happy with my exam results.

8 Open answers

> ### LANGUAGE NOTE – VERB AND NOUN COMBINATIONS
>
> Where other languages use just a verb to express an idea, English sometimes uses a combination of verb and noun, e.g. *have breakfast, go swimming*. Encourage students to record and learn these as one item.

Exercise 7 page 21

- Pre-teach *relatives* and *(to do) the washing up*. Ask students to read the instructions, then model the task by asking one or two students: *How often do you do homework at the weekend?* when the student responds, *Always*, say: *So, write 'always' in column 1.*

Exercise 8 page 21

- Before students start speaking, practise the questions they have to ask: *How often do you do homework at the weekend? How often do you visit relatives at the weekend?*

Exercise 9 page 21

- Ask a few students to tell the whole class 3–4 things they found out about their partner.

➡ Lesson outcome

Ask students: *What was this lesson about?* in the hope of eliciting: *adverbs of frequency* and having a laugh together at this sophisticated term. Accept an answer in the students' own language, or answers such as *how often* or *always*, etc. Ask students to say one adverb of frequency each until you've elicited them all. Draw students' attention to the lesson statement: *I can talk about daily routines.*

2E READING
Kung fu

LESSON SUMMARY ● ● ● ○ ○

Reading: an interview; true or false
Vocabulary: parts of the body
Listening: a song
Topic: sport and culture

SHORTCUT *To do the lesson in 30 minutes, ask students to read the text for the first time at home, and possibly do task 4.*

➡ Lead-in 2 minutes

- Ask students to take pieces of scrap paper and write down any names of parts of the body they know. Allow 30–60 seconds. Ask everybody to read one word from their list until there are no more new words. Tell them they are going to learn more names of parts of the body.

Exercise 1 page 22

- Point to the photo. Ask: *What sport is this?* Elicit the name of the sport, and confirm that word used in English is *yoga*. Ask students to label the parts of the body in the picture. Allow the use of dictionaries. Monitor students' progress and stop after most of them have finished. **Fast finishers** can use the dictionary to label a few more parts of the body.

KEY

1 mouth	6 neck	11 hands	16 feet
2 nose	7 shoulders	12 stomach	17 toes
3 eyes	8 chest	13 back	
4 head	9 fingers	14 knees	
5 ears	10 arms	15 legs	

Exercise 2 page 22 🎧 1.35

- Play the recording for the students to check their answers, and then again for them to repeat. Pay attention especially to the pronunciation of the final /z/ (not /s/) in *arms, eyes, ears, fingers, legs, shoulders* and *toes*, and to the reduced vowel /ə/ in the final syllables in *shoulders* and *stomach*.

Exercise 3 page 22

- Students test each other on the words.

Exercise 4 page 22

- Draw students' attention to the photographs. Ask: *What is this text about?* Elicit: *kung fu*, or just *martial arts*. Read the introductory paragraph aloud. Explain that first you want students to read the text quickly and do a simple task. Read the reading tip as a class. Allow 2 minutes for students to read the interview and do the task.

KEY

3 is true.

Exercise 5 page 23

- Allow two minutes. You can make it a race, if you think this will motivate your students.

KEY

legs, arms, stomachs, hands, feet

Exercise 6 page 23

- Students now read the text a second time, more carefully, and answer more detailed questions. Make sure dictionaries are available. As part of vocabulary work, you can ask a sporty student to demonstrate *press-ups*!
- When checking the answers, ask: *Why? Why not?* and require students to quote specific sentences from the text. With a **stronger class**, ask for more details, e.g. *David wants to teach Kung Fu in Britain. – What else does he want to do?*

KEY

1 F	2 F	3 T	4 F	5 F	6 T

OPTIONAL ACTIVITY

Ask students: *Would you like to train like David? Why?/Why not?* Try to elicit some reasons *why* and some *why not*. Then explain the meaning of the title: *No pain, no gain*. (You can do this part in the students' own language if you think your students will understand better.) Explain that it is a proverb, and that *pain* doesn't necessarily mean physical pain, but effort, difficulty or sacrifice. Ask if they agree with this statement.

Exercise 7 page 23

- Especially with a **weaker class,** remind students what the structure of a question in present simple is:
  (question word +) *do*/*does* + subject (the person) + infinitive
- Circulate and monitor, helping weaker students. Go over answers as a class.

KEY

1 Where does David come from?
2 What does he study in China?
3 What do they/the kung fu students have for breakfast and for dinner?/ What do they eat?
4 Why does he like the afternoons?
5 When do they have dinner?

CULTURE NOTE – KUNG FU FIGHTING

Kung Fu Fighting was sung by Carl Douglas, a Jamaican singer, in the 1970s. Since then there have been several remixes of the song.

Exercise 8 page 23 🎧 1.36

- Tell students they are going to listen to a song about kung fu.
- With a **stronger class**, start with books closed, ask students to listen and try to hear some words or phrases. Play the song once, ask for any words or phrases they heard, then proceed to the next step.
- Ask students to read the gapped lyrics and the glossary first, then point out the task. Play the whole song through once, then play it again stopping after each gap to check.

KEY

1	are	4	knows	7	Start
2	fight	5	says	8	makes
3	are	6	take		

ADDITIONAL SPEAKING TASK

Ask which students in the class do or have done a sport fairly seriously and intensively. It would be ideal if there were no less than 50% of such students: each of them could then work with one less sporty partner. If sportspeople are scarce, students can work in groups of three: one sportsperson and two interviewers. The task is to prepare an interview.

- Groups decide if the interview will be about the sportsperson's usual training routine and lifestyle, or about a camp he/she has been to. In the latter case, they have to imagine that he/she is still at the camp and is being interviewed there.
- Groups look through the questions in the interview with David and in exercise 7 and decide which of them will be relevant to their interview.
- Interviewers prepare some questions of their own. The sportsperson helps them by suggesting what would be interesting to ask about. Remind them they can also look for inspiration in lesson 2C. Circulate and monitor, helping with vocabulary and checking if questions are grammatically accurate.
- Interviewers ask their questions and the sportsperson answers. Monitor this activity quite closely, helping with language, but also selecting the most attractive-sounding interviews to be acted out in front of the class. If there are two interviewers, make sure each of them asks some questions.
- A few groups act out their interviews in front of the class. Give feedback on strengths and weaknesses.

➡ Lesson outcome

Ask students: *What have we studied today?* Accept any relevant answers (including single words), but try to elicit: *parts of the body*. Ask everyone to close their books and say one word for a body part in turn; they mustn't repeat words that have already been said. Draw students' attention to the lesson statement: *I can understand a magazine article about sport.*

2F EVERYDAY ENGLISH
Giving an opinion

LESSON SUMMARY ● ● ● ○ ○

Functional English: phrases to express likes and dislikes
Listening: short dialogues; listening for specific information
Speaking: talking about likes and dislikes
Grammar: object pronouns
Topic: people

SHORTCUT *To do the lesson in 30 minutes, set the second exercise in the Grammar Builder as homework and keep the performances in exercise 9 brief.*

➡ Lead-in 2 minutes

- With books closed, ask a student the two questions which will appear in the dialogue in exercise 1: *Do you like music?* and, *Who's your favourite singer?* Ask one or two other students: *Do you like (the singer mentioned by the first student)? Which singer do you like?* and so on. Say: *Today we are going to talk about likes and dislikes.*

Exercise 1 page 24   1.37

- Ask students to open their books, look at the photos and read the instructions. Play the recording and ask the question in exercise 1.

KEY

Eminem

Exercise 2 page 24

- Students do the exercise individually. Help **weaker students**: if someone doesn't understand the meaning of one of the phrases, say it to them in a tone of voice showing a critical/neutral/enthusiastic attitude.

KEY

bad	quite good	good
He's terrible.	He's all right.	I love it.
I can't stand it.	She's not bad.	She's great.
I hate them.	They're OK.	They're brilliant.
It's awful.		

Exercise 3 page 24   1.38

- Play the recording once for students to check their answers to exercise 2. Then play it again pausing after each phrase for students to repeat: first individually, then chorally. Encourage students to say the phrases with real, or even exaggerated, feeling: *I can't stand it* with disgust, *She's great* with enthusiasm, *They're OK* with a shrug, etc.

Exercise 4 page 24

- Monitor as students do the task individually, then check as a class and write answers on the board.

KEY

1 her   2 it

For further practice of object pronouns, go to:

Grammar Builder 2F: Student's Book page 110

KEY

9 Open answers

10 1 We don't know them.   4 She hardly ever phones me.
      2 I can't find her.   5 They never listen to us.
      3 I don't like him.   6 Do you like it?

CULTURE NOTE – CELEBRITIES

Avril Lavigne is a Canadian born singer song-writer now living in the USA. She became famous at the age of 17 when her album *Let Go* reached the US Top 10 in 2002. Her music is a mixture of pop and skater punk.

Robbie Williams is one of Britain's most successful singer song-writers. He was a member of the boy band *Take That* and went solo in 1996.

Eminem is an American rapper. He is famous for his lyrics, which have been described as modern-day poetry, but which are controversial because of their offensive content.

Angelina Jolie is an American actress famous for her role as Lara Croft in *Tomb Raider,* and Mrs Smith in *Mr and Mrs Smith*. She is married to Brad Pitt.

Exercise 5 page 24

- Illustrate the function of the object pronouns by writing an example on the board, e.g.: *He is great. – I like **him**. **They** are awful. – I hate **them**.*
- Ask a few students the question in the example, *What do you think of Robbie Williams?* Elicit appropriate responses. Students then proceed to talk in pairs.

Exercise 6 page 24   1.39

- Ask students to read the instructions and the three statements. Play the dialogues once, stopping after each one to check the answer.

KEY

1 a   2 b   3 a

Transcript 1.39

1

Jenny	Do you like sport?
Chris	Yes, I do.
Jenny	What's your favourite sport?
Chris	Volleyball.
Jenny	Volleyball? Really? I hate volleyball. It's so boring!
Chris	So, what do you like, then?
Jenny	I like athletics.
Chris	Urgh. Athletics is awful.
Jenny	And I like cycling.
Chris	Yes, I like cycling, too.

2

Kylie	Are you interested in computer games?
Jeff	Yes, I am.
Kylie	I love *The Sims*. It's brilliant.
Jeff	It's OK, I suppose. But I don't really like it.
Kylie	What games do you like?
Jeff	I love *Tomb Raider*.
Kylie	Really? I can't stand it.
Jeff	And *Grand Theft Auto* is great.
Kylie	Yeah, it's brilliant.

3

Grace	Is that a fashion magazine?
Charlie	Yes, it is. I'm really interested in fashion.
Grace	Me too. Who's your favourite designer?
Charlie	Armani.
Grace	Really? I don't like Armani clothes.
Charlie	Look at these jeans – they're Diesel. Do you like them?
Grace	Let me see … Not really. I don't like Diesel jeans. But I like those sunglasses.
Charlie	Are they Ray-Bans?
Grace	Yes, they are. I love Ray-Bans.
Charlie	Me too.

Exercise 7 page 24   1.40

- First students try to fill in the gaps without listening again. When most of them have finished, or have done as much as they can, play the recording to check / complete the answers. Get students to repeat the sentences (play the recording stopping in the right place), or model the pronunciation yourself.

KEY

1	What	3	interested	5	really
2	like	4	OK	6	Who

Exercise 8 page 24

- Explain to students that they are now going to talk about their favourite hobbies. Point to the chart and the prompts. Ask pairs to prepare conversations. Encourage **stronger students** to write prompts or notes rather than whole dialogues. Circulate and monitor.

Exercise 9 page 24

- Several pairs act out their conversations. Remind students to speak loudly and clearly. If they are expressing strong opinions, encourage them to speak with feeling.

➡ Lesson outcome

Ask students: *What did we talk about today?* Elicit: *opinions, likes and dislikes* or *what we like and don't like.* Ask: *Can you remember some phrases which you can use to say you like someone/something very much? That you don't like something? That something is not bad?* Elicit as many of the relevant phrases as you can; insist on correct intonation. Draw students' attention to the lesson statement: *I can express my likes and dislikes.*

Notes for Photocopiable activity 2.2

Your likes and dislikes

Pairwork

Language: likes and dislikes, present simple (third person)
Materials: one copy of the worksheet per student (Teacher's Book page 126)

- Students work individually to write the name of something or someone that they either love or hate, for each category.
- Elicit the language from lesson 2F exercise 2 for expressing likes and dislikes onto the board.
- Demonstrate the activity by writing on the board the name of a film. Elicit the question: *What do you think of ...?* Answer using the language from Lesson 2F e.g. *It's awful – I can't stand it!*
- Students take it in turns to ask their partners: *What do you think of ...?* They tick the appropriate box for each answer.
- Conduct an open class feedback, asking students to tell the class about their partner, e.g. *Ania quite likes Coldplay.*

2G WRITING
An announcement

LESSON SUMMARY

Writing: an announcement
Reading: announcements; reading for specific information
Grammar: imperatives
Topic: People

SHORTCUT *To do the lesson in 30 minutes, set the writing task as homework. With a weaker class, have the students write a draft in class and a finished version at home.*

➡ Lead-in 2–3 minutes

- Draw students' attention to the announcements on page 25. Say: *We've got two announcements here. What are they for? What are they telling you to do?* (Elicit *film club, chess club* or *come to film club, play chess.*) Briefly find out by a show of hands who prefers chess, and who likes films.

Exercise 1 page 25

- Find out whether any students go to clubs.

Exercise 2 page 25

- Students read and work out the answers individually. Circulate and help. After checking the answers with the whole class, ask: *Which club would you prefer to go to?* With a **stronger class**, the discussion can go on: *Why? What kinds of films do you like? Do you play chess well? Who do you play with?*

KEY

	film club	chess club
1	Thursday at four o'clock	Tuesday at six o'clock
2	at Lauren's house	in Gino's Café
3	watch and talk about DVDs	play chess
4	meet to decide the next 4 films	have a competition
5	Lauren White	Lewis Connor

Exercise 3 page 25

- Read the *Learn this!* box. Make sure students understand the meaning of *imperative*. You can explain in the students' own language.

KEY

Come (to film club)! Play (chess)
Call Lauren White Phone Lewis Connor today
Use (your head) **Negative:** Don't wait.

Exercise 4 page 25

- Students can do the task individually and check with their partners, or do it in pairs. Go over answers with the whole class.

KEY

1 Come 4 Meet 7 Don't forget
2 Play 5 Learn
3 Don't stay 6 Visit

For further practice of imperatives, go to:

Grammar Builder 2G: Student's Book page 110

KEY

1 f 2 e 3 d 4 c 5 b 6 a

Exercise 5 page 25

- This could be done in pairs. Allow students to work with someone with shared interests. Doing this stage in pairs means the writing will probably also be done together and so will have to be done in class.

Exercise 6 page 25

- Circulate and help with any special vocabulary. Encourage **fast finishers** to invent more information than the chart requires.

Exercise 7 page 25

- If students invented a club in pairs, the writing is better done in class. Otherwise it can be set as homework. Remind students of the resources they've got: the two model announcements, and possibly vocabulary from the rest of unit 2 (free-time activities). Encourage creative students to produce attractive posters to put on the walls.

ALTERNATIVE WRITING TASK

If the previous writing task was done in class, this one can be set for homework. Ask students to imagine they want to organise an event (this word will probably need explaining, but it may be explained through the examples) – a party, a disco, a concert for people from school. They are going to write an announcement about this event.

With a **weaker class**, you may want to photocopy the table below and hand it out to students. With a **stronger class,** you may show the table on an OHP and discuss the points to include, or write the main points and sentence openings on the board.

Points	Useful language
What event?	Come to _____
Activities	Play ____ / Dance _____ / Listen _____ / See _____ / Buy ____ / Eat ____ / _____ There will be _____
Time	When? On _____ at _____
Place	Where? In/At _____
How to join	Tickets? /Phone _____ ? / Just come

➡ Lesson outcome

Ask students: *What have we talked about today?* Elicit: *announcements* or *clubs* Elicit a few phrases that can be used in an announcement. Draw the students' attention to the lesson statement: *I can write an announcement for a club.*

LANGUAGE REVIEW 1–2

1 1 a   2 a   3 b   4 b   5 a

2 1 wives   3 photos   5 buses
    2 husbands   4 potatoes   6 families

3 1 basketball   3 gymnastics   5 photography
    2 computer games   4 ice skating   6 rollerblading

4 1 studies   3 goes   5 live
    2 play   4 watches   6 gets up

5 2 She doesn't sit next to Pete. She sits next to Sue.
    3 I play the piano. I don't play the guitar.
    4 He doesn't go swimming. He goes cycling.
    5 They come from France. They don't come from Spain.
    6 She teaches music. She doesn't teach sport.
    7 He doesn't speak English. He speaks Italian.

6 1 Where do you live? f
    2 Does he like sport? c
    3 What does she study? a
    4 How do you get to school? d
    5 Does she get up early? b
    6 Do you know Lucas? e

7 2 She's hardly ever late for school.
    3 I often play computer games.
    4 He never does his homework on the bus.
    5 It's usually cold in January.
    6 School always finishes at quarter past four.
    7 We sometimes have lunch at school.

8 1 How   2 Where are   3 Have you got
    4 How old is

9 1 c   2 a   3 e   4 b   5 d

SKILLS ROUND-UP 1–2

1 paragraph 1 – a a Hungarian in the UK
    paragraph 2 – b people from abroad in the UK
    paragraph 3 – b people from abroad in the UK

2 1 c   2 c   3 b   4 b   5 b   6 c

Transcript 1.40

Narrator	Márton is at his home in London. He lives there with five other young people. One of them is Anna, from Portugal.
Anna	Hi, Márton. How are you?
Márton	Oh, hi Anna. I'm fine, thanks.
Anna	Márton, this is my sister, Claudia.
Márton	Hi, Claudia. Nice to meet you.
Claudia	Nice to meet you too. Where are you from?
Márton	I'm from Miskolc.
Claudia	In Hungary?
Márton	Yes. It's in the east of Hungary.
Claudia	Have you got any brothers or sisters?
Márton	Yes, I have. I've got two sisters.
Claudia	Really? How old are they?
Márton	They're only 10 and 14. They live in Hungary, with my parents.
Claudia	Oh, I see. So you're here in England on your own.
Márton	Yes, that's right. What about you? Do you live in London?
Claudia	No, I don't. I live in Portugal.
Anna	Claudia is here on holiday. She wants to see London.
Claudia	And see my sister!
Márton	Well, have a good holiday. London is a great place!
Claudia	Yes, I know. My sister loves the shops …
…	
Narrator	It's quarter to ten on Monday morning. Márton is at the hotel. He starts work at ten o'clock.
Dave	Hi! You're early today.
Márton	Oh, hi, Dave. How are you?
Dave	Fine thanks.
Márton	Is the hotel busy today?
Dave	Yes, it is. We've got twenty new visitors from Spain. They're here for a conference. [PHONE RINGS] Sorry, Márton. [PICKS UP PHONE] Hello, reception? Yes, of course. No problem. Goodbye. [REPLACES PHONE]
Márton	What's that? A new CD?
Dave	Yes – it's The Scissor Sisters.
Márton	Oh right. Who?
Dave	The Scissor Sisters. Do you like music?
Márton	Yes, I do. But I don't know the Scissor Sisters. Are they good?
Dave	I love them! Who's your favourite singer or band?
Márton	I really like U2.
Dave	Really? Urgh. I can't stand them!

3 Anna is d   Claudia is b   Dave is a

4 1 Miskolc   3 10 and 14   5 U2
    2 Yes, two sisters   4 Yes, I do.

5–6 Open answers

EXAM For further exam tasks and practice, go to Workbook page 24. Procedural notes, transcripts and keys for the Workbook can be found on the *Solutions* Teacher's Website at www.oup.com/elt/teacher/solutions

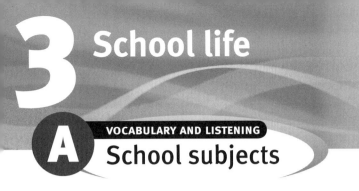

3 School life

A VOCABULARY AND LISTENING
School subjects

THIS UNIT INCLUDES ● ● ● ●

Vocabulary • school subjects • in the classroom • prepositions of place
• parts of a school • directions • capital letters
Grammar • there is/there are • have to
Speaking • talking about subjects and timetables • describing a classroom
• giving directions
Writing • a description
WORKBOOK pages 26–32

LESSON SUMMARY ● ● ● ● ● ●

Vocabulary: school subjects, classroom vocabulary
Listening: short dialogues; recognizing the situation
Speaking: talking about the school timetable
Topic: school

SHORTCUT *To do the lesson in 30 minutes, skip exercise 7.*

➡ Lead-in 2 minutes

- Ask students: *How many lessons have you got today? What lesson did you have before English? What lesson do you have next? Is today a good school day or a bad one? Why?* and announce: *Today we're going to talk about school subjects.*

Exercise 1 page 28

Students do the matching exercise individually or in pairs.

KEY
See transcript 1.42

Exercise 2 page 28 🎧 1.42

- Play the recording once for students to check their answers to exercise 1. Play it a second time, pausing after each item and asking students to repeat first individually, then chorally.
- If students' pronunciation needs correcting, keep repeating the word/phrase yourself so that they have a model to imitate. Pay particular attention to *technology* and *chemistry*.

Transcript 1.42

1 music	6 information and communication technology (I.C.T.)
2 English	7 art and design
3 maths	8 geography
4 religious education (R.E.)	9 history
5 Spanish	10 biology

Not illustrated: chemistry   design and technology (D.T.)
French   German   physical education (P.E.)   physics

Exercise 3 page 28

- Chat with students about which subjects they study at school. Especially with a **stronger class**, you may tell students that we also say to *take* or *do* a subject.

CULTURE NOTE – SUBJECTS

There are some points to note about subjects in English schools.

R.E.: In the British system R.E. includes knowledge about many different religions.

Design and Technology varies in different schools in Britain. If the school has the facilities, it may include practical skills such as woodwork, otherwise a school may choose to focus more on the design element. It is a creative subject but also involves aspects of engineering.

Art and design is a practical subject. Students learn art skills and have the opportunity to work with different media, such as photography, pottery, fabrics, etc. It may include an art history component in some schools.

For further practice of school subjects, go to:

Vocabulary Builder (part 1): Student's Book page 130

KEY

1 **Monday:** Lesson 1 is Spanish. Lesson 2 is music. Lesson 3 is P.E. Lesson 4 is art and design. Lesson 5 is French. Lesson 6 is I.C.T. Lesson 7 is D.T. Lesson 8 is German.
Tuesday: Lesson 1 is English. Lesson 2 is maths. Lesson 3 is geography. Lesson 4 is R.E. Lesson 5 is history. Lesson 6 is biology. Lesson 7 is chemistry. Lesson 8 is physics.
2 Open answers

Exercise 4 page 28

- Students read the instructions, the box and the example. To make sure everyone understands what the exchange should sound like, ask a student: *Do you like biology?* After eliciting an answer, ask another student: *What about you? Do you like biology?* After receiving an answer, ask two students to ask and answer about the next subject in the box, chemistry. Ask students to work in pairs, go through the whole list of subjects in exercise 1 and take turns to express an opinion on each (unless it's a subject they don't study.)

Exercise 5 page 28 🎧 1.43

- Explain that students are going to hear seven short extracts of lessons and their task is to understand what lesson it is and write the name of the subject in the timetable (explain *timetable* – the simplest way may be to point to the one in the book and say something like: *This is a timetable: eight forty-five to nine thirty, maths. Nine thirty-five to ten twenty... something else, maybe English or biology. That's a school timetable.*) Make sure everyone knows what they're supposed to do. Say you are going to play the recording twice. Read the listening tip aloud.
- Play the recording once pausing very briefly between the extracts, so that students can write down their answers. The second time stop after each extract and check answers.
- Finally, you can ask students if they think this is a good or a bad timetable. Why do they think so?

KEY

1 maths		4 P.E.		7 chemistry
2 French		5 geography		
3 music		6 I.C.T.		

36   Unit 3 • School life

Transcript 1.43

Lesson 1

Teacher   OK, settle down. Now, open your books at page 43. Let's check your homework. Question 1, Sonia.
Sonia   Yes?
Teacher   What's the answer?
Sonia   The answer to …
Teacher   Question 1!
Sonia   Is it 4, 763, 976?
Teacher   No, the correct answer is ten.
Sonia   Oh.

Lesson 2

Teacher   Bonjour! Asseyez-vous!
Class   Huh?
Teacher   Asseyez-vous!
Belinda   That means 'sit down'.
Teacher   Merci, Belinda.

Lesson 3

Teacher   OK, now listen to this. Do you know the composer?
Sonia   Is it Mozart?
Teacher   No, it isn't. Any other ideas? No?
Luke   Chopin?
Teacher   Excellent. Yes, it's Chopin.

Lesson 4

Teacher   OK, so do you all know the rules of basketball?
Class   Yes. Yes.
Teacher   Great! So, now we need two teams.
Jack   Boys against girls!
Class   Yes!
Teacher   OK. Boys against girls!

Lesson 5

Teacher   OK, today's lesson is about Africa. What do you know about Africa. Jack?
Jack   Is it in Australia?
Teacher   Jack! Africa is a continent.
Jack   Oh.
Teacher   Can you name any countries in Africa?
Belinda   Egypt?
Teacher   Good!

Lesson 6

Teacher   Good, now … can everybody see a computer?
Class   Yes. Yes.
Teacher   Today's lesson is about the Internet – how it works, why it's important …
Jack   Yes! I win!
Teacher   What's that, Jack?
Jack   Oh, sorry. Nothing.
Teacher   Is that a computer game?
Jack   No, it's a … er … it's a website.
Teacher   Hmm. Well, just pay attention.

Lesson 7

Teacher   Good. Now, add the red liquid to the mixture. Just a very small amount – one or two millilitres. And be careful because …

Exercise 6 page 28

- Before students start writing the timetables, agree on a template: will the lesson starting and finishing times be the same as in exercise 5, or the same as in your school? Students write their dream timetables. As an **optional activity**, you can also ask everyone, or just **fast finishers** to write a 'horror timetable' – the worst timetable for a day they can imagine.

Exercise 7 page 28

- For this activity, each student needs to sketch a blank timetable (of the kind agreed on for the previous exercise) on a loose sheet of paper. Students work in pairs – preferably not with their best friends, who might be able to guess their choices of lessons. They ask and answer questions as in the example. Emphasise that they should try to write down each other's timetables without looking at them.

For further practice of classroom vocabulary and prepositions of place, go to:

Vocabulary Builder (part 2): Student's Book page 130

KEY

3
1	blind	7	clock	13	CD player
2	window	8	board	14	CDs
3	plant	9	shelves	15	table
4	notice board	10	books	16	bin
5	TV	11	cupboard	17	chair
6	poster	12	computer	18	desk

4   Open answers

5
1	opposite	4	in front of	7	under
2	between	5	next to	8	near
3	behind	6	in	9	on

6   Open answers

➡ Lesson outcome

Ask students: *What did we talk about today?* Elicit: *school* or *subjects*. Ask everyone to say one useful word they learned. Accept all answers mentioning lexical items which appeared in the lesson. Draw students' attention to the lesson statement: *I can talk about my school subjects.*

3B GRAMMAR *there is/there are*

LESSON SUMMARY ● ● ● ○ ○

Grammar: *there is/there are*
Vocabulary: names of furniture and objects; prepositions of place
Speaking: asking and answering questions about your bedroom; saying where things are.

SHORTCUT   *To do the lesson in 30 minutes, do exercises 6 and 7 as a class, and set the Grammar Builder as homework.*

➡ Lead-in 2–3 minutes

- Ask students to take a loose sheet of scrap paper each and write down at least five things they can see in the classroom. Allow 30–45 seconds. Ask 5–7 students to say one word from their list. Choose two of the words they give and write on the board:
There is a _____ in this room.
There are _____ _____ in this room. (plural noun with a number)
- Say: *Today we are going to work on sentences like these, with there is …/ there are …*

Exercise 1 page 29

- Ask students to open their books and look at the photo on page 29. Where do they think this classroom is? With a **stronger class**, get the students to describe what they see in the photo.

KEY

It's in India.

Exercise 2 page 29

- As students read, you may need to explain *noticeboard, large,* and possibly *motivation*.

Exercise 3 page 29

- Complete the table as a class. Go through each of the different forms on the blackboard. Use translations if necessary.

KEY

1 There are	3 There aren't	5 Are there
2 There isn't	4 Is there	

Exercise 4 page 29

- Make sure students understand that they are supposed to make *true sentences about the photo*. Do the first three sentences as a class. In a **weaker class**, you may want to do the whole exercise together, but make sure weaker students get a chance to produce some answers!

KEY

1 There are some boys.	5 There isn't a noticeboard.
2 There isn't a teacher.	6 There isn't a TV.
3 There isn't a computer.	7 There aren't any shelves.
4 There aren't any posters.	8 There are five girls.

LANGUAGE NOTE – *BOARD*

If students get confused, explain that *board* is a general term to describe either a *blackboard,* which is written on with chalk or a *whiteboard,* which is written on with ink that can be washed off. A *noticeboard* (as in exercise 1), as the name suggests, has posters and notices pinned onto it.

Exercise 5 page 29 🎧 1.44

- Play the recording once. Check if students are sure of all the answers now. If they are not, play it again.

Exercise 6 page 29

- Ask students to read through the sentences in exercise 4 again and tick the ones that are true for your classroom. Ask them to read out *only the ones that are true*. **Fast finishers** or **stronger classes** can modify the sentences that are false to make them true.

For further practice on there is / there are, *go to:*

Grammar Builder 3B: Student's Book page 112

KEY

1 1 There are	4 There's	7 There's
2 There's	5 There are	8 There's
3 There are	6 There are	

---

2 1 There isn't a computer in the room.
   2 There aren't 650 students in the school.
   3 There aren't two possible answers.
   4 There isn't a teacher in the classroom.
   5 There isn't a table next to the door.
   6 There aren't three plants near the window.
   7 There aren't five shelves near the board.
   8 There isn't a bin under the desk.

3 3 Is there a notice board? No, there isn't.
   4 Are there any students? Yes, there are.
   5 Is there a clock? Yes, there is.
   6 Is there a table? No, there isn't.
   7 Are there any CDs? No, there aren't.
   8 Are there any blinds? Yes, there are.

Exercise 7 page 29

- If students did not do Vocabulary Builder (part 2) in lesson 3A, it would be helpful if dictionaries were available. Circulate and help **weaker students** build the questions.

KEY

3 Is there a	7 Are there any	11 Is there a
4 Is there a	8 Is there a	12 Is there a
5 Are there any	9 Are there any	13 Are there any
6 Is there a	10 Are there any	14 Is there a

Exercise 8 page 29

- Before asking students to do the activity, demonstrate the meaning of the prepositions in the box using the bin and your desk (or another pair of objects): *Now the bin is **under** my desk ... now it's **in front of** the desk ... now it's **on** the desk ...* You may repeat the activity with the students calling out the right prepositions the second time.
- Do the first 4–6 sentences in open pairs; then let students do the rest in closed pairs.

Exercise 9 page 29

- You may encourage students to sketch plans of their bedrooms as they talk about them. Start with an outline of the room with just the window(s) and the door marked. Student A asks: *Are there any chairs in your bedroom?* Student B answers: *Yes, there is one chair in front of my desk, and the desk is next to the window,* at the same time drawing the desk and the chair. When the plan of Student B's bedroom is complete, Student B starts asking questions and Student A answers and draws. Demonstrate how to do the activity by sketching the outline of your bedroom or study on the board and inviting students to ask questions.

➡ Lesson outcome

Ask: *What did we learn today?* Elicit: *there is ... there are ...* and/or *prepositions* and/or *names of furniture*. Ask everyone to say one new word they learned. Draw the students' attention to the lesson statement: *I can describe what is in a room.*

Notes for Photocopiable activity 3.1

Spot the difference

Pairwork

Language: *there is, there are*, prepositions of place, classroom objects

Materials: one copy of the worksheet per pair of students (Teacher's Book page 127)

- Quickly elicit the vocabulary for objects in the classroom and prepositions of place, by pointing at the objects.

- Divide students into pairs and give out the worksheets. Tell students that they must not look at their partner's picture. Explain that they both have a picture of the same scene but there are six differences. Demonstrate the activity by drawing attention to the example sentences and ask two students to read them out.
- Students describe their pictures and ask questions about their partner's picture in order to find the differences. When they find a difference, they mark it with a cross.
- The activity continues until most pairs have found the six differences. Elicit the differences from the class.

KEY

In picture A the teacher is in front of the board. In picture B the teacher is next to a student.
In picture A the CD player is on the teacher's desk. In picture B it's on a shelf next to the board.
In picture A there is a TV. In picture B there isn't a TV.
In picture A there are two boys next to the computer. In B there is a girl next to the computer.
In picture A there is a bin near the door. In picture B the bin is near the computer.
In picture A there are no posters. In picture B there are two posters.

3C CULTURE
Schools in England

LESSON SUMMARY ●●●●●●

Reading: factual text; secondary education in England
Listening: two students talking about their schools
Speaking: discussing schools
Topic: school

SHORTCUT *To do the lesson in 30 minutes, ask students to read the text for the first time and do exercise 2 at home.*

➡ Lead-in 2 minutes
- Write *school* on the board. Ask students: *In your country, how old are children when they go to school? Is it compulsory for them to go to school?* (explain the meaning of 'compulsory'). *How long do you have to go to school? How many years of school are compulsory?* Introduce the topic of the lesson by saying: *Today we are going to read and talk about school and education in England.*

Exercise 1 page 30
- Explain the vocabulary in the chart. Students calculate how many years of compulsory education there are in England.

KEY
11

CULTURE NOTE – *COLLEGE*
College in the American school system means university. In England the term has several meanings.

Some universities, notably Oxford and Cambridge and a few of the other older universities have a collegiate system, whereby the university is made up of separate colleges.

Higher education institutes that are not universities may also be called colleges, e.g. the Oxford College of Further Education. These institutions provide education to students over 16 who may be doing AS levels or vocational qualifications, but also for adults who have decided to study later in life.

Some public schools may also call themselves *colleges*, e.g. Eton College or Winchester College.

Exercise 2 page 30
- Ask students to read the title. Introduce the task and ask students to read the five headings. Ask which two they think are the extra ones that will not be used. Students do the task. Check answers with the whole class.

KEY
1 b   2 e   3 a

LANGUAGE AND CULTURE NOTE – SCHOOLS
Students often say *public school* instead of *state school*. A *public school*, in Britain, despite the name, is in fact a very exclusive private school. The term started in the nineteenth century to describe a school that was publicly managed as opposed to privately owned by teachers. The most famous public schools are Eton [iːtən] (attended by Princes William and Harry) and Harrow [hærəʊ], for boys, and Cheltenham Ladies' College [tʃeltənəm] and Roedean, [rəʊdiːn], for girls. The students often live at the school during term time. The schools put a strong emphasis on discipline, sport and religion.

In the USA, however, *public school* is the same as *state school*.

Exercise 3 page 30
- Students read for detail. **Fast finishers** may write corrected versions of the false sentences. Allow students to compare answers in pairs, then check with the whole class. After every sentence ask if it is true about the students' own country and if not, what is. With a **weaker group**, you might ask students to write 7 sentences about their country modelled on the sentences in the exercise and read them aloud.

KEY
1 T   2 F   3 F   4 T   5 F   6 T   7 T

Exercise 4 page 30 🎧 1.45
- Tell students they are going to hear two teenagers talking about their schools. Ask them to read the three statements. Play the recording once and check how many students know the answer. If fewer than a half do, play the recording again. Ask for the right answer.

KEY
1 is correct

Transcript 1.45

Nick   Hi, my name's Nick and I go to Abingdon School. It's a big private school near Oxford, in the middle of England. It's a very old school – about 700 years old. There are about 800 students here, and about 100 teachers. There are only boys – there aren't any girls. Some boys live at home and just come to school for lessons, like in a normal school, but I live in the school during the term. I go home for the holidays of course. All the boys wear a uniform – that's special clothes. The uniform is a dark blue jacket, light blue shirt, grey trousers, black shoes and socks, and a tie. We work very hard but I like my school. I want to do A-levels and then go to university.

Stephanie   Hi, I'm Stephanie and I'm at Oaklands School in London. It's a state secondary school in the east of London. It's a mixed school, for boys and girls. There are about 600 students in the school, and some of them come from different countries – there are lots of Pakistani, West Indian, Indian and Chinese students here. There are 89 teachers. I come to school five days a week. Lessons start at 9 and finish at 4. We wear a uniform at my school. I don't like the uniform – it's a green T-shirt or sweatshirt and a grey skirt – trousers for the boys, of course. School's not bad, but I want to leave after my GCSEs and get a job.

Exercise 5 page 30 🎧 1.45

- Ask students to read the chart. Play the recording through once. The second time, pause after Nick. Check if most students have got the answers, then play Stephanie's part. Allow them to confer in pairs. Check answers as a class.

KEY

	Nick	Stephanie
Name of school	Abingdon	Oaklands
Private or state	private	state
Number of students	800	600
Number of teachers	100	89
Mixed (boys and girls?)	no	yes
Wants to leave when?	after A-levels	after GCSEs

Exercise 6 page 30

- Check that students understand the terms *state school* and *private school*.
- Go around the room and listen as students ask and answer the questions.

OPTIONAL ACTIVITY

After students have asked and answered the questions in exercise 6 in pairs, you can ask them to prepare a 30-second presentation about their school. Suggest they can start their presentations with *I go to ...* or *Welcome to ...* Allow 2 minutes to prepare. They can write if they wish. Have 3–5 students say their mini-presentations in front of the class.

Exercise 7 page 30

- As students fill in the chart, circulate, monitor, and help. After they have finished, ask a few questions, for example: *How old are children when they go to nursery school?*

→ Lesson outcome

Ask students: *What have we talked about today?* Elicit: *school in England (and in our country).* Ask students for vocabulary from the lesson – ask everyone to say one word related to schools and education that they learned. Draw students' attention to the lesson statement: *I can talk about different school systems.*

LESSON SUMMARY ● ● ● ● ●

Grammar: *have to*
Speaking: talking about an ideal school
Reading: gapped text

SHORTCUT *To do the lesson in 30 minutes, do exercise 5 orally as a class and skip exercise 8.*

→ Lead-in 2 minutes

- Think of one rule that most students dislike at your school and one thing they like, for example: *We have to be at school at 8 o'clock every day. We don't have to wear uniforms.*
- Write the two sentences on the board, accompanied by an unhappy and a happy face. Circle the words *have to* and ask *What do you think 'we have to' means? What do you think 'don't have to' means?* Elicit translations. Conclude: *Today we are going to talk about things we have to do and things we don't have to do at school.*

Exercise 1 page 31

- As students read the text about Summerhill, be prepared to answer questions about this unusual school.

CULTURAL NOTE – SUMMERHILL SCHOOL

Summerhill School was founded by A S Neill in 1921. It has 69 students, aged from five to seventeen, many of whom come from abroad (especially Japan, Korea and Taiwan). The school's underlying philosophy is that children learn best when they are free from pressure. The British Government tried to close the school in 1999 since it did badly in a government inspection, but the school appealed against the decision and won.

Exercise 2 page 31

- With a **weaker class,** allow 30–45 seconds for students to look through the *Learn this!* box, but complete it as a class, making sure that weaker students also get a chance to contribute. With a **stronger class,** let students complete the box individually or in pairs, then check with the whole class. Point out the third person singular –s again, emphasising that it's the same –s as in *goes, likes, does,* etc.

KEY

1 have to   2 don't have to   3 Does   4 does

LANGUAGE NOTE – *HAVE TO* VS. *MUST*

Students may have come across *must* before and may ask you about it. If so, explain that it means the same as *have to*. It is not advisable to go into the differences between *must* and *have to* at this level. *Have to* is more common in everyday conversational English.

Exercise 3 page 31

- Students work on the exercise individually or in pairs.

KEY

1	has to, don't have to	4	have to
2	don't have to	5	have to
3	have to	6	doesn't have to

Exercise 4 page 31 🎧 1.46

- Play the recording once for students to check their answers to exercise 3, then again, stopping after every sentence and asking a few students to repeat it individually. Make sure they use the weak form of *to* in *have / has to*.

For further practice on have to, *go to:*

Grammar Builder 3D: Student's Book page 112

KEY

4
1	do the washing	4	cook dinner
2	make breakfast	5	tidy his/her bedroom
3	go to the supermarket	6	clean the house

5
2 Suzie doesn't have to tidy her bedroom.
3 Mark has to clean the house.
4 Suzie doesn't have to clean the house.
5 Mark and Suzie don't have to cook dinner.
6 Mark and Suzie have to do the washing.
7 Suzie has to make breakfast.
8 Suzie has to go to the supermarket.
9 Mark doesn't have to go to the supermarket.

6
2 Does Suzie have to tidy her bedroom? No, she doesn't.
3 Does Mark have to clean the house? Yes, he does.
4 Does Suzie have to clean the house? No, she doesn't.
5 Do Mark and Suzie have to cook dinner? No, they don't.
6 Do Mark and Suzie have to do the washing? Yes, they do.
7 Does Suzie have to make breakfast? Yes, she does.
8 Does Suzie have to go to the supermarket? Yes, she does.
9 Does Mark have to go to the supermarket? No, he doesn't.

7 Open answers

Exercise 5 page 31

- Check that everyone understands *compulsory* (they may remember it from lesson 3C). Do the first two examples orally as a class, to make sure everyone understands what they need to do. With a **stronger class**, you can do the whole exercise orally.

Exercise 6 page 31

- Emphasise that this is supposed to be an *ideal* school (so that the students don't miss the point). Students complete the description individually. Check answers with the whole class by having students read the text aloud.

KEY

1	don't have to	3	have to	5	don't have to
2	don't have to	4	don't have to	6	don't have to

Exercise 7 page 31

- Allow 5 minutes for pairs to work on their descriptions (possibly more, if the students are feeling very creative). Circulate and help with vocabulary.

Exercise 8 page 31

- Either one student from each pair forms a new pair with a different partner, or pairs get together forming groups of four. If you don't have a number of students that's divisible by 4, the last odd pair or even group of three can be divided, each student joining a different group (so there will be some groups of 5).
- Alternatively, pairs could just read their descriptions to the whole class.

OPTIONAL ACTIVITY

Ask students to write 3–4 sentences about the rules in their family, e.g. *I have to be at home at ...* or *I have to clean my room*. Tell them to look back at Unit 1E, page 13 – the vocabulary there will be helpful. Circulate and help. Students get into groups of three and compare the rules in their homes. If there's time, they can then report back to the class about any similarities or differences.

➜ Lesson outcome

Ask students: *What did we talk about today?* Try to elicit *have to,* but accept all answers relevant to the content of the lesson. Briefly practise the grammar by eliciting the different forms, affirmative, interrogative and negative. Draw students' attention to the lesson statement: *I can describe my ideal school.*

Notes for Photocopiable activity 3.2

Find someone who ...

A class survey

Language: *have to* (questions, short answers, and 3rd person singular), present simple
Materials: one copy (half the worksheet) per student (Teacher's Book page 128)

- Explain that students are going to ask and answer questions to complete a class survey. They need to change the sentences on the worksheet into questions. Elicit the first few questions e.g. *Do you have to work at the weekend?* and pre-teach vocabulary as necessary (e.g. *baby-sit*).
- Demonstrate the activity by asking a student the first question. Encourage them to reply with a short answer, e.g. *Yes, I do.* or *No, I don't.* If the student answers: *No, I don't,* move onto the next student. When a student answers *Yes, I do,* ask the follow-up question: *Where do you work?*
- Students move around the class asking and answering questions. They write the name and answer in the spaces provided. Tell them they must write another student's name only once. (This is to ensure they speak to as many of their classmates as possible.)
- When a few students have finished ask everyone to sit down and have a class feedback session. E.g. *Barbara has to work at the weekend. She works in a shop.*

3E READING
High flyers

LESSON SUMMARY ● ● ● ○

Reading: an article; reading for specific information
Vocabulary: rooms and facilities in a school
Topic: school

SHORTCUT *To do the lesson in 30 minutes, ask students to read the text for the first time at home and to do exercise 2 in advance. Alternatively, do exercises 3, 7 and 9 as a class.*

- Ask a few students: *How far do you live from school? (How many kilometres?) How long does it take you to get to school? (How many minutes or hours?)* If some of your students come from another town or village, you can ask: *How often do you go home?* Explain: *Today we are going to read about students in Australia who live very far from school.*

Exercise 1 page 32

- First, students work in pairs; each chooses one of the photos and describes it. Circulate and listen. Ask a few students who did well to describe their photos to the whole class. Choose them so that every photo is described at least once. Point out the strong points of the description (good use of vocabulary, good ideas, good sentence structures).

Exercise 2 page 32

- Read the reading tip aloud and check understanding.
- Now ask students to do exercise 2 as quickly as possible. See who can do it under 1 minute!

KEY

1 20 million people
2 over 1000
3 once or twice a year

Exercise 3 page 32

- Tell students they are now going to work out the meaning of some words from the text, without using a dictionary. The definitions in the exercise are not in the same order as the words in the text. Allow 3–5 minutes. Ask students how many words they managed to work out the meaning of. If someone hasn't got all the words, they can now check with a partner or look at the Wordlist.

KEY

1 on their own	4 takes place	7 once
2 enormous	5 twice	
3 borrow	6 post	

Exercise 4 page 32

- Ask students to go back to page 13 and re-read the reading tip there. When checking answers, ask students to point to specific sentences in the text where the answer is contained.

KEY

1 b 2 b 3 a 4 b 5 b 6 b

Exercise 5 page 33

- Ask students to look at the vocabulary in box. Do they know any of the words? If they do, encourage them to try and do some of the questions without looking words up. After they've done as much as they can, let them consult the Wordlist or use their dictionaries.

KEY

1 library	6 gym
2 canteen	7 corridor
3 playing field	8 computer room
4 classroom	9 hall
5 staff room	10 stairs

Exercise 6 page 33 🎧 1.47

- Play the recording once for students to check their answers to exercise 5, then again pausing after each word and asking students to repeat individually and chorally. Pay attention to stress in the compound nouns: *classroom, computer room, staff room, playing field* – each of them is pronounced as one word with stress on the first element.

Exercise 7 page 33

- With a **weaker class**, you can tell students there are only 3 of the words in the text. With a **stronger class**, you can ask if they can remember without looking!

KEY

classroom, library, playing fields

Exercise 8 page 33

- Students work in pairs. Ask them to copy the chart onto a loose sheet of paper so that they have plenty of space to write. Explain *advantages, disadvantages, compare*. With a **stronger class**, tell the students they have to add at least five ideas of their own (on whichever side).

Exercise 9 page 33

- Put the pairs together in groups of four. If there is an odd number of pairs, one will have to split, joining different groups. Students exchange ideas. At the end, bring the class together to share views. Did most people agree about what the advantages and disadvantages of studying at home are? How many think there are more advantages/ disadvantages?

→ **Lesson outcome**

Ask students: *So, what did we do today?* Elicit something like: *We read about Schools of the Air.* Ask everyone to say one piece of information or one new word they learned from the lesson. Draw students' attention to the lesson statement: *I can understand and react to an article about schools.*

3F EVERYDAY ENGLISH
Giving directions

LESSON SUMMARY ● ● ● ● ○

Functional English: directions
Listening: following directions
Speaking: giving directions
Topic: school

SHORTCUT *To do the lesson in 30 minutes, spend less time practising pronunciation and limit the number of performances in exercise 8 .*

→ **Lead-in** 2 minutes

- Ask students to recall some of the names of places in a school from the last lesson: *library, canteen, staff room, computer room,* etc. Ask a few questions about your own school, for example: *Where is the … (e.g. library) in our school? Which floor: first or second?* Elicit the floor and possibly some other information, e.g. *Next to the … (computer room)*
- Inform the class: *Today, we're going to learn to say where places are and how to get there.*

Exercise 1 page 34 🎧 1.48

• Ask students to look at the pictures and name the places they see: *corridor, stairs, staff room*, etc. Then ask them to read the task. Play the recording once, allow 30–45 seconds for students to complete answers, and check.

KEY

1 B   2 E   3 A   4 D   5 C

Exercise 2 page 34 🎧 1.48

• Before students read the dialogue in pairs, play the recording one more time, pausing to practise the pronunciation of the phrases: *Excuse me*, and *Where's that?* all the instructions (*Go up the stairs*, etc.) *Thanks very much, You're welcome.* Ask students to repeat individually and chorally, focusing on intonation: encourage them to copy the intonation in the recording as closely as they can. Finally, play it a third time without stopping, to give students a model of the whole, and ask them to read it in pairs.

Exercise 3 page 34

• Students work individually. Circulate and see how well they're doing. Students can compare answers in pairs. To check, ask one student to show the route to the class.

Exercise 4 page 34 🎧 1.49

• Explain to students that they are now going to do the same thing as in the previous exercise – follow someone's route on the plan – but they will only hear the directions, not read them. Reassure them that you will play the recording as many times as they need to hear it. Make sure everyone knows where the starting point is. Play the material all the way through once, then again, pausing briefly after each dialogue, then ask students if they need to hear any of the dialogues again. Replay any parts of the recording as necessary until most students have got most of the answers.

KEY

1 computer room   3 toilets   5 Head teacher's office
2 library   4 gym

Transcript 1.49

1

Boy Excuse me. Do you know where the [beep] is?
Girl Yes, I do. It's on this floor.
Boy Oh, right.
Girl Go along this corridor and turn left. Turn left again at the end and it's on your left, opposite the canteen.
Boy Thanks!

2

Girl Excuse me. Where's the [beep]?
Boy Go upstairs to the first floor.
Girl Where are the stairs?
Boy Oh, OK. Go along this corridor and turn left. The stairs are just opposite. Go up to the first floor.
Girl OK
Boy Then turn right. It's the second door on the left.
Girl Thanks!
Boy You're welcome.
Girl Thanks very much!

3

Boy Excuse me. Where are the [beep] ?
Girl They're on the first floor. Go along this corridor and turn left. Go up the stairs and turn left at the top. They're on your left.
Boy Thanks very much.

4

Girl Excuse me. Can you tell me where the [beep] is, please?
Boy Yes, of course. Go along this corridor and turn left. Go past the stairs, along to the end of the corridor, and turn right.
Girl OK …
Boy It's the door on your left.
Girl Thanks very much!

5

Girl Excuse me. Where's the [beep] ?
Boy Go along this corridor and turn right. And you're there! Good luck!

Exercise 5 page 34 🎧 1.50

• Tell students they are going to hear another dialogue. Ask them to read the questions. Play the recording twice. Allow students to compare answers in pairs, then check with the whole class.

KEY

1 To the canteen   3 Four
2 He wants to have lunch   4 The canteen is closed

Transcript 1.50

Oliver Excuse me. Where's the canteen?
Boy 1 Go along the corridor. Turn left.
Oliver Thanks!

…

Oliver Hmm. Oh, excuse me.
Girl 1 Yes.
Oliver Is the canteen near here?
Girl 1 The canteen?
Oliver Yes. I want to have lunch.
Girl 1 No, the canteen is in the other part of the school.
Oliver Oh. Where's that? I'm new here.
Girl 1 Go outside. Turn right. Then, let me see. Go through the doors. And you're there!
Oliver Thanks.

…

Oliver Excuse me. Where's the canteen?
Boy 2 Go past the library. Turn right, and it's opposite the computer room.
Oliver … past the library …. turn left – no, right …

…

Oliver Is the canteen near here?
Girl 2 Yes, go up the stairs …
Oliver Up the stairs?
Girl 2 Yes. Turn left and it's next to the staff room, on the right.
Oliver Thank you.

…

Oliver At last! Excuse me. Is this the canteen?
Woman Yes, it is. But it's closed. Sorry.
Oliver Oh no!

Exercise 6 page 34 🎧 1.51

• Play the sentences one by one, asking students to repeat chorally. Then play them again, pausing and asking some students to repeat individually. Focus on intonation.

Exercise 7 page 34

• Students prepare their dialogues. Circulate and monitor. Note some common errors and discuss them with the whole class so that students can include the corrections in their final version. Select the best dialogues for acting out in front of the class (clear pronunciation, funny content, some attempt at acting).

Exercise 8 page 34

- Three or four pairs act out their conversations to the whole class. Give feedback – comment on strengths and correct a few errors in the target language.

➡ Lesson outcome

Ask students: *What have we talked about today?* Elicit *giving directions* or equivalent. Ask everyone to give one word or phrase they learned from the lesson. Draw students' attention to the lesson statement: *I can understand and give directions.*

3G WRITING
A description

LESSON SUMMARY ● ● ● ○ ○
Writing: a description
Reading: a description
Vocabulary: a review of vocabulary from the unit
Topic: school

SHORTCUT *To do the lesson in 30 minutes, set the writing as homework, or do exercises 5 and 6 as a class and have students write a first draft in class.*

➡ Lead-in 2 minutes

- Ask students: *What information do you need when you come to a new school?* Accept any relevant answers, but try to elicit some of the *Where is ...* type and some of the *What time ...* type. Do not insist on grammatical accuracy. Tell students that they are now going to read a description which gives this information to a new student, and then they're going to learn to write a description.

Exercise 1 page 35

- Exercise 1 and 2 can very well be done simultaneously. The photos help students understand the content of the description and put the parts in the correct order. Students work individually, then check the answers as a class.

KEY
4 – 2 – 1 – 3

Exercise 2 page 35

- Ask students to match the photos with three parts of the description in exercise 1. Students do the task. Check answers as a class.

KEY
A 3   B 1   C 2

Exercise 3 page 35

- Students answer the questions individually or in pairs. Check as a class.

KEY
1 8.45	3 Next to the gym	5 At 3.30
2 10.20	4 On Tuesdays at 1.45	6 Early, at 2.30

Exercises 4 and 5 page 35

- Tell students they are now going to look at the use of capital letters in English. Read the writing tip aloud, asking for English examples of *months, names, languages/ nationalities, towns and countries*. Put some examples on the board or appoint a student to do it. Then ask the question: *Which rules are different in your language?*

Exercise 6 page 35

- Allow students 2 minutes to do the exercise, then ask 2–3 students who write clearly to come to the board (simultaneously) and write down the answers. You may put the numbers 1, 2, 3, 4, 5 on the board in a column so that the volunteers know where to write the sentences. As a class, look at the answers and correct any errors.

KEY
1 The new school year starts on Monday 6th September.
2 Your first lesson on Thursday is history.
3 Our Spanish teacher is from Lima in Peru.
4 My brother James and I go to Eton College.
5 Our geography teacher's name is George White.

Exercise 7 page 35

- Suggest to students that they should choose the four bullet points they are going to write about based on two criteria: (1) which information is most relevant in the context of their school, and (2) for which point they can think of some good vocabulary to show off.

Exercise 8 page 35

- Say that the description should begin with a title or introduction: this could be one or two sentences saying what the description is about, for example: *I go to X school.* or *This is some information about my school, X school in ... .*
- Students write their descriptions.

ALTERNATIVE WRITING TASK

Imagine you are setting up your own, ideal school. Write a description of the timetable and the weeks' activities. Include some information about three of these subjects:

- what times lessons start and finish
- how many lessons there are on each day/in each week
- where the lessons take place
- which subjects aren't studied at your school, and why
- what extra studies and activities are on the timetable
- what the food is like, how and where it is served

Say why students like your school.

➡ Lesson outcome

Ask students: *What have we learned about today?* Elicit: *description*, or *writing a description*. Elicit a few phrases that can be used in a description. Draw the students' attention to the lesson statement: *I can write a description of my school.*

TOPIC ● ● ● ○ ○
Sport

➤ Lead-in 2minutes

- Discuss issues related to listening with students. Ask them if they like listening tasks, if they think listening is easier or more difficult than reading, and what can make listening difficult (e.g. the people may speak too fast for you, if you miss something you cannot go back, it's difficult to listen and write at the same time (if there is a task), there may be background noise, the quality of the recording may be bad). Ask students if they have any strategies that they use to make listening easier. Share ideas as a class.

Exercise 1 page 36

- Students look at the photo and do the task. Check understanding by saying: *The man is a …? And he's got a …? And he's wearing* (point to your clothes to communicate the meaning of *wearing*) *a …? And this* (draw a wave on the board) *is a …?*

Exercise 2 page 36 🎧 1.52

E Listening: multiple-choice statements

- Read the Listening tip with the whole class. After reading point 2, emphasise that it is important not to stop listening – you can think about what's in the exercise on the page later, but you can't hear the recording later.
- Say you are moving on to the exam task. Ask: *So, what should you do first?* Elicit: *Read the questions and the multiple choice answers.* Allow a minute for students to read.
- Play the recording twice. Ask students to compare answers in pairs. Ask which ones they agreed and disagreed about. Discuss the answers to the questions that caused some doubts in more detail, possibly playing the relevant sections of the recording again.

KEY

1 A	2 C	3 B	4 A	5 C	6 C	7 A

Transcript 1.52

Interviewer	I'm here to meet 16-year-old Joshua Stevens. He is the new under-eighteens British surfing champion. Hello, Josh. Pleased to meet you.
Joshua	Hello. Pleased to meet you, too.
Interviewer	Josh, what do you do when you're not on a surf board?
Joshua	Well, I'm still at school. I have to take my exams next year.
Interviewer	That's tricky. What do you do when you're not at school?
Joshua	That's easy! If I'm not at school, then I want to be out on the waves. I live in north Devon, and we usually have great surfing waves there.
Interviewer	Tell me, Josh, about a typical day in your life.
Joshua	OK. In the summer, I get up early, and go surfing for a couple of hours before breakfast. Then, I go to school.
Interviewer	Do you work hard at school?
Joshua	Oh, yes, very hard. And if it's good day for surfing, I try to do my homework at lunchtime, so that I have more time at the beach after school.
Interviewer	Do you go to the beach every day after school?
Joshua	Yes, usually, if the waves are good.
Interviewer	Even in the winter?
Joshua	In the winter I don't go surfing before breakfast because it's too dark, but I go after school if I can. It's a bit cold in winter, but I wear a wetsuit, and the waves are usually great.

Interviewer	And what do you do at the weekends?
Joshua	Well, I go to the beach! In fact, all my family go. We are all members of the local surf club. My mum and dad love surfing, too. So does my little sister. She has her first competition next month. All our friends are at the club. It's great fun.
Interviewer	When is your next competition?
Joshua	We have a club competition next week. But in two months time it's the world championships, and I want to do well!
Interviewer	Good luck for that, Josh!
Joshua	Thanks very much.

Exercise 3 page 36

- Ask students: *Do you like presents? Do you like getting presents or giving presents? Is it difficult to choose a present for someone?* Then ask them to do the task in pairs or groups of three. Circulate and help with vocabulary. Let students share ideas as a class. Which presents are the most popular?

Exercise 4 page 36 🎧 1.53

- Read the Speaking exam task as a class.
- Tell students they are going to hear a candidate doing the task in the exam. Ask them to read the instructions for the listening task.
- Play the recording through once, then again, stopping after each gap to check.

KEY

1 Why don't	4 shall	7 what about
2 think	5 Let's	8 idea
3 like	6 exciting	

Exercise 5 page 36

E Speaking: situational role-play

- Read the list of phrases with the whole class.
- Students do the exam task in pairs. They can then switch roles and do the same task again, or switch roles to do the optional task. For this task, pre-teach *organise, invite, take (him/her) out to …*

OPTIONAL ACTIVITY

Speaking: situational role-play

You are visiting a friend in London. She has suggested going shopping.

- Reject the suggestion and give a reason.
- Suggest doing something else.
- Suggest where and when you could meet.

(The examiner starts the conversation.)

➤ Lesson outcome

Ask students: *What did we do today?* Elicit: *listening*, *speaking*, and *negotiating*. Ask students if they remember any of the good advice about doing listening tasks. Elicit some of the phrases for suggesting and responding to suggestions.

TOPIC ● ● ○ ○ ○
School

➡ Lead-in 3 minutes

- Tell students you are going to briefly revise vocabulary related to school: names of subjects, places, people, things you do at school, etc. Ask everybody to think for about 30–45 seconds and try to remember as many words as they can. Then ask everybody in turn to say one word related to the topic of school. They must not repeat words which have already been said. If someone cannot think of a word or repeats a words that's already been mentioned, they are out. The winner is the last person (or three people) that is/ are left.

Exercise 1 page 37

- Ask students to read the rubric. Challenge them to find the answer in less than 20 seconds! Ask everyone to put their hand up when they have got the answer. Check when all or nearly all the hands are up, but not later than 30 seconds.

KEY

Yes

Exercise 2 page 37

E Reading: multiple-choice statements

- Read the Reading tip as a class. After point 2, say you can also note the number of the question in the margin next to the relevant passage.
- Ask students to read the exam task and the seven multiple-choice statements. Make sure everyone understands them.
- Students do the task individually and compare answers in pairs. Check with the whole class.
- Ask students to justify their answers by reading the relevant parts of the text.

KEY

1 B	3 C	5 B	7 C
2 C	4 A	6 A	

Exercise 3 page 37

- Ask students to try and list as many subjects as they can without looking in unit 3. When they cannot remember any more, they can refer back to it. Pairs compare lists in groups of four and ask and answer about their favourite subjects.

Exercise 4 page 37 🎧 1.54

- Ask students to read the Speaking exam task and explain they will hear a candidate doing it. Ask them to read the instructions for the exercise and make sure everyone understands what they are supposed to listen for.

Transcript 1.54

Examiner	Can you tell me about your school? How many students are there?
Blanka	There is about 800 students in the school.
Examiner	Really. And what subjects do you study?
Blanka	We study about ten subject. English, Czech, maths, biology, physics, geography, history, computing, art and P.E.
Examiner	And what's your favourite subject?
Blanka	Um, that's a difficult question! I like the biology and maths, but my favourite subject is physics.
Examiner	Can you tell me about the timetable? When do lessons start, and finish?
Blanka	We start at eight o'clock, and lessons finish at half past three o'clock.
Examiner	And, how long is the lunch break?
Blanka	An hour, from twelve o'clock to one o'clock.

- Tell students there is one mistake in each of the sentences 1–4. Students do the task individually and compare answers in pairs. Check with the whole class.

KEY

1 There **are** about 1,000 students in the school.
2 We study about ten subject**s**.
3 I like biology and maths.
4 Lessons finish at half past three.

Exercise 5 page 37

E Speaking: situational role-play

- Students do the Speaking exam task in pairs. They can then switch roles and do the same task again, or switch roles to do the optional task.
- Get a few pairs to perform in front of the class.

OPTIONAL ACTIVITY

Speaking: situational role-play

There's a group of foreign students visiting your school. One of them has asked you a few questions. Tell him /her

- what your next two lessons are,
- which subjects you like,
- where the canteen is.

(The examiner starts the conversation.)

➡ Lesson outcome

Ask students: *What did we do today?* Elicit: *reading with multiple-choice statements, speaking.* Ask several students to say one thing they learned from the lesson – either an exam tip or a piece of lexis.

4 Time to party!

THIS UNIT INCLUDES ● ● ○ ○

Vocabulary • clothes • adjectives • musical instruments • types of party
• free-time activities • prepositions of time
Grammar • present continuous • can/can't • adverbs
Speaking • describing clothes • talking about the clothes you wear
• making arrangements
Writing • a party invitation
WORKBOOK pages 34–40

A VOCABULARY AND LISTENING
Clothes

LESSON SUMMARY ● ● ● ● ○

Vocabulary: clothes, colours
Listening: descriptions of people's clothes
Speaking: describing a person's clothes
Topic: people

SHORTCUT *To do the lesson in 30 minutes, set the Vocabulary Builder as homework.*

➡ Lead-in 2 minutes
• Bring in an item of clothing which you imagine students may know the name of, e.g. jeans or a sweater, preferably in a surprising colour. Have a conversation along these lines with the class: *What are these?* (Elicit: *Jeans.*) *Are they blue jeans?* (Elicit: *No, orange!*) *Today we are going to talk about clothes (point to the clothes you're wearing) and colours. Look around! Do you know any other names of clothes or colours that anyone is wearing here today?* Elicit any names of clothes and/or colours.

Exercise 1 page 38
• Ask students to open their books and continue working on clothes vocabulary, using the picture. They can use the Wordlist if they wish.

KEY

1	shirt	6	shoes	11	sweatshirt
2	jacket	7	boots	12	jeans
3	dress	8	skirt	13	trainers
4	top	9	blouse	14	T-shirt
5	trousers	10	cap		

Not illustrated: shorts jumper socks tie
tracksuit bottoms

LANGUAGE NOTE – CLOTHES

Jeans and *trousers* are always plural in English.

Clothes is also always plural, e.g. *I bought some clothes today.* If we want to make it singular we have to talk about a specific item, e.g. *I bought a shirt today.*

A *top* can be a shirt, t-shirt or blouse. It is mainly used for women's clothes. A *blouse* is only worn by women.

Exercise 2 page 38 🎧 1.57
• Play the recording through once for students to check their answers to exercise 1, then again pausing after each item for them to repeat chorally and individually.

Exercise 3 page 38
• In pairs, students take turns to identify the colours in the picture.

KEY

1	green	6	brown	11	brown
2	purple	7	black	12	blue
3	pink	8	orange	13	white
4	grey	9	red	14	yellow
5	black	10	white		

Exercise 4 page 38
• This game can also be played in groups of three, with one student asking questions and the others trying to recall the answers. You may specify a number of questions (e.g. 5 or 6) to be asked by one student; after that, students switch roles.

For further practice of clothes vocabulary, go to:

Vocabulary Builder (part 1): Student's Book page 131

KEY

1 🎧 2.05

1	a blue top	6	blue tracksuit bottoms
2	a black and white dres	7	grey trousers
3	a purple blouse	8	an orange and yellow T-shirt
4	brown boots	9	a pink shirt
5	red shorts	10	a green tie

2 as above

3–4 Open answers

Exercise 5 page 38
• With a **stronger class**, encourage students to produce more than one sentence for each person they describe. Circulate and monitor. Identify a few particularly well-written sentences (detailed observations, a good range of vocabulary, correct and natural-sounding structure) and ask students to read them aloud.

Exercise 6 page 38 🎧 1.58
• Tell students they are going to listen to four teenagers talking about their clothes. Ask them to read the task.
• Play the recording through once, then stop after each speaker to check answers.

KEY

David and Fiona have to wear a uniform

Transcript 1.58

1 David

Int.	What do you usually wear to school?
David	We have to wear a uniform, so it's always the same! It's a green jacket, white shirt and green tie, and black trousers.
Int.	And what do you wear when you go out with friends?
David	I usually wear trousers or jeans, and a sweatshirt or a jumper.

2 Maria

Int.   What do you usually wear to school?

Maria   It depends. Sometimes I wear jeans, trainers and a top. Sometimes I wear a skirt and a blouse.

Int.   And what do you wear when you go out with friends?

Maria   The same things really – jeans or a skirt. If it's a special occasion I sometimes wear a dress.

3 Peter

Int.   What do you usually wear to school?

Peter   I wear tracksuit bottoms and trainers.

Int.   And what do you wear with them? A shirt?

Peter   Yes, sometimes, or just a T-shirt.

Int.   And what do you wear when you go out with friends?

Peter   I usually wear a T-shirt and a jacket, and jeans.

4 Fiona

Int.   What do you usually wear to school?

Fiona   I wear the school uniform – grey skirt, white blouse and a blue jacket.

Int.   And what do you wear when you go out with friends?

Fiona   I usually wear jeans and a top, sometimes a jacket if it's cold.

Exercise 7 page 38   🎧 1.58

- Ask students to read the instructions and the sentences. Make sure everyone understands they are to listen out for names of clothes. Play the recording again. Stop after each speaker and check if students need to hear it one more time.

KEY

1 trousers, jumper	3 T-shirt, jeans
2 skirt, dress	4 top, jacket

Exercise 8 page 38

- With a **stronger group,** or a group where a lot of people are interested in clothes, encourage students to include some details in their descriptions of clothes. Provide a model by describing what you wear, e.g.: *Around the house, I often wear old black tracksuit bottoms and my favourite old T-shirt, which is blue, with Snoopy on it.*

Exercise 9 and 10 page 38

- This can be a bit sensitive. Use your judgement to decide whether this activity may cause any nastiness (mocking someone's unfashionable clothes, etc.) in a particular group. If there is such a risk, decide on the most appropriate procedure. Students could write the descriptions, but not read them aloud or you could decide which ones will be read aloud after having seen them.

For work on adjectives (opposites), go to:

> **Vocabulary Builder (part 2):** Student's Book page 131

KEY

5	1 old – young	7	easy – difficult
	2 fast – slow	8	cold – hot
	3 bad – good	9	expensive – cheap
	4 quiet – loud	10	ugly – beautiful
	5 small – big	11	late – early
	6 new – old		

6 small, big, new, old, expensive, cheap, ugly, beautiful

7	1 expensive	5 easy		8	slow
	2 cheap	6 difficult		9	cold
	3 young	7 fast		10	hot
	4 old				

8 Open answers

➡ Lesson outcome

Ask: *What did we talk about today?* Elicit: *clothes.* Ask everyone to say one name of an item of clothing. Draw students' attention to the lesson statement: *I can describe what someone is wearing.*

Notes for Photocopiable activity 4.1

Pronunciation pelmanism

Pair or group game

Language: pronunciation – vowel sounds, clothes and colours
Materials: one copy of the worksheet per pair or group of three to four students (Teacher's Book page 129)

- Give each pair or group a set of cards and ask them to spread them out on the desk face up. Ask them to put the words into pairs with matching vowels, e.g. *pink and orange.* (N.B. for words with more than one syllable they should find a match for the underlined syllable.) Go through the answers as class and then play a game of *pelmanism* as follows.

- Students shuffle the cards and spread them out face down. Students take it turns to turn over any two cards. If they match, the student keeps them and has another turn. If the cards don't match, he /she must turn them back over. The cards must stay in exactly the same place. The game continues until all the cards have been matched. The student with the most cards is the winner.

Alternative procedure

- Omit the first stage if you think your students can go straight into the game of *pelmanism.*

4B GRAMMAR
Present continuous

LESSON SUMMARY ● ● ● ● ○

Grammar: present continuous

Speaking: describing what people in a picture are doing

> **SHORTCUT** *To do the lesson in 30 minutes, set exercise 8 and Grammar Builder as homework.*

➡ Lead-in 2–3 minutes

- Remind students: *We have already studied one English present tense. Do you remember what it was called?* Elicit: *present simple.* You may wish to quickly go over the affirmative, negative and question forms. Say: *English has more than one present tense and today we are going to see why, or what for. The present simple is used to talk about things that happen regularly. Today, we are going to look at a present tense used to say what's happening now.* (You can say all of this in the students' own language.)

Exercise 1 page 39 🎧 1.59

- Students keep their books closed. Tell them they are going to listen to a phone conversation between Jane and Alan. Put the questions from the exercise on the board: *Where's Jane? Where's Alan?* Let students listen to the dialogue first without following the transcript in the book. Then tell them to open the books and play the recording a second time. Check answers as a class.

KEY

Jane is at home.
Alan is at Sarah's party.

Exercise 2 page 39

- Explain: *Jane and Alan are using the new tense, the present continuous tense, to say what they are doing now, at this moment: I'm not having a good time. I'm sitting in the living room.* Ask students to look at the first sentence in the chart in the book. Elicit the forms of *be*. Now ask students to complete the exercise in the book. Check as a class. With a **weaker class**, write the completed sentences on the board.

KEY

1 leaving	3 watching	5 are you
2 is	4 'm not	

Exercise 3 page 39

- Students may not be aware which vowels are long and which are short. For the time being just give the example of /ɪ/: in words where the letter *i* is not pronounced /aɪ/ (which is long), it is a short /ɪ/, as in *swim–swimming*.
- With a **weaker class**, write at least one example of each spelling on the board, e.g. *watch–watching, have–having, sit–sitting*.
- Some students may give *boring* as a present continuous form. Point out the *a* before *boring* in the sentence *It's a boring documentary.*

KEY

Verb + -*ing*: doing
Verbs ending in -*e*: having, dancing, leaving
Verbs ending in short vowel + consonant: sitting

Exercise 4 page 39 🎧 1.60

- Explain to students that they are going to hear some sound effects. They have to decide what's happening. Ask them to read the verbs first to know what kind of sounds they are listening out for. Play the recording through once. Play it a second time stopping after each sound and write the answers on the board. Do not talk about the answers yet, as students will need to write the full answers in exercise 5.

KEY

1 b	2 d	3 f	4 c	5 a	6 e

Transcript 1.60

Sound effects:
1 a girl singing
2 two people chatting
3 a woman doing gymnastics
4 a boy shouting to his friends
5 a guitar being played well
6 a man eating noisily

Exercise 5 page 39

- Students write sentences individually or in pairs. When they've finished, play the sounds one more time, pausing after each one and asking someone to read the sentence that describes it.

KEY

1 She's singing.	4 He's shouting.
2 They're chatting.	5 He's playing the guitar.
3 She's doing gymnastics.	6 He's eating.

Exercise 6 page 39

- Students write individually. Check with the whole class.

For further practice of the present continuous, go to:

Grammar Builder 4B: Student's Book page 114

KEY

1	1 is	3 are	5 is
	2 am	4 is	6 are
2	1 studying	3 writing	5 reading
	2 doing	4 swimming	6 having
3	1 are swimming	3 are doing	5 are having
	2 is studying	4 am reading	6 is writing

4
1 I'm not working.
2 Tom and I aren't dancing.
3 Kate isn't sitting next to Paul.
4 David and Lucy aren't listening to music.
5 Martin isn't wearing brown shoes.
6 I'm not walking to town.
7 The sun isn't shining.
8 We aren't chatting to Robert.

5
2 Are Fred and Sue playing computer games?
3 Is Sarah doing gymnastics?
4 Are you phoning your friend?
5 Is he driving to Oxford?

6
2 Are Wendy and Pam going cycling? Yes, they are.
3 Are you using that computer? No, I'm not.
4 Is Pam getting up? No, she isn't.
5 Are Cathy and Steve cooking? No, they aren't.
6 Is Harry doing the washing up? Yes, he is.

Exercise 7 page 39

- With a **strong class,** you may ask students to do it as a memory game: students look at the picture for a minute, then one of them closes the book and the other quizzes him/her about what the people in the picture are doing. Students switch roles after a specified number of questions (e.g. 5). With a **weaker class**, make sure students read the verbs first and know what they mean.

Exercise 8 page 39

- After writing the descriptions, students may read them to one another in pairs or groups of three and identify the person who's being described.

OPTIONAL ACTIVITY

Tell students they are going to mime some activities. (Explain *mime*, or repeat the instructions in the students' own language. You could also demonstrate.) The question for others to guess will be: *What am I doing?* Ask everyone to think of three activities they could mime – allow 30 seconds to 1 minute for preparation. If you have a small class, everyone in turn mimes one or two activities in front of the class (they have to prepare more so that ideas are not repeated.) and asks: *What am I doing?* If you have a bigger class, get students to do it in groups of 4–5.

→ Lesson outcome

Ask students: *What did we work on today?* Elicit: *The present continuous.* Ask: *What is the present continuous used for?* Elicit: *To say what's happening at the moment.* You can say this first part in the students' own language; then ask a few questions in English: *What are you doing now? Are you listening to me?* Any answers are good, of course, but insist on correct present continuous forms. Draw student's attention to the lesson statement: *I can describe what is happening in a picture.*

4C CULTURE
Music festivals

LESSON SUMMARY ● ● ● ● ●
Reading: a text about three music festivals
Listening: a song: *I am sailing*
Speaking: speaking about music festivals
Topic: Sport and culture

SHORTCUT *To do the lesson in 30 minutes, ask students to read the text for the first time and do exercise 2 at home.*

→ Lead-in 2 minutes

- Before students open their books, write these questions on the board: *What kind of music do you like? Do you go to concerts? (What kind of concerts?) Do you go to music festivals? (Which ones?)*
- Ask students to stand up. Everyone must interview 3 people – excluding the person who always sits next to them.
- When students sit down, ask a few of them to report what they have discovered. Try to find out if anyone has been to a music festival. Introduce the topic of the lesson.

Exercise 1 page 40

- Tell students they are going to talk about the photo in a moment, but first invite them to read the speaking tip. Read it aloud and explain *foreground* and *background*.
- Ask students to read the words in the box and look up any unknown ones in the Wordlist. Read the words aloud. Repeat *audience* a few times and ask a few students to repeat. Make sure they pronounce the *au* as /ɔː/ not /aʊ/.
- Ask students to describe the photo in pairs: one person starts, says 2–3 sentences, the other adds 2–3 more. Circulate and monitor. Pick 2–3 students whose descriptions were good for different reasons and ask them to repeat their descriptions to the whole class. Comment on the strengths. Correct errors in the use of the present continuous.

Exercise 2 page 40

- Students read the text quickly. Read the names of the festivals aloud so that they will know how to pronounce them, the first two are: Glastonbury /ˈglæstənbəri/, WOMAD /ˈwəʊmæd/. Check answers with the whole class.

KEY
1 The International Dance and Music Festival in Rexburg, Idaho
2 Glastonbury Festival
3 WOMAD

Exercise 3 page 40

- Students read through the questions. You may need to explain *take place, stand for* and *last*. If these are new, make sure students write them down, because they are going to need them. Students read the text in more detail and answer the questions. Check answers as a class. Make sure students understand the meaning of *about 150,000*. You may point out Idaho on the map if you have a map of the USA in your room.

KEY
1 On a farm in the south-west of Britain.
2 About 150,000.
3 'World of Music, Arts and Dance'.
4 In different countries.
5 In Rexburg, Idaho
6 Two weeks.

Exercise 4 page 40

- Ask students to work in groups of 3–4. The groups list the musical festivals they know in their country, and try to remember what they know about them. Share information as a class.

Exercise 5 page 40 🎧 1.61

- Tell students they are going to hear the song *I am sailing*. Ask if anyone knows it. Ask students to close their books. Play the song once. Ask if anyone can repeat any words or phrases at all. Ask students to open their books and read the task and the gapped lyrics. Play the song once or twice again for students to do the task.

KEY

1	I am sailing	3	passing	5	trying
2	I am flying	4	I am dying	6	We are sailing

CULTURE NOTE – *I AM SAILING*
I am sailing is the biggest selling hit by British singer-songwriter, Rod Stewart, who is now in the fifth decade of his singing career.

Exercise 6 page 40

- Students read the three sentences and say which one they think is an accurate interpretation of the song. Then ask them to talk in groups of three and try to come up with some titles of songs with a similar message.

KEY
b

➡ Lesson outcome

Ask students: *What have we talked about today?* Elicit: *music/music festivals.* Ask students what they learned about music festivals. Elicit some of the vocabulary from the lesson – especially *take place, last, stand for* and the words from exercise 1. Draw students' attention to the lesson statement: *I can describe a photo and talk about music festivals.*

GRAMMAR
4D can and adverbs

LESSON SUMMARY ● ● ● ○ ○

Grammar: *can* and adverbs
Listening: an interview
Speaking: talking about skills and abilities

SHORTCUT *To do the lesson in 30 minutes, set the Grammar Builder for homework.*

➡ Lead-in 2 minutes

• Think in advance about some students in your class who are known to have a skill such as a sport, playing an instrument or speaking an unusual language. Before the lesson, write two to three statements about those skills on the board, e.g.: *Ana can play the guitar. Simon can jump on his bike.* Point to the first statement and read it aloud, maybe also indicating the person with your hand. Then point to yourself and say: *I can't play the guitar.* Ask a student: *Can you play the guitar?* (Elicit: *Yes/No*, don't insist on *Yes, I can* at this stage.) Repeat the procedure with the second sentence. Circle the word *can* in the two sentences on the board and ask: *So, what does 'can' mean?* Elicit the correct translation. Conclude by saying: *Today we're going to talk about what we can and can't do.*

Exercise 1 page 41

• Draw students' attention to the photo. Ask if anyone knows the person in it and can say something about her.
• Students read the text and answer the two questions.

KEY

1 *Buffy the Vampire Slayer*
2 martial arts, ice skating, rollerblading

CULTURE NOTE – *BUFFY THE VAMPIRE SLAYER*

Buffy the Vampire Slayer is a hugely successful cult American TV series, which was broadcast between 1997 and 2003, about a young woman with supernatural powers who tries to lead a normal life.

Exercise 2 page 41

• As students complete the *Learn this!* box, circulate and look over their shoulders to see if they're getting it right. With a **weaker class**, you may want to write the answers on the board. Ask students to look for examples of affirmative, negative and interrogative sentences in the text.

KEY

1 can't   2 Can

Exercise 3 page 41

• Do the first 2–3 sentences as a class. Students do the rest individually. Check as a class.

KEY

1 can't drive	4 can't speak	6 can't swim
2 can't dance	5 can count	7 can't talk
3 can play, can do		

Exercise 4 page 41

• The word *adverbs* came up when *adverbs of frequency* were studied in lesson 2D. Find out if students remember what it means. Try to elicit a translation. Read the *Learn this!* box with the whole class. Have students translate the examples into their own language. Point out the spelling change in *easy – easily.* Point out that it is the same change as in *I study – He studies.*
• Do sentences 2 and 3 of the exercise as a class. Students continue individually. Check as a class. With a **weaker class**, write answers on the board.

KEY

1 slowly	3 early	5 well
2 carefully	4 late	6 easily

For further practice of can *and adverbs, go to:*

Grammar Builder 4D: Student's Book page 114

KEY

7
1 I can't swim.
2 We can speak English.
3 William and Mary can rollerblade.
4 Anne can't sing.
5 Charles and Elizabeth can't use a computer.
6 Philip and I can cook.
7 Edward can't do gymnastics.
8 You can play the piano.

8 Can Clare and Beth ride a bike? Yes, they can.
Can Rob play volleyball? No, he can't.
Can Clare and Beth play volleyball? Yes, they can.
Can Rob speak Italian? Yes, he can.
Can Clare and Beth speak Italian? No, they can't.

9 early – late   quietly – loudly
fast – slowly   well – badly

10
1 late	3 well	5 fast
2 quietly	4 early	6 slowly

Exercise 5 page 41 🎧 1.62

• Students read the instructions and the phrases in the table. Play the recording twice (or more, if students indicate they need to listen again). Check. If someone has ticked 2, 3 or 7, explain (or better still, have another student explain) that Andrea can do those things, but not *quickly, fluently* or *well*.

KEY

Tick 1, 5, and 6.

Transcript 1.62

Boy	Can I ask you some questions, Andrea?
Girl	Sure.
Boy	OK. Can you dance well?
Girl	Yes, I can. I love dancing.
Boy	Can you type quickly?
Girl	No. I can type, but really slowly!
Boy	OK, next question. Can you speak Russian fluently?
Girl	Russian? No! I know a few words, but I can't speak it fluently.
Boy	Can you remember names easily?
Girl	No! I'm terrible with names. I always forget them.
Boy	Can you run fast?
Girl	Yes, I can. I do a lot of sport – and I'm good at athletics.
Boy	Can you whistle loudly?
Girl	Yes, I can. Listen. [WHISTLE]
Boy	Yes, that's loud! Can you play an instrument well?
Girl	Um, not really. I can play the guitar, but not very well.
Boy	Can you eat chocolate slowly?
Girl	No, I can't. I love chocolate. I always eat it really quickly.

Exercise 6 page 41

- Students get to think about themselves and relate the target language to their own experience.

Exercise 7 page 41

- Students talk in pairs. Circulate and listen. If some students are saying very little, you may ask additional questions, e.g. :
  S1: *Can you play an instrument well?*
  S2: *Yes.*
  T: *What instrument can you play?*
- You can also get into little conversations with **fast finishers**, pushing them to say more and give details.

Exercise 8 page 41

- Students report back to the class. If your group is big (15+), this stage may be too long. Ask them to tell the class only the 3–4 most interesting things about their partner.

➡ Lesson outcome

Ask students: *So what did we talk about today?* Elicit: *can/ I can/ What we can do.* Ask a few students to say a few things they can and cannot do. You may end by saying: *I hope you can all say some of the things you can do!* Draw students' attention to the lesson statement: *I can say how well I can do something.*

4E READING
It's party time!

LESSON SUMMARY ● ● ● ○ ○ ○

Reading: an article; reading for gist and for specific information
Speaking: speaking about music and parties; describing a picture
Vocabulary: musical instruments
Topic: People

SHORTCUT *To do the lesson in 30 minutes, ask students to read the text for the first time at home.*

➡ Lead-in 2 minutes

- Ask students: *Do you like going to parties? What do you like doing at a party? Do you like organising parties?*
- Write on the board: *At a good party, there is ...* – ask students to suggest ways of finishing this sentence (orally, no preparation).
- Say: *Today, we are going to read and talk about parties.*

Exercise 1 page 42

- Tell students they're going to describe a photograph. Read the speaking tip aloud. In pairs, ask students to describe the photo of the woman using the questions in exercise 1. Then have one or two students describe the photo to the whole class.

Exercise 2 page 42

- Ask students to read the reading tip first. Allow 1–2 minutes for them to read through the text quickly. Check answers.

KEY

1 She organises parties.   2 Yes, she does.

Exercise 3 page 42

- Students read the text a second time and do the task. Check answers with the whole class.

KEY

1 b   2 c   3 a   4 b   5 c

Exercise 4 page 42

- Allow 4–5 minutes for students to find the words. When checking the answers to question 3, point out that *hard* and *fast* can also be adjectives, e.g. *a hard bed, a hard exam, a fast car*; but in this sentence they are adverbs: she has to work *hard* and she has to work *fast*. This is important, as it shows students that a word only achieves its full meaning in context. You may even want to write the examples on the board with the headings *adjectives* and *adverbs*. Students work individually, then compare answers in pairs. Finally, check with the whole class.

KEY

1 parrot, elephant   3 (to work) hard, fast
2 dress, shoes   4 castle, house

Exercise 5 page 43

- Students do the matching exercise in pairs. Dictionaries should be available, or they can use the Wordlist. When checking, pay attention to pronunciation, especially the /eɪ/ in *bass*, the /aɪ/ in *violin*, the stress in *guitar* and *saxophone*.

KEY

1 violin   4 piano   7 trumpet
2 cello   5 drums   8 bass guitar
3 guitar   6 saxophone

Exercise 6 page 43

- When checking, explain the difference between a grand piano and an upright piano.

KEY

guitar, grand piano

Exercise 7 page 43 🎧 1.63

- Play the recording once without stopping, then a second time pausing after each instrument to check answers. It's supposed to be a fun exercise, so don't worry too much if some students get very few answers right, and don't push them – it's probably because they're not musical, not because they can't cope with the English.

KEY

1	guitar	4	cello	7	bass guitar
2	drums	5	piano	8	violin
3	saxophone	6	trumpet		

LANGUAGE NOTE – AMERICAN ENGLISH

In British English we say e.g. *play the guitar, play the piano*, etc. In American English *the* is omitted.

Exercise 8 page 43

- Students can work in pairs or groups of three. The answer to question 1 will be short and straightforward in most cases, but if you've got some serious music lovers in your class, answering number 2 may take forever! Allow it if the students are enjoying themselves and using English. You might even turn it into a competition: which group can list the largest number of musicians each playing a different instrument?

ADDITIONAL SPEAKING EXERCISE

- Ask students to go back to the text and underline or highlight all the unusual parties that are mentioned:
  - a Hawaiian party with guitars, palm trees and parrots
  - a historical party in a castle
  - an 'India' party with elephants
  - a 'winter' party with ice and snow and skating
  - a party where everything is red

- In groups of three or four, ask students to discuss:
  - Which party would they like to go to? – Why?
  - Which party would they like to have for their 18th birthday? – Why?

- Circulate and monitor, asking additional questions if needed.

- The groups now split into pairs. Tell them to imagine they are party planners and they have to sell the parties they organise to customers. Each pair chooses one party they are going to advertise. They find all the vocabulary that will help them describe the party in the best possible terms, and prepare a 1-minute talk.

➡ Lesson outcome

Ask students: *What did we talk about today?* Accept any relevant answers, but try to elicit something like: *parties* and *music*. Ask everyone to say one new word they learned in the lesson (they should not repeat words). Draw the students' attention to the lesson statement: *I can understand a magazine article and describe photos.*

4F EVERYDAY ENGLISH
Making arrangements

LESSON SUMMARY ● ● ● ● ●

Functional English: making arrangements
Vocabulary: *let's*, prepositions of time, collocations: activities
Grammar: present continuous for future use
Listening: dialogues
Speaking: making arrangements
Topic: people

SHORTCUT *To do the lesson in 30 minutes, set the Grammar Builder as homework, and have fewer pairs act out their dialogues in front of the class.*

➡ Lead-in 2 minutes

- Put this question to the class in general: *Have you got any plans for this afternoon? (or for the weekend?)* Point to yourself: *I'm going to the British Council library.* (or whatever it is you're doing – give true information). Now ask a specific student: *Are you doing anything this afternoon, Joanna?* Accept any relevant answer, e.g. *Go to cinema*, but if a student produces *I'm going... (to the cinema, shopping*, etc.) say: *Very good!*
- Announce the topic of the lesson: *Today we're going to talk about making arrangements.*

Exercise 1 page 44 🎧 2.01

- Ask students to read the instructions, the box and the dialogue. Students do the task individually and compare answers in pairs. Play the recording twice – first without stopping, then pausing after each gap to check. While checking, work a bit on intonation in the phrases: *This is Harry, What about Tuesday? Let's meet, See you there.*

KEY

1	This	3	can't	5	meet
2	want	4	What	6	See

LANGUAGE NOTE – USAGE

Point out that *I'm afraid* means *I'm sorry but* in this context and is used to refuse invitations or give bad news.

The word *then* at the end of a sentence has a similar meaning to *so* at the beginning of a sentence. For example, A *I can't come on Tuesday.* B *Let's go on Wednesday then.* B's sentence is similar to: *So let's go on Wednesday.*

Exercise 2 page 44

- Read the *Learn this!* box with the whole class. Then let students read the dialogue again.

KEY

I'm playing volleyball. Are you doing anything?
Let's meet outside the bowling alley.

Exercise 3 page 44

- Allow 30–45 seconds for students to study the *Free-time activities* box. They should know what they want to say before they start speaking. Circulate and listen. If time allows, have one or two pairs act out their dialogue in front of the class.

For further practice of the present continuous for future, go to:

Grammar Builder 4F: Student's Book page 114

KEY

11 1 are (you) doing   3 are going   5 is working
    2 am staying   4 are (you) going   6 am meeting

Exercise 4 page 44   🎧 2.02

- Allow 30–45 seconds for students to read the *Prepositions of time* box. Then tell them they are going to hear three conversations between friends who arrange to meet. The task is to write down in the chart details of the activities the friends arrange to do together. Check answers. If students have written *Saturday* or *2 o'clock*, accept it, as it is correct, but ask them to add the prepositions.

KEY

Activity	Day	Time
1 go to the disco	tomorrow (evening)	at 8 o'clock
2 play football in the park	on Saturday	at 2 o'clock
3 go for a coffee	on Sunday	at 3 o'clock

Transcript 2.02

1
Vicky   Hi Steven. This is Vicky. How are you?
Steven   Fine thanks. And you?
Vicky   I'm fine. What are you doing tomorrow evening?
Steven   Nothing in particular. Why?
Vicky   I'm going to the disco with Jake. Do you want to come?
Steven   Thanks, I'd love to. What time are you going?
Vicky   At about eight o'clock.
Steven   OK. Let's meet outside the disco at eight.
Vicky   Fine. See you there.
2
Tom   Hello
Andy   Hi Tom. This is Andy.
Tom   How are you?
Andy   Fine. Listen, are you doing anything on Saturday?
Tom   I'm going shopping in the morning, but I'm free in the afternoon.
Andy   I'm going to the park with Liam and Ben to play football. We're meeting at two o'clock. Do you want to come?
Tom   Yes, great idea.
Andy   OK. See you in park at two.
Tom   Great. See you there.
3
Kate   Hello. Kate here.
Sarah   Hi Kate. This is Sarah.
Kate   Do you want to go for a coffee on Saturday morning?
Sarah   I'm afraid I can't. I'm going shopping with my sister. What about the afternoon?
Kate   Sorry, I'm busy then. I'm visiting my grandparents.
Sarah   I'm free on Sunday afternoon. Are you doing anything then?
Kate   No, I'm free too.
Sarah   Then let's go for a coffee on Sunday. What time?
Kate   Three o'clock at the cafe?
Sarah   Fine. See you there.

Exercise 5 page 44   🎧 2.03

- Students complete the sentences. In a **weaker class,** play the recording while they're doing it, stopping after each sentence. Then check. In a **stronger class**, let students do the task looking at the rules and using their memory, then play the recording to check.

KEY

1	–	4	in	7	on
2	at	5	at		
3	on	6	on		

Exercise 6 page 44

- Students work on their conversations. Circulate and monitor, correcting errors and doing some pronunciation practice if needed. Practise pronouncing these tone units: *I'd love to. – Great idea. – I'm afraid I can't. – I'm busy then.*
- Get students to practise speaking without writing their dialogues down.

Exercise 7 page 44

- Depending on time and on students' patience, have 3–5 pairs act out their dialogues in front of the class. Pick students who speak loudly and clearly and/or whose dialogues have something interesting or funny about them. You may ask them to sit back to back so that they cannot see each other – as when talking on the telephone.

➡ Lesson outcome

Ask students: *What have we looked at today?* Elicit: *making arrangements (arranging to meet); prepositions of time (at five o'clock, in the morning, on Monday, tomorrow evening).* Draw students' attention to the lesson statement: *I can make arrangements to meet somebody.*

Notes for Photocopiable activity 4.2

Let's meet next week

A class mingle
Language: making arrangements, free-time activities, present continuous, prepositions of time
Materials: one copy of the worksheet per student (Teacher's Book page 130)

- Give a copy of the worksheet to each student and explain that they are going to make arrangements for next week.
- Brainstorm leisure activities onto the board. Ask students to choose six activities and write them down in note form in different places in the diary. They may do a maximum of two activities in one day.
- Ask students to go around the class and find somebody to do each activity with them. They should also organise a place and a time to meet. A typical dialogue should be:
  A *Hi, Ela. Do you want to go swimming on Tuesday afternoon?*
  B *I'm afraid I'm going for a coffee with Karolina.*
  A *OK. What about Wednesday?*
  B *Good idea.*
  A *Let's meet at 3 o'clock outside the swimming pool.*
- When students have agreed to do an activity together, they should write the other student's name and the time of meeting in the correct place in their diary. They repeat the activity until they have found somebody to do all of their activities with.

4G WRITING
An invitation

LESSON SUMMARY ● ● ● ● ●
Writing: an invitation
Reading: invitations
Grammar/vocabulary: *can* for requests
Topic: home

SHORTCUT *To do the lesson in 30 minutes, set the writing as homework.*

➡ Lead-in 2 minutes

• Write *invitation* on the board. Ask who knows what it means. (Accept a translation.) Have a chat with the class about invitations. Ask: *When you're having a birthday party, do you write invitations? Who does? How about your eighteenth birthday, would you like to have written invitations / invitations on paper then? How about a party at school, should there be invitations? What do you think – is a written invitation a very formal thing?*
• Conclude: *Today we are going to work on writing invitations.*

Exercise 1 page 45

• Look at the photo with the whole class, but ask individual students to answer the questions. Try to get them to describe the photo in as much detail as possible.

Exercise 2 page 45

• Students should have not trouble with the task itself, so encourage them to look up all the types of parties in the Wordlist or their dictionaries. After you've checked the answers, ask additional questions: *Which types of parties did you have in the last year? Was it a good party? Did you write invitations? Did anyone have a fancy dress party? What did you wear?* etc.

KEY

1 fancy dress party   3 end-of-term party
2 birthday party

Exercise 3 page 45

• Students study the *Learn this!* box. The word *request* needs to be explained. Go over the texts again.

KEY

Can you invite Mandy, please?
Can you bring some CDs, please?
Can you bring something to eat or something to drink?

LANGUAGE NOTE – POLITENESS

Students often think that if they use the word *please*, then they are being sufficiently polite when they make a request. However, it is necessary to use the question *Can you ... ?* e.g. *Can you help me, (please)?* Not ~~Please help me.~~ or ~~Help me, please.~~

Exercise 4 page 45

• Students read the invitations again. While checking, you may point out that time and place do not necessarily have to

come in this order; you can also state the place first and the time afterwards.

KEY

1 the event   4 the place
2 the day   5 extra information or request
3 the time

Exercise 5 page 45

• Allow 30–45 seconds, then go through the openings and endings as a class.

KEY

Hi / Dear   See you soon.
                   Love
                   Cheers

Exercise 6 page 45

• Read the writing tip together. With a **weaker class**, you may provide the following additional information on the board:
  – wrong verb form
  – 2 x spelling mistakes
  – wrong preposition
  – one word to delete
• When students have identified the errors and thought of ways of correcting them, discuss the answers with the whole class and write the correct versions on the board.

KEY

We're **having**   **on** Saturday   you can ~~to~~ come
Christmas   **house**

Exercise 7 page 45

• Allow about two minutes for students to read through the instructions and guidelines. You may wish to discuss what extra information there could be.

Exercise 8 page 45

• Students proofread each other's work. As an **optional activity,** they could write replies to each other's invitations, refusing them politely, explaining why they cannot come and suggesting meeting some other time. (This can be done even if the main writing activity was set as homework, but it relies on everyone or nearly everyone bringing their invitations promptly. If some students don't do that, they can write replies to the invitations in the book.)

ALTERNATIVE WRITING TASK

Together with some friends, you are organising an event at school (a show, concert, bazaar). Write an invitation to the parents. Information to include:

• type of event
• when (day and time)
• where
• a request for parents to come in large numbers

➡ Lesson outcome

Ask students: *What did we work on today?* Elicit: *invitations.* Elicit a few phrases that can be used in an invitation. Draw students' attention to the lesson statement: *I can write an invitation to a party.*

1 1 music
2 physics
3 chemistry
4 religious education
5 information and communication technology
6 geography

2 1 tracksuit   4 jeans   7 jumper
2 trousers   5 boots   8 sweatshirt
3 trainers   6 skirt

3 2 There isn't a gym but there is a playing field.
3 There is a computer room but there isn't a library.
4 There aren't any DVDs but there are some videos.
5 There is a cinema but there isn't a museum.
6 There is a café but there aren't any restaurants.

4 2 Sue and Jenny have to walk to school.
3 Karen doesn't have to do a lot of homework.
4 My dad has to get up early.
5 My grandparents don't have to work.
6 Their mum has to cook dinner every night.

5 2 Do Sue and Jenny have to walk to school? Yes, they do.
3 Does Karen have to do a lot of homework? No, she doesn't.
4 Does my dad have to get up early? Yes, he does.
5 Do my grandparents have to work? No, they don't.
6 Does their mum have to cook dinner every night? Yes, she does.

6 1 is dancing   3 is swimming   5 isn't listening
2 aren't eating   4 am writing

7 2 Jack and Sarah can speak Italian.
3 I can do martial arts.
4 My sister can't cook.
5 His cousins can't swim.

8 2 She's singing well.
3 They're playing football badly.
4 He speaks Chinese perfectly.
5 She's dancing beautifully.

9 1 opposite   3 corridor
2 stairs   4 left

10 1 d   2 b   3 e   4 c   5 a

1 1 two kilometres   3 £90
2 11 a.m. to 11 p.m.

2 1 c   2 c   3 b   4 a   5 b   6 c

Transcript 2.04

Narrator   It's Friday morning. Márton is arriving for work at the Arcadia Hotel. Dave, the receptionist, is there.
Dave   Good morning! How are you?
Márton   I'm fine, thanks. And you?
Dave   Oh, I'm fine. Márton, are you working in the restaurant this evening?
Márton   No, I'm not. I have a free evening. Why?
Dave   Do you want to work some extra hours? It's the Friday night party here at the hotel. We need more people to work in the bar.
Márton   Oh … OK. Yes.
Dave   You don't have to. It's just an offer.
Márton   No, I want to. I need the money!
Dave   Great!

Márton   What time?
Dave   Can you be here at 8 o'clock?
Márton   Sure, no problem.
Dave   OK. See you later.
…
Narrator   It's 8 o'clock in the evening.
Dave   Hi, Francesca!
Francesca   Hi, Dave. Are you working?
Dave   Yes, of course. Are you here for the party?
Francesca   That's right. Where is the bar?
Dave   Go along this corridor and turn right. Then go down the stairs. The bar is on your left.
Francesca   OK, thanks. See you later.
Dave   Bye.
Márton   Hi, Dave. Am I late?
Dave   No, you aren't. It's 8 o'clock now.
Márton   Is the party in the bar?
Dave   Yes, it is. Just follow Francesca!
Márton   Who?
Dave   My friend, Francesca.
Márton   I don't know her.
Dave   She's walking along the corridor. Look!
Márton   Is she wearing jeans?
Dave   No, that isn't her. She's wearing black trousers and a white T-shirt.
Márton   Oh, I can see her. Is she English?
Dave   No, she isn't. She's Italian. She's from Milan. She's really nice.
Márton   Yes. She is.
…
Narrator   It's now 10 o'clock. Everybody is enjoying the party. Márton is working in the bar. He's making cocktails.
Márton   Oh, hi Dave. How are you?
Dave   Fine. Márton, this is my friend, Francesca.
Márton   Nice too meet you!
Francesca   Nice to meet you too. Where are you from?
Márton   I'm from Hungary. What about you?
Francesca   I'm from Italy – Milan.
Customer   Er, excuse me. Are you serving cocktails?
Márton   Oh, sorry. Just a minute.
Francesca   Hey, see you later.
Márton   Yes … see you later. Sorry – I can't talk now. I'm working.
Francesca   Do you work here every evening?
Márton   No, I don't. I'm working tonight because …
Customer   Excuse me!
Márton   Sorry, sorry. What can I get you?
Francesca   Bye!
Márton   Bye!

3 1 c   2 e   3 a   4 d   5 f   6 b

4 1 He needs the money.   4 She's there for the party.
2 At 8 o'clock.   5 Black trousers and a white top.
3 He's working.   6 He's working.

5–6 Open answers

EXAM For further exam tasks and practice, go to Workbook page 42. Procedural notes, transcripts and keys for the Workbook can be found on the *Solutions* Teacher's Website at www.oup.com/elt/teacher/solutions

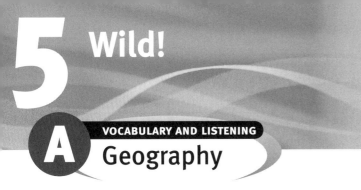

5 Wild!

A VOCABULARY AND LISTENING
Geography

THIS UNIT INCLUDES ● ● ○ ○
Vocabulary • geographical features • continents • adjectives for measurement
• wildlife • outdoor activities • prepositions of place • holiday accommodation
Grammar • comparative adjectives • superlative adjectives • *would like*
Speaking • asking and answering quiz questions • giving opinions
• talking about National Parks • asking for information
Writing • a description of an animal • a postcard
WORKBOOK pages 44–50

LESSON SUMMARY ● ● ● ○ ○
Vocabulary: geographical features and geographical names
Listening: a quiz
Grammar: the use of articles with geographical names
Speaking: asking and answering quiz questions
Topic: nature and the environment

SHORTCUT *To do the lesson in 30 minutes, set Vocabulary Builder (part 1) as homework.*

➡ Lead-in 5 minutes

• If you have access to a large physical map of the world, display it in the classroom. Ask students if they can name any of the things on it (you can explain what you mean by saying: *for example, this is an ocean* and pointing to one).

Exercise 1 page 48

• Students label the pictures with words from the box. Some of the words will have already been mentioned; for others use dictionaries or the Wordlist.

KEY

1	island, sea	5	rainforest	9	beach
2	river	6	forest	10	waterfall
3	mountains, valley	7	ocean		
4	desert	8	hill		

Not illustrated: lake

Exercise 2 page 48 🎧 2.06

• Play the recording once without stopping for students to check their answers.
• Play the recording again, pausing after each word and asking different students to repeat individually.
• Try to make sure that *mountains* is pronounced /ˈmaʊntɪnz/ not /ˈmaʊnteɪnz/, and that *valley* is /ˈvæli/ not /ˈvæleɪ/. Also pay attention to the reduced vowel /ə/ in unstressed syllables in *island, desert, ocean,* etc.

Exercise 3 page 48 🎧 2.07

• After students have completed the names of the places, play the recording once for them to check. Then play it again, pausing and asking students to repeat first chorally, then individually, paying attention to pronunciation, especially intonation.
• Draw students' attention to the *Look out!* box with rules for the use of articles with place names. N.B.: The aim is to make students aware of those rules, so that they may notice examples and with time build the habit of correct usage. It would be unrealistic and unhelpful to expect elementary level students to memorise such rules and to use articles accurately at this stage.

KEY

1	the Amazon Rainforest	5	the River Ganges
2	the Baltic Sea	6	the Sahara Desert
3	the island of Tasmania	7	Lake Superior
4	the Tatra Mountains		

Exercise 4 page 48 🎧 2.08

• If you have a map of the world in the classroom, walk up to it and point out the continents as their names are spoken on the recording. Ask students to repeat individually.
• Point out that the 'Au' in *Australia* is /ɒ/ not /aʊ/. The same is true about *Austria. North America* and *South America* are tone units (pronounced as single words).

Exercise 5 page 48

• Model the activity by asking one student the question in the book: *Where is the Amazon Rainforest?* You can help by pointing at the map.
• Students can ask and answer questions in closed pairs, but if you want more control over their performance at this stage, it can also be done in open pairs across the class.
• There is a potential problem with is/are: *Where ~~is~~ the Tatra Mountains?* With a **stronger class**, simply correct the error if it occurs. With a **weaker class**, write: *Where is …? Where are …?* on the board before or while asking the model question and ask what the difference is.

For further practice of geography vocabulary, go to:

Vocabulary Builder (part 1): Student's Book page 132

KEY

1	1	hill	5	sea	8	waterfall
	2	lake	6	valley	9	forest
	3	river	7	island	10	desert
	4	beach				

2	1	North America	3	Europe	5	Asia
	2	South America	4	Africa	6	Australia

3 2 Spain is in Europe.
3 Brazil is in South America.
4 Canada is in North America.
5 Nigeria is in Africa.
6 India is in Asia.
7 Argentina is in South America.
8 Finland is in Europe.

Exercise 6 page 48 🎧 2.09

• Play the questions once without stopping, then pausing after each one to check. When everyone is sure what the questions are, allow 2–3 minutes for students to answer in pairs.

KEY

1	Europe	3	ocean	5	islands
2	River	4	Desert	6	Lake

Exercise 7 page 48 🎧 2.10

• Play the whole quiz to allow students to check their answers. Check that everyone is sure what the answers are.

KEY

See transcript 2.10

Transcript 2.10

QM Welcome to the Geography Quiz. Our first contestant is Kevin from London. Are you ready, Kevin?

Kevin Yes.

QM OK. Here's the first question. Are the Rocky Mountains in North America or Europe?

Kevin They're in North America.

QM That's correct. Well done. Here's the next question: Which sea does the River Danube flow into – the Black Sea or the Mediterranean?

Kevin Is it the Mediterranean? ... I think it's the Mediterranean.

QM No, that's the wrong answer. The Danube flows into the Black Sea. OK. Question 3. Which ocean is between America and Asia?

Kevin That's easy. It's the Pacific Ocean.

QM That's right – the Pacific Ocean. Are you ready for the next question?

Kevin Yes.

QM OK. Here it is. Where's the Gobi Desert – in Africa or Asia?

Kevin The Gobi Desert. Mmm. I'm not sure.

QM Have a guess.

Kevin Asia?

QM That's right. It's in China. Question five. Can you name two islands in the Mediterranean Sea?

Kevin Mallorca – that's in the Mediterranean. I often go there on holiday.

QM Lucky you! Can you name another island?

Kevin Corsica.

QM Well done. They're both in the Mediterranean Sea. You've got four points, Kevin. Now for the last question. In which continent is Lake Victoria?

Kevin Lake Victoria. It's in Australia, I think.

QM Is that your final answer?

Kevin Yes, Australia.

QM Oh, dear, Kevin. Lake Victoria is in Africa.

Kevin Oh, yes, of course!

QM You've got four points! Well done, Kevin!

Exercise 8 page 48

- This can be done in pairs or groups of three, and it's essential that there should be an even number of pairs/groups. It would be helpful to have a big map of the world on the wall and/or atlases for each team.
- Students write questions. Circulate and help.

Exercise 9 page 48

- Each pair or group gets together with another and they quiz each other. Circulate and supervise, paying special attention to the pronunciation of place names.

For work on adjectives of measurement, go to:

Vocabulary Builder (part 2): Student's Book page 132

- Read the *Learn this!* box with the class. In a **stronger class**, elicit examples using the adjectives presented in the box. Focus the students on exercise 4. If necessary, students can work in pairs to work out or look up the meaning of the adjectives.

KEY

4 1 How long is the lake?   4 How old is the boy?
    2 How wide is the lake?   5 How tall is the boy?
    3 How deep is the lake?   6 How heavy is the boy?

5 1 old   3 wide   5 tall
    2 high   4 long

- Point out to students that we usually use *tall* for people, but *high* for mountains. Focus their attention on the units of measurement used in the sentences in exercise 5. You could

ask students to close their books, and dictate the same sentences, this time gapping the units, e.g. *Mount Rysy is 2499 _____ high.*

KEY

6 Open answers.

→ Lesson outcome

Ask students: *What have we talked about today?* Elicit: *geography / places / geographical names.* Ask: *Can you give me some words for geographical features?* Praise the students who come up with the more sophisticated ones, such as *waterfall* or *valley.* Draw students' attention to the lesson statement: *I can talk about places around the world.*

5B GRAMMAR
Comparative adjectives

LESSON SUMMARY ● ● ○ ○ ○

Grammar: comparative adjectives
Speaking: comparing things

SHORTCUT *To do the lesson in 30 minutes, set the Grammar Builder as homework.*

→ Lead-in 2 minutes

- Ask two students of very different height to stand up. Ask: *Who is taller?* Indicate *tall* and *taller* with your hands and arms. You can give another example, e.g. two rulers or pencils: *long – longer.* Ask students to say what *taller* and *longer* are in their own language. Introduce the subject of the lesson: comparative adjectives, and ask for the equivalent in the students' own language.

Exercise 1 page 49

- Ask students to look at the photos of the two elephants. Ask: *Do you know which is the African and which the Asian elephant?* If someone volunteers an answer, you ask: *Why?* or *How do you know?* (Unless you think the student would have great difficulty giving an answer in English.)
- Ask all students to read the text in exercise 1, then ask: *So, was (student's name) right? Which is the African elephant?*

KEY

1 African elephant   2 Asian elephant

Exercise 2 page 49

- Focus students' attention on comparative forms by pointing to the elephants and saying: *The Asian elephant is big, but the African elephant is bigger.* Explain that comparative adjectives are constructed in several different ways in English and that all those ways are presented in the box in exercise 2.
- Students fill in the table with comparative adjectives. Circulate and monitor. Go over the answers with the whole class. With a **weaker class**, you may want to write the answers on the board or show them on an OHP.

KEY

1 larger   3 more intelligent
2 heavier   4 better

LANGUAGE NOTE – COMPARATIVE ADJECTIVES

There isn't a fixed rule about exactly which adjectives take –er and which take *more*. In general –er is used with one-syllable adjectives and two-syllable adjectives ending in –y. With most other two-syllable adjectives *more* is used, e.g. *more boring*, *more careful*. There are several two-syllable adjectives where both are possible, e.g. *cleverer*, *more clever* and *friendlier*, *more friendly*. At this level, however, it is useful to focus only on the general guideline, as given in the coursebook, that long adjectives need *more*.

Exercise 3 page 49 🎧 2.11

- Play the recording, pausing after each sentence and asking several students to repeat individually. If some of them produce /ər/ instead of /ə/, point out that the *r* is silent. N.B. The word *than* in the two sentences also has the weak vowel /ə/.

Exercise 4 page 49 🎧 2.12

- Make sure students understand what they have to do in this exercise. Play the first sentence twice and ask which words end in /ə/. If few students seem to have identified all the words, play the sentence again. Ask a few students to repeat first the individual words, then the whole sentence. Repeat the procedure with the second sentence.

KEY

1 River, Volga, longer
2 America, further, Australia, Asia

Exercise 5 page 49

- Students read the instructions. Do the first sentence with the whole class as an example (with a **weaker class** do the first three sentences). Students compare answers in pairs first. Check with the whole class.

KEY

1	wider	4	bigger	7	heavier
2	further	5	faster		
3	more intelligent	6	more expensive		

Exercise 6 page 49

- As students ask and answer the questions, monitor their work, paying attention to the pronunciation of weak vowels.
- In case anyone should be in doubt: the Pacific is wider, Saturn is further from the sun, Russia is bigger, gold is more expensive, and water is heavier than ice. Questions 3 and 5 may generate some discussion.

For further practice of comparative adjectives, go to:

Grammar Builder 5B: Student's Book page 116

KEY

1	1	higher	4	wetter	7	taller
	2	easier	5	friendlier	8	later
	3	bigger	6	nicer		
2	1	noisier	4	further	7	heavier
	2	shorter	5	hotter	8	larger
	3	wider	6	better		
3	Open answers					

Exercise 7 page 49

- If you have a map of the world in the room, indicate the Atacama Desert and Death Valley. Students read the instructions and do the exercise individually. With a **weaker class**, start with the whole class, then allow time for individual work. Ask different students to read one sentence each.

KEY

1 The Atacama Desert is colder than Death Valley.
2 The Atacama Desert is drier than Death Valley
3 Death Valley is further from the sea than the Atacama Desert
4 Death Valley is higher than the Atacama Desert.
5 Death Valley is hotter than the Atacama Desert
6 Death Valley is wetter than the Atacama Desert.

Exercise 8 page 49

- Invite students to think of places they've been to. Were they beautiful? boring? hot? As students work in pairs while you circulate and monitor. Ask a few pairs with the most imaginative ideas to report them to the class.

➡ Lesson outcome

Ask students: *What have we talked about today?* Try to elicit: *comparative adjectives* or *comparing things,* or *big and bigger*, but accept any answer that refers to the content of the lesson. Briefly revise comparative forms, asking different students to supply them, e.g. *wide – ?*. Draw students' attention to the lesson statement: *I can make comparisons.*

5C CULTURE National Parks

LESSON SUMMARY ● ● ● ● ●

Reading: National Parks
Listening: descriptions; matching
Speaking: talking about national parks
Topic: nature and the environment

SHORTCUT *To do the lesson in 30 minutes, ask students to read the text for the first time as homework beforehand.*

➡ Lead-in 2 minutes

- Write *National Parks* on the board and say this is going to be the topic today. Ask: *What kind of things can you see in national parks?* Accept any sensible answers, e.g. *trees, animals*, but try to elicit some of the vocabulary from lesson 5A. Then say: *Today we are going to find out about some national parks in Britain, Ireland, Australia and Canada.*

Exercise 1 page 50

- Read through the phrases in the box. Ask students to describe the photo in pairs. Ask one student who is not very strong, but reasonably confident, to repeat their description to the whole class; then ask who would like to add something. Elicit as complete a description as you can.

Exercise 2 page 50

- Tell students they are going to read a text about the Lake District National Park in England. Use the picture in the article to point out the location of Lake District.
- Ask students to read through the text fairly quickly first and do the task in exercise 2. You might even set a time limit of 1–2 minutes. Go over answers with the whole class.

KEY

1 C   2 A   3 B

CULTURE NOTE

William Wordsworth /wɜːdzwɜːθ/ is one of the most popular of all English poets. He was one of the poets who started the Romantic Movement in English poetry. Most of his poems are about the beauty of nature and many of them describe the countryside of the Lake District. His most famous poem is *Daffodils*.

Beatrix Potter /bɪatrɪks pɒtə/ wrote children's books about the adventures of animals, including *Peter Rabbit*, *Tom Kitten*, and *Jemima Puddle-Duck*. She also painted the illustrations of the books, which are still popular with children today. She was born in London but spent most of her life in the Lake District. In 2006 *Miss Potter*, a biographical film was released, starring Renee Zellweger and Ewan McGregor.

Exercise 3 page 50

- Students now have to read the text more carefully. It would be good to have dictionaries available; otherwise they can use the Wordlist. Go over answers with the whole class.

KEY

1 F   2 F   3 F   4 T   5 F   6 T

Exercise 4 page 50

- Ask students to read through the list of outdoor activities in the box and see how many words they know or can understand. Ask them to look up the rest.
- Students do the task individually, compare what they found in pairs, then report back to the whole class. Confirm what they say, using the verb *go*: *Yes, you can go walking and climbing there* ... (to reinforce the use of *go* with activities)
- Point out the silent *b* in *climbing* and have several students repeat the word.

KEY

walking, climbing, swimming, sailing

Exercise 5 page 50

- In this task students relate the vocabulary to their own experience. Ask them to imagine they are going to have some foreign visitors who are really interested in outdoor activities. Students confer and generate ideas in pairs or groups of three. After that, you can take on the roles of several visitors and say: *I really love cycling and especially mountain biking. Where should I go?* or *I like swimming, sailing ... What's a good place to go?* etc.

Exercise 6 page 50 🎧 2.13

- Draw students' attention to the photos of three national parks. Tell them they are going to hear three speakers from different countries talking about their favourite national parks. Point out the task. Tell them they will hear the recording twice. Play it once without stopping, then stopping after each speaker to check answers.

KEY

1 C   2 A   3 B

Transcript 2.13

1

Hi, I'm Sandra and I'm from Adelaide, in Australia. There are lots of great National Parks in Australia. My favourite is the Great Barrier Reef National Park. It's on the east coast of Australia. There are lots of little islands, with fantastic beaches. People go swimming and surfing there, and of course you can go diving and see beautiful fish.

2

Hi, I'm Liam and I'm from Dublin in Ireland. My favourite National Park is the Killarney National Park. It's in the west of Ireland. There are three beautiful lakes where people go sailing and fishing. There are also rivers and forests with lots of interesting animals. I sometimes go there with my family in the summer and we go walking.

3

Hi, I'm Maria and I'm from Calgary, in Canada. I love skiing so my favourite National Park is Banff National Park. It's in the Rocky Mountains in the west of Canada. There are fantastic mountains where people go skiing and snowboarding. But it isn't just winter sports – I go cycling with my friends and go canoeing on the lakes. It's a great place for a holiday.

Exercise 7 page 50 🎧 2.13

- Play the recording once more without stopping, and then again stopping after each speaker to check answers. Students may need reminding what *natural features* are.

KEY

Great Barrier Reef National Park: little islands, surfing; diving
Killarney National Park: lakes, rivers; fishing
Banff National Park: mountains; snowboarding, cycling

Exercise 8 page 50

- Allow time for this activity. It can be done in several ways:
  A The simplest – students talk in pairs while you monitor.
  B Students work in groups – preferably with team-mates of their own choice – and decide on one national park they're going to describe in some detail; each team then speaks in front of the whole group. You can repeat the foreign visitor scenario: you are a foreigner who would like to know about national parks you might visit in this country.
  C If you feel your students are up to it, you may ask everyone to prepare a 1-minute talk about a national park of their choice at home and present it in front of the class. This could also be done in teams of two.

➡ Lesson outcome

Ask students: *What have we talked about today?* Elicit: *National Parks.* Elicit some vocabulary from the lesson. Praise the students who come up with the more sophisticated items. Draw students' attention to the lesson statement: *I can describe a National Park.*

5D GRAMMAR
Superlative adjectives

LESSON SUMMARY ● ● ● ○ ○

Grammar: superlative adjectives
Speaking: expressing opinions
Listening: quiz questions

SHORTCUT *To do the lesson in 30 minutes, set the Grammar Builder for homework.*

➡ Lead-in 2 minutes

- Ask students: *What is the fastest car in the world? What is the best film of this month? What is the most beautiful animal in the world?* Write on the board: *the fastest, the best, the most beautiful* and ask students for translations. Explain: today we are going to talk about superlative adjectives (elicit a translation).

Exercise 1 page 51

- Draw students' attention to the photos and ask them to prepare to talk about them using the words in the box. Some of the words may be new. With a **weaker class**, explain *grow, shelter* and anything else that poses problems. With a **stronger class**, encourage the use of the Wordlist. Allow a minute for preparation. First have students talk about the photo in pairs, then ask 2 or 3 to tell the whole class what they said.

Exercise 2 page 51

- Ask students to read the first sentence of the text. Ask: *What is the text about?* (Antarctica) *Why is the climate extreme?* (Because it's cold/the coldest place in the world.)
- Students read the text for the first time. When they have finished, ask: *So, in what ways is the climate of Antarctica extreme?* (Elicit: *It's the coldest, the wettest and the driest.*)
- Now ask students to read the instructions for exercise 2. Students read the text for a second time to identify the superlative forms.

KEY

1 the coldest	3 the lowest	5 the driest
2 the worst	4 the wettest	6 the most difficult

Exercise 3 page 51 🎧 2.14

- Draw students' attention to the *Learn this!* box and ask them to compare it with the box on comparative adjectives on page 49. Discuss the differences and similarities. As students complete the box, look over their shoulders to make sure they get the spelling right. Play the recording to check answers and practise pronunciation. With a **weaker class**, you may want to write the answers on the board or show them on an OHP.

KEY

1 the largest	3 the hottest	5 the worst
2 the heaviest	4 the most difficult	

Exercise 4 page 51

- Students individually complete the sentences and decide if they think they are true. Check with the whole class. As different students read the sentences aloud, you may ask them for true versions, e.g.
  Student: *I'm the funniest person in the class.* – *Not true.*
  Teacher: *So who is the funniest person in the class?*

KEY

1 the funniest	4 the best
2 the hottest	5 the most exciting
3 the most important	6 the most difficult

For further practice of superlative adjectives, go to:

Grammar Builder 5D: Student's Book page 116

KEY

4 2 the highest	5 the nicest	8 the furthest
3 the easiest	6 the worst	
4 the wettest	7 the funniest	

---

5 (Answers will vary)
  2 Who's the most intelligent person in your family?
  3 What's the most popular food in your country?
  4 Who's the most famous actor in your country?
  5 What's the most important school subject?
  6 What's the most boring sport?

6 2 France is hotter than Britain, but Spain is the hottest.
  3 Harry is more intelligent than Dave, but Robert is the most intelligent.
  4 Magazines are cheaper than books, but newspapers are the cheapest.
  5 History is more interesting than science, but music is the most interesting.
  6 Kate is friendlier than Steve, but Wendy is the friendliest.
  7 New York is larger than London, but Tokyo is the largest.
  8 *The Simpsons* is better than *Malcolm in the Middle,* but *Friends* is the best.

Exercise 5 page 51

- Make sure students understand they have to do two things: complete the questions and choose the right answers.

Exercise 6 page 51 🎧 2.15

- Play the recording to check the answers. With a **weaker class**, write all the adjective forms on the board; with a **stronger class**, you may still want to write *furthest* and *biggest*.

KEY

1 the furthest a	4 the longest a	7 the biggest b
2 the deepest c	5 the fastest a	
3 the most intelligent c	6 the largest b	

Transcript 2.15

1 Oslo is further north than Ottawa, but Reykjavik is the furthest north – 2,874 km from the North Pole.
2 The deepest Ocean in the world is the Pacific. The Mariana Trench near the Philippines is more than 11,000 metres deep.
3 Dogs and dolphins are very intelligent animals but the most intelligent animals are chimpanzees.
4 All three rivers are more than 6,000 kilometres long. The Amazon and the Yangtze are both about 6,400 kilometres, but the longest is the Nile, which is more than 6,800 kilometres.
5 The lion is very fast, but the cheetah is the fastest animal in the world. It can run at 110 kilometres per hour.
6 The largest land animal is the elephant. However, the blue whale is much bigger and is the largest and heaviest animal in the world. They can be 30 metres long and weigh 130 tonnes.
7 The three largest continents are Africa, Asia and North America. But which is the biggest? The answer is Asia – it's 45 million square kilometres.

Exercise 7 page 51

- Before students start asking and answering, emphasise that we always say *who* for people, *what* for things. Do the first two or three questions in open pairs to make sure they are getting it right. At the end of the activity bring the class together to compare ideas.

KEY (Answers will vary)

1 Who's the most beautiful actress in the world?
2 What's the most interesting city in your country?
3 What's the best programme on TV?
4 Who's the worst singer in the world?
5 What's the easiest subject at school?
6 Who's the best football player in the world?
7 Who's the funniest actor on TV?

➡ Lesson outcome

Ask students: *What have we talked about today?* Try to elicit: *superlative adjectives* or a translation, but accept any answer that refers to the content of the lesson. Briefly revise superlative forms, asking different students to supply them. Draw students' attention to the lesson statement: *I can describe people and things using superlative adjectives.*

Notes for Photocopiable activity 5.1

How much do you want to bet?

Pairwork
Language: comparatives, superlatives and articles
Materials: one copy of the worksheet per pair of students (Teacher's Book page 131)

- Divide students into pairs and give each pair a copy of the worksheet. Ask students to go through the sentences ticking whether they think they are correct or incorrect. Next they bet between 10 and 100 points on their sentences and write the number in the BET column. Explain that if they bet correctly on the sentence, they win that amount. If they bet incorrectly, they lose it.
- Go through the sentences. If necessary, to avoid cheating, let the students correct another pair's worksheet.
- At the end, students add up their total winnings and losses (gains minus losses). The pair with the highest score wins.
- Correct the incorrect sentences as a class.

KEY

1 The Nile is the longest river in the world.
2 You are the funniest student in the class.
3 correct
4 Mount Everest is the highest mountin in the world.
5 New York is colder than Florida.
6 correct
7 correct
8 Geography is easier than maths.
9 correct
10 correct
11 Football is the most popular sport in the UK.
12 July is hotter than April.
13 correct
14 Russia is the biggest country in the world.
15 correct

5E READING
Dangerous!

LESSON SUMMARY ● ● ● ● ○ ○

Reading: an article; reading for detail
Vocabulary: animals
Speaking: describing animals
Topic: nature and the environment

SHORTCUT *To do the lesson in 30 minutes, ask students to read the text for the first time at home, and possibly to do exercise 1.*

➡ Lead-in 2–3 minutes

- Ask students to remember as many names of animals as they can. Everybody in turn has to say one. If someone cannot think of an animal or repeats a name that's already

been mentioned, they are out. The activity usually continues until there is only one person left – the winner, but you can stop at two or three winners if you wish.

Exercise 1 page 52

- Draw students' attention to the photographs. Ask if they can name any of the animals. Then ask them to do the task, using dictionaries or the Wordlist if they need to.

KEY

1	tiger	5	mosquito	9	elephant
2	whale	6	eagle	10	bear
3	snake	7	jellyfish	11	shark
4	lion	8	hippo		

Exercise 2 page 52 🎧 2.16

- Play the recording once for students to check their answers and a second time to practise pronunciation. Pay attention to the weak vowel /ə/ in *elephant, lion, tiger,* etc.

Exercise 3 page 52

- Students classify the animals, then compare in pairs and add more. Check with the whole class. Write the additional ideas on the board.

KEY

Land: bear, elephant, hippo, lion, snake, tiger
Sea: jellyfish, whale, shark
Air: eagle, mosquito

Exercise 4 page 52

- Introduce the topic of the reading text by asking: *Which animals do you think are the most dangerous?* Elicit a few responses, then direct students' attention to the text. Ask them to read it once and a) match the photos and the paragraphs; b) find out which is the most dangerous animal in the world and why. Allow 3–4 minutes to read. Check answers with the whole class.

KEY

A Hippos (photo 2)
B Box jellyfish (photo 3)
C Mosquitoes (photo 1)
The mosquito is the world's most dangerous animal, because it spreads malaria.

Exercise 5 page 52

- Make sure students understand the meaning of *noun, verb,* and *adjective.* Elicit some examples. If the names of parts of speech are new to your students, write them on the board together with the examples. Show students how it's possible to tell from context if an unknown word is a noun, verb or adjective, and also to tell something about its meaning. You can use the following examples. Write the sentences on the board, then ask the leading questions. You can explain and discuss this in the students' own language if necessary.
- *Hummingbirds live in South America. – What part of speech is 'hummingbirds'?* (Noun.) *How do we know that?* (It is the subject of a sentence; a verb comes after it; the sentence tells us where hummingbirds live.) *What can we guess about its meaning? Are hummingbirds people? Animals? Machines?* (They must be living creatures, as they live somewhere. The second half of the word is *–birds*, so they may be a kind of bird.)
*Our dog always **barks** at the postman. – What part of speech is 'barks'?* (Verb.) *How do we know that?* (From its

position – after the subject and 'always', and from the form, with the third person singular –s, which agrees with the word *dog*.) *Can you guess what it means? What can a dog do to a postman?*
*They have a **vicious** dog. It attacks everyone. What part of speech is 'vicious'?* (adjective) *How do we know that?* (Because of its position between 'a' and a noun; it describes the noun.) *Does it mean a good dog or a bad dog?*

Exercise 6 page 52

- After the practice in exercise 5, you can ask the students to do the same with the five highlighted words in the text. As you go over the answers with the class, ask additional questions to reinforce the vocabulary: *Michał, is your dog aggressive? Ania, do you like Garfield cartoons?* etc.

KEY

1 aggressive (adj.) 3 population (n.) 5 insect (n.)
2 tentacles (n.) 4 cartoons (n.)

Exercise 7 page 52

- Students read the instructions. Make sure they understand that the sentences should be completed using information from the text. Point out the irregular plural of *box jellyfish*. Ask individual students to read the answers aloud.

KEY

1 Mosquitoes 4 box jellyfish 7 box jellyfish
2 Box jellyfish 5 hippos
3 Hippos 6 Mosquitoes

Exercise 8 page 52

- Check with the whole class. As students read their answers aloud, pay attention to the pronunciation of the weak vowel /ə/ in *million* and *thousand*. Point out the absence of the plural *s* in forms such as *three million*.

KEY

1 The body of the box jellyfish is about 20 centimetres long.
2 Mosquitoes give malaria to over 300 million people a year.
3 Some hippos are 3,000 kg.
4 About 3 million people die of malaria every year.
5 Forty percent of the world's population are in danger of malaria.
6 The box jellyfish has got about 60 tentacles.

Exercise 9 page 52

- With a **weaker class**, go over the phrases in the box together. Students may write the descriptions in pairs. With a **stronger class**, encourage the use of dictionaries and the Wordlist. As students write their descriptions, circulate and help. You could also have stronger students sit with weaker ones and help them.

Exercise 10 page 52

- Encourage students to read loudly and clearly. Correct pronunciation mistakes if they affect communication.

ADDITIONAL SPEAKING ACTIVITY

Ask students to work in groups of three or four. Tell them they are preparing a TV programme about dangerous animals. They have to warn tourists about hippos, box jellyfish and mosquitoes – one person will present each animal. They have to tell viewers where the animals live, why they are dangerous, and suggest ways of staying safe. One person will have to introduce the program.

Stage 1: Students prepare what they're going to say. Put these phrases on the board:
Good morning , this is …   *Beware of …*
Today we want to tell you about …   *Don't go near …*
If you're going to …   *Don't go swimming …*
Circulate and help. If students' descriptions of the animals are largely quoted from the text, that is OK. Reading new language aloud, carefully and clearly, is also useful practice.

Stage 2: In their teams, students practise delivering their talks. They can read, but emphasise that they have to read clearly, fluently and expressively. Circulate and help with pronunciation.

Stage 3: Each team in turn presents its programme to the class. Set up a good place for them to do it: a table or two in front of the board, facing the class, with three or four chairs.

Stage 4: Provide some feedback: quote the best sentences or phrases, or examples of particularly effective pacing and intonation. Correct a few errors, especially those which occurred more than once and were made by more than one person.

➡ Lesson outcome

Ask students: *What have we talked about today?* Elicit: *animals* or a similar answer. Elicit examples of new vocabulary. Accept any words from the lesson, but praise the students who come up with the more sophisticated ones. Draw students' attention to the lesson statement: *I can understand an article about animals.*

LESSON SUMMARY ● ● ● ○ ○

Listening: dialogues
Speaking: asking for information
Grammar: *would like*
Topic: shopping and services

SHORTCUT *To do the lesson in 30 minutes, set exercise 7 in the Grammar Builder as homework, and have fewer pairs act out their dialogues in front of the class.*

➡ Lead-in 2 minutes

- Inform the class of the lesson objectives. Ask a few students: *Do you ever go to the zoo? Do you ever go to museums? Do you like going to zoos?/ to museums? What do you need to know before you go?* (Try to elicit the idea of opening hours and ticket prices, in any form, but preferably in English.)

Exercise 1 page 54 🎧 2.17

- Draw students' attention to the photos. Say they are going to hear a phone conversation: a girl is calling the Bronx Zoo (in New York) to ask for some information.
- Play the recording once, asking students to complete the dialogue. Then play it a second time, asking them to concentrate on the intonation. Pause after the four phrases which were missing and ask students to repeat them first chorally, then individually. Make sure they repeat them as single tone units. Model the intonation if necessary.

KEY

1 How can I help you? 3 And what time do you close?
2 What time do you open? 4 How much does it cost to get in?

Exercise 2 page 54

• Read the *Learn this!* box together. Elicit the example of *would like* from the dialogue in exercise 1.

KEY

I'd like some information about the zoo, please.

For further practice of the use of would like, *go to:*

Grammar Builder 5F: Student's Book page 116

KEY

7 1 Would you like 3 Would you like 5 I'd like
2 Do you like 4 I'd like 6 Would you like

8 Open answers

Exercise 3 page 54

• First ask students to read the dialogue in pairs in the form in which it appears in the book. Then they read it again, substituting different names of museums and different times and prices. Ask one or two pairs to perform for the class.

Exercise 4 page 54 🎧 2.18

• Tell students they are going to hear another phone call. Allow 1–2 minutes to read the task and think about the listening tip. Elicit the meaning of *last entry*. Play the recording. Ask students if they need to hear it again. Students compare answers in pairs first, then check as a class.

KEY

Tickets: Adults $14, Children $8, Students $10
Opening hours: 10.00–17.45 **Last entry:** 17.00

Transcript 2.18

Clerk Good afternoon. American Museum of Natural History. How can I help you?
James Oh, hello. Can you give me some information about the museum?
Clerk Sure. What would you like to know?
James What are your opening times?
Clerk We open at 10 and close at quarter to six. But we don't sell tickets after five o'clock.
James How much are the tickets?
Clerk It's $14 for adults and $8 for children under 12.
James How much is it for students?
Clerk For students it's $10.
James OK, thanks very much.
Clerk You're welcome. Have a nice day.
James Bye.

Exercise 5 page 54 🎧 2.18

• Play the recording one or two more times for students to complete the questions and match the replies. Check, paying attention to the pronunciation of whole tone units.

KEY

1 Can, give **b** 3 How much **d**
2 What, times **a** 4 students **c**

Exercise 6 page 54

• In pairs, ask students to imagine that one of them works in one of the museums in your town or a nearby city and the other is a visitor looking for information. Encourage them to choose a real museum. Pairs prepare and practise their dialogues.

Exercise 7 page 54

• Ask 2–6 pairs act out their dialogues to the class. Comment on any recurring errors, praise good performances.

➡ Lesson outcome

Ask students: *What have we talked about today?* Try to elicit: *asking for information* or a similar answer. Elicit some of the questions practised in the lesson. Draw students' attention to the lesson statement: *I can ask for and give information.*

5G WRITING
A postcard

LESSON SUMMARY ● ● ● ● ●

Writing: a postcard
Reading: postcards
Grammar/vocabulary: prepositions of place
Topic: nature and the environment

SHORTCUT *To do the lesson in 30 minutes, set the writing as homework.*

➡ Lead-in 2 minutes

• Write *postcards* on the board. Have a chat with students about writing holiday postcards. Use these questions: *Do you ever write holiday postcards? Who do you write to? How much do you write?*
• Conclude: *Today we are going to work on writing postcards.*

Exercise 1 page 55

• Draw students' attention to the postcard photos and the two texts. When checking answers, you may ask: *Where is Mallorca?* If you have a map of the British Isles in your room, you can point out the location of Loch Ness.

KEY

1 Scotland 2 Mallorca

Exercise 2 page 55

- This can also be done as a jigsaw reading activity: one student in each pair reads the Mallorca card, the other the one from Scotland; they answer the questions and then exchange information. Later ask everyone to read the card they haven't yet read and go over the answers as a class.

KEY

Sally's card:

1	In Scotland.	4	In a youth hostel.
2	They think it's great.	5	Loch Ness.
3	Not very good.	6	They go walking in the mountains.

Dan and Kate's card:

1	In Mallorca.	4	At a campsite in a small village.
2	They think it's lovely.	5	The beach near the campsite.
3	Fantastic.	6	They go swimming and Kate goes sailing.

Exercise 3 page 55

- Students write the phrases. With a **weaker class**, you could write them on the board as well.
- *Wish you were here!* is a fixed expression typically used in postcards. Encourage students to learn it as an expression rather than worry about grammatical issues such as why we use *were* when it's in the present.

KEY

1 It's lovely here and the weather is fantastic.
2 Wish you were here.
3 See you next week.

Exercise 4 page 55

- Draw students' attention to the box with prepositions of place. Ask a few students questions like: *Do you prefer being at the seaside or in the mountains? Or maybe near a lake?*
- Ask students to find the expressions with prepositions in the two postcards they have read.

KEY

We're in Mallorca.   We're at a campsite in a small village.
the beach near the campsite
We're in Scotland   We're in a youth hostel near Loch Ness.
in the mountains

Exercise 5 page 55

- Draw students' attention to the photos at the bottom of the page. Say: *These are different kinds of accommodation – places where you can stay.* (Write *accommodation* on the board.) Ask students to do the matching exercise, using dictionaries. Check with the whole class. Ask a few students questions like: *Do you prefer staying in a villa or at a campsite? Would you like to stay in a cottage like this?*

KEY

Italy – Villa   Las Vegas – hotel   Ireland – campsite
Spain – apartment   Finland – cottage
Austria – youth hostel

Exercise 6 page 55

- Set up the writing activity. Have students read the writing tip and tell them it is very, very important to always *think first*, before they write anything! Invite them to look at the photos and choose one place. Then ask them to imagine the actual holiday, considering the points listed in the task. Encourage them to note down some vocabulary for each of the points.

Exercise 7 page 55

- The actual writing is best set as homework. To make it more attractive and realistic, you can ask students to use real postcards (they can be the cheap variety with no photograph) and to address the cards to their classmates – everyone to the person directly before them on the class list. (The first person writes to the last one.) In the next lesson, the cards can be 'delivered' and read.

ADDITIONAL WRITING TASK

You're on holiday in your favourite place in your country. Write a postcard to friends from the USA, which will make them want to visit the place in the future. Information to include:

- Say where you are, what kind of place it is and where it lies. (*it is a … in the north of … / near …*)
- Say what kind of accommodation is available. (*I'm staying in a … but you can also stay in …*)
- Say what a tourist can do there (*We go swimming, etc.*) *every day. You can also … here …*)
- Encourage them to come. (*Come …/ Can you come …?*)

➡ Lesson outcome

Ask students: *What did we look at today?* Elicit: *postcards* or *holidays*. Elicit any useful tips students have learned. Draw students' attention to the lesson statement: *I can write a postcard describing a place.*

Notes for Photocopiable activity 5.2

Wild!

Mind map

Language: vocabulary from Unit 5
Materials: one copy of the worksheet per pair of students (Teacher's Book page 132)

- In this activity students work in pairs to complete a mind map which groups together words in topics related to the theme *Wild*. Explain that learning words in topic groups in this way helps the brain to store new words and will help students remember them. They should be encouraged to start topic vocabulary pages in their notebooks and to add to them as they meet words throughout the course.
- You could set the activity as a race.

KEY

Geographical features:
Land desert beach hill island mountains rainforest valley
Water lake ocean river sea waterfall
Animals:
Types of animal eagle bear hippo jellyfish shark snake tiger whale
Parts of an animal's body legs tail tentacles wing
Adjectives fast aggressive dangerous fast intelligent large rare
Weather cold dry hot wet
Activities bird-watching canoeing climbing cycling diving horse riding mountain biking sailing
Accommodation cottage campsite youth hostel

TOPIC ● ● ● ● ●
People

➡ Lead-in 2 minutes
- Discuss going out with students. Where do they like going? Who do they usually go out with? What do they wear? How often do they go out?

Exercise 1 page 56
- Students ask and answer in pairs. Circulate and monitor. At the end ask students if they think there is a connection between the clothes people like and the music they listen to.

Exercise 2 page 56 🎧 2.19
E Listening: matching statements to speakers
- Read the listening tip as a class. Emphasise that when doing a listening task students should be familiar with all the questions / statements in the exercise before the recording is played, so that they know exactly what they're listening for.
- Play the recording twice. Ask students to compare answers in pairs. Ask them if they want to listen to any of the speakers again and replay whatever is required. Check answers as a class.

KEY
1 C   2 F   3 A   4 B   5 D

Transcript 2.19
1
I'm a black jeans and T-shirt person. I always wear jeans and denim jackets and big black boots. You can probably tell that I like American rock music. My favourite T-shirt is a black and white one that I got from an Aerosmith concert. That was a good night. Great music.

2
I like casual, comfortable clothes. I like big trousers and long cotton shirts or jumpers. I usually wear trainers during the day. If I go out in the evening, I'll probably wear the same thing! But I'll put shoes or boots on instead of trainers. I like listening to R'n'B music, and I like going to clubs that play that kind of music, but I can't dance very well.

3
I wear jeans and T-shirts during the day, but if I go out in the evening, I like to dress up. I like skirts and dresses and nice shoes with quite high heels. But my shoes have to be comfortable, because I like dancing. I usually go out to a club with good dance music, and stay on the dance floor for as long as possible.

4
I am comfortable in long skirts and dresses. I usually wear boots with them in the winter and flip-flops or sandals in the summer. If I go out in the evening, I just change my dress. I'm a classical music student, but I also really like blues and some folk music. There's a great blues bar near the university that I go to with my friends.

5
I love rap music, and I love the clothes that go with it. When I go out, I wear narrow jeans with a big belt, white trainers or high heels, a brightly-coloured top or T-shirt and lots of jewellery. I like to go out clubbing with my friends. We dance for hours and hours. It's amazing.

Exercise 3 page 56
- Students read the instructions and the statements about the photos. In pairs, students match the descriptions to the photos.
- Check the answers with the class.

KEY
1 Photo 1
2 Both
3 Both
4 Photo 2
5 Photo 2

Exercise 4 page 56
- Ask students to look more closely at photo 1. Explain that they are going to learn how to describe a person's position in a photo. This will help them discuss photos in an exam situation.
- Students do the task and compare answers in pairs.

KEY
1 a   2 d   3 b   4 c

Exercise 5 page 56
- Students build on the previous exercise and describe the people in the photos in greater detail. Circulate and monitor. Ensure students are able to clearly state which person they are talking about.

Exercise 6 page 56
E Speaking: picture-based discussion
- Read the speaking tip with the class. Explain that when they have two photos, they need to be able to talk about things that are similar and things that are different in each one. The tip box has some useful phrases for discussions of this kind.
- Read the exam task as a class and check understanding.
- Allow students two or three minutes to prepare. In pairs, students take it in turns to speak about the photos for 1–2 minutes. Their partner listens.
- Listen to students, and see if they are using the phrases from the speaking tip box correctly.
- At the end, discuss the task with the students. Did they find it easy or difficult? How do they feel about talking on their own rather than as part of a conversation? Was the preparation time useful? Discuss ideas around the class.

➡ Lesson outcome
Ask students: *What have we done today?* Elicit: *listening with a matching task* or equivalent and *describing photos* or *talking about going out*. Elicit some information about the tasks and tips.

Get ready for your EXAM 6

Nature and the environment

➡ Lead-in 3-4 minutes

- Brainstorm vocabulary related to nature: for example, ask everyone to give the name of an animal, then ask where each of the animals lives; ask for some names of landscape features (remembered from unit 5), e.g. *lake, mountain*.

Exercise 1 page 57

- Tell students they are going to read about blue whales. Check if everyone remembers the word *whale*. Say blue whales are the biggest whales and elicit a translation.
- Ask students to read the sentences and decide if they are true or false in pairs. Do not go over the answers – students will find them in the text.
- Ask students to read the text quickly to find out if their answers were correct.

KEY

1 T	2 F	3 T	4 F

Exercise 2 page 57

E Reading: completing a text

- Ask students to read the rubric and to re-read the reading tip on page 17 (in *Get Ready for your exam* 2). Remind them that in a matching exercise there is always an extra item or items that do not belong anywhere.
- Students work on the task individually. Check as a class. As you go over the answers to the matching exercise, ask students to answer the questions with information from the chosen paragraphs.

KEY

A 2	C 3	E 1	G 6
B 5	D 7	F –	H 4

Exercise 3 page 57 🎧 2.20

- Ask students if they remember a situation when somebody suggested going out and they refused. Did they thank the person? Did they give a reason?
- Study the expressions for refusing invitations, then play the recording. Ask students to repeat individually and chorally, paying attention to pronunciation.

Exercise 4 page 57

- Read the task with the class. The controlled practice can be done in open pairs with the whole class: choose a pair of students, preferably sitting quite far apart, to do one mini-dialogue of suggestion and refusal. Then repeat with another pair.
- If you feel students need more practise, allow them to continue in closed pairs. Circulate and monitor as students talk. Listen for any errors in the target language and discuss these as a class at the end.

Exercise 5 page 57

- Read the information. Students do the exercise individually and compare answers in pairs.
- Ask students to read out their answers and check as a class.

KEY

1 at, on	3 at	5 –, at
2 –, at	4 in, at, in	

Exercise 6 page 57

E Speaking: situational role-play

- Read the speaking exam task. Students do the task in pairs. They can then switch roles and do the task again. Ask some students to perform the task in front of the class. Elicit feedback from the class focusing on good points and also correcting any persistent mistakes.

Exercise 7 page 57

- Read the tip. Students work in pairs. You may wish to ask them to describe the photo in pairs, bringing together all the language they have practised. Then one student asks the two questions and the other one answers, after which they change roles and the first student answers the questions. Circulate and monitor. Have 2–3 students answer the questions in front of the whole class (and 2–3 others describe the photo if they were practising it at this stage). Discuss the strong and weak points of each answer.

➡ Lesson outcome

Ask students: *What have we done today?* Elicit: *reading and completing a text* or equivalent and *role-plays, inviting,* or *refusing and accepting invitations* or equivalent. Elicit some information about the tasks and tips.

6 Out and about

THIS UNIT INCLUDES ● ● ● ●
Vocabulary • places in town • time expressions • sequencing words
Grammar • past simple: *be* and *can* • past simple affirmative (regular verbs)
Speaking • talking about places in town • retelling a story
• telephone English • saying phone numbers
Writing • a tourist information leaflet • phone messages
WORKBOOK   pages 52–58

A VOCABULARY AND LISTENING
In town

LESSON SUMMARY ● ● ● ● ●

Vocabulary: places in town
Listening: short dialogues
Speaking: talking about the location of places in town
Topic: Travel and tourism

SHORTCUT *To do the lesson in 30 minutes, set questions 1–3 in Vocabulary Builder (part 1) as homework and keep exercise 7 brief.*

➡ Lead-in 2 minutes

• Say: *Today, we are going to talk about places in town. Can you name any places in our town?* Students will probably know a few names in English, and a further few might be names of companies owning office buildings. If students are stuck for ideas, offer a few prompts, e.g. *What's near our school? Where do you often go at weekends?*

Exercise 1 page 58

• Ask students to look at the map. Can they name some of the places? Ask them to do the task in pairs, using the Wordlist.

KEY

1	park	9	tourist information office
2	cinema	10	theatre
3	church	11	car park
4	town hall	12	police station
5	post office	13	art gallery
6	museum	14	railway station
7	library	15	bank
8	department store	16	bus station

Exercise 2 page 58 🎧 2.21

• Play the recording once for students to check their answers. Then play it again pausing after each item and asking them to repeat chorally and individually. With a **weaker class**, ask for translations to check they understand. With a **stronger class**, you may wish to ask some additional questions, e.g. *What can you do there? Is there one in our town? Where is it?*

Exercise 3 page 58

• Students do the exercise individually or in pairs. Check with the whole class.

KEY

1	railway station	5	park	9	theatre
2	library	6	bus station	10	art gallery
3	post office	7	car park		
4	tourist information office	8	cinema		

Exercise 4 page 58 🎧 2.22

• Tell students they are going to hear 8 short conversations happening in some of the places listed in exercise 1 and they have to guess which place it is. Say they will hear the recording twice. Play it through once without stopping; the second time, stop after each place and ask for answers.

KEY

1	car park	5	post office
2	art gallery	6	railway station
3	theatre	7	library
4	tourist information office	8	bus station

Transcript 2.22

1	**Man**	Go on ... go on ... There's lots of space behind the car.
	Woman	We're very near to that blue car.
	Man	Which blue car?
	Customer	That one.
	Man	Oh, dear. Sorry.
2	**Boy**	What is it?
	Girl	I don't know. I can see a face, I think.
	Boy	That's not a face. It's a tree.
	Girl	Is it? Well I like the colours.
	Boy	I don't.
3	**Actor**	To be or not to be. That is the question. Whether 'tis nobler in the mind to suffer ...
	Girl	Look at his trousers. Aren't they funny!
	Boy	Ssshhh!
4	**Tourist**	Good morning. Do you have a map of London, please?
	Clerk	Yes, here you are.
	Tourist	Thanks. And I'd like some information about Buckingham Palace, please ...
5	**Customer**	I want to send this postcard to the USA. How much is it?
	Clerk	55p, please.
6	**Girl**	Quick! there's the train. Don't miss it!
	Boy	Oh, no! I haven't got a ticket yet!
7	**Boy**	There's a really good book here.
	Girl	Really? What is it?
	Boy	It's called ...
	Librarian	Sshhhh!
8	**Boy**	I'd like a ticket to Liverpool, please.
	Clerk	Single or return?
	Boy	Single, please.
	Clerk	That's £20, please.
	Boy	What time's the next bus?

For further practice of places in town, go to:

Vocabulary Builder (part 1): Student's Book page 133

KEY

1	1	d	3	g	5	a/c/f	7	e
	2	a/c/f	4	b/h	6	h/b	8	a/c/f

2	1	bus station	5	railway station
	2	town hall	6	art gallery
	3	car park	7	police station
	4	post office	8	tourist information office

3
1 library
2 church
3 art gallery
4 park
5 car park
6 post office
7 theatre
8 museum

4 Open answers

Exercise 5 page 58

• Ask students study the pictures illustrating the prepositions *between, near, next to* and *opposite*. Elicit translations to check understanding, then move on to the speaking activity. Monitor, paying attention to pronunciation.

Exercise 6 page 58

• Encourage students to make use of all the language on the page – the box with names of places and the prepositions, and possibly words from other lessons (e.g. *zoo* or *museum* from Unit 5). Encourage the use of different sentence structures – there are three models in the exercise, and with a **weaker class** you might specify: *Write six sentences built like the sentences in the book: two like the first one, two like the second one and two like the third.*

Exercise 7 page 58

• Allow a minute for students to prepare some descriptions. As they work in pairs, circulate and monitor. At the end, bring the class together and ask a few students to perform.

For work on words that go together, go to:

Vocabulary Builder (part 2): Student's Book page 133

KEY

5 catch a train, go for a walk, park a car, visit a museum, order a pizza
go to a night club, have a good time, pay for a ticket, speak to a friend, take a boat trip

6
1 order a pizza
2 goes to a night club
3 take a boat trip
4 catch a train
5 go for a walk
6 park a car
7 speaking to a friend
8 having a good time

7
1 for
2 to
3 to
4 at
5 at
6 from
7 of
8 in
9 for
10 with
11 in
12 from

➡ Lesson outcome

Ask students: *What have we talked about today?* Elicit: *places in town/ our town.* Ask: *Can you give me some words for places in a town?* Accept all answers, but praise the students who come up with the more sophisticated ones, such as *town hall*. Draw students' attention to the lesson statement: *I can say where places are in my town.*

GRAMMAR
6B Past simple: *be* and *can*

LESSON SUMMARY ● ● ○ ○ ○ ○

Grammar: past simple of *be* and *can*
Listening: a dialogue
Speaking: talking about skills and abilities in the past

SHORTCUT *To do the lesson in 30 minutes, do exercise 4 as a class and limit exercise 8 to one sentence per person. Set the Grammar Builder as homework.*

➡ Lead-in 2-3 minutes

• Say: *Today, we begin to talk about the past. For example: I am at school now, but at 8 o'clock last night I wasn't at school. I was at home. Where were you at 8 o'clock last night?* (Don't expect a full sentence in reply: *At the cinema* is very good.) *I can swim now, but when I was 5 years old, I couldn't swim. Could you swim when you were 5 years old?* (Again, *Yes / No* is enough.)

• Write on the board: **past simple** *be: I was at home last night. can: I could swim when I was 10.*

• Conclude: *Today, we're going to study the past tense of the verbs* be *and* can.

Exercise 1 page 59 🎧 2.23

• Before students open their books, tell them they are going to listen to a phone conversation between Cathy, who is on holiday in the United States, and Tom, who's at home. Ask the two questions from exercise 1. Play the recording once, then tell students to open their books and follow the dialogue in the book as you play it a second time. Elicit answers to the questions.

KEY

1 in Boston
2 in New York

LANGUAGE NOTE – *WHAT ... LIKE*?

The question *What ... like?* frequently confuses students because they aren't used to seeing *like* being used as a preposition, as it is here. Watch out for responses such as, *It's like amazing.*

Exercise 2 page 59

• Students fill in the table and compare answers in pairs. Check with the whole class. If you have an OHP, you can display the completed chart on a transparency.

KEY

1 was	6 was	11 could
2 were	7 wasn't	12 couldn't
3 wasn't	8 Were	13 Could
4 weren't	9 were	14 could
5 Was	10 weren't	15 couldn't

Exercise 3 page 59

• Students do the exercise individually or in pairs. Check with the whole class.

KEY

1 were	4 weren't	7 weren't
2 wasn't	5 wasn't	8 wasn't
3 was	6 were	

For further practice of past simple, be *and* can, *go to:*

Grammar Builder 6B: Student's Book page 118

KEY

1
2 Joe and Helen were in Bratislava on Wednesday.
3 Joe wasn't in Paris on Tuesday.
4 Helen was in Liverpool on Saturday.
5 Joe was in Moscow on Thursday.
6 Joe and Helen weren't in Liverpool on Friday.
7 Helen wasn't in Budapest on Monday.

2 2 Where was Helen on Tuesday? She was in Paris.
   3 Was Helen in Budapest on Wednesday? No, she wasn't.
   4 Was Joe in Stockholm on Saturday? No, he wasn't.
   5 Were Joe and Helen in Bratislava on Thursday? No, they weren't.
   6 Where were Helen and Joe on Wednesday? They were in Bratislava.
   7 Where was Joe on Thursday? He was in Moscow.
   8 Were Joe and Helen in Liverpool on Saturday? Yes, they were.

3 1 couldn't go
   2 couldn't find
   3 couldn't finish
   4 couldn't understand
   5 couldn't hear
   6 couldn't listen
   7 couldn't sleep
   8 couldn't play

Exercise 4 page 59

- Read the example and do sentence 2 with the whole class to make sure everyone knows what they have to do. After students have finished, check with the whole class. Ask: *Which of these people do you know?*

KEY

1 Budhia Singh could run marathons when he was three.
2 Maria Sharapova could play tennis when she was four.
3 Vanessa Mae could play the violin and piano when she was five.
4 Michael Schumacher could drive when he was four.
5 Sergey Karjakin could play chess when he was four.
6 W.A. Mozart could write music when he was five.

CULTURE NOTES

Born in India in 2002, **Budhia Singh** is the world's youngest marathon runner. At the age of three and a half he ran 60 km in six and a half hours. He has become famous and appeared in a number of television commercials. In 2006 he was ordered by the government to stop running because of fears for his health.

The tennis player and model, **Maria Sharapova,** was born in Siberia in 1987, but moved to the US at the age of seven. In 2004 she won Wimbledon at the age of seventeen. In 2007 she was ranked the top seeded (and highest-earning) female tennis player.

Born in Singapore in 1978 and now living in Britain, **Vanessa Mae** /meɪ/ is a classical and pop violinist. She became a worldwide phenomenon in her mid teens when she created a new kind of 'fusion music'.

The German Formula One racing driver, **Michael Schumacher**, won the Grand Prix seven times. He retired as a driver in October 2006.

Sergey Karjakin from Ukraine became the youngest person ever to receive the title of chess *grandmaster* at the age of twelve.

Wolfgang Amadeus Mozart was born in Austria, in 1756. He was a child prodigy, composing when he was five and performing for the Austrian empress when he was six. He was taught by his father, Leopold Mozart, a professional musician and scholar, who took Wolfgang and his sister on a musical tour, playing to the courts of Europe, when Wolfgang was six. His first opera, *Bastien und Bastienne*, was produced when he was twelve. Mozart died in 1791 leaving 600 different compositions in a wide range of musical forms.

Exercise 5 page 59

- Make sure everyone knows what *because* means. Read the example and do sentence 2 with the whole class to make sure everyone knows what they have to do. Students work individually and compare answers in pairs. After they have finished, check with the whole class.

KEY

1 I couldn't go to school because I was ill.
2 I couldn't read my book because it was dark.
3 She couldn't swim because the water was very cold.
4 We couldn't eat our dinner because we weren't hungry.
5 I couldn't speak to Kevin because he wasn't home.
6 They couldn't play tennis because it was wet.
7 I couldn't sleep because I wasn't tired.
8 They couldn't buy alcohol because they weren't 18 years old.

Exercise 6 page 59

- Read the example and do sentence 2 with the whole class to make sure everyone knows how to build the questions. After students have finished, ask them to read the questions aloud. Work on pronunciation.

KEY

1 Could you read when you were four?
2 Could you write your name when you were two?
3 Could you walk when you were one?
4 Could you count to ten when you were three?
5 Could you speak English when you were twelve?
6 Could you ride a bike when you were ten?
7 Could you swim when you were four?

Exercise 7 page 59

- Tell students to pay attention and remember the most interesting things they find out about their partner, as they will have to report them to the class.

Exercise 8 page 59

- Ask students to just tell the class the 2–3 most interesting things about their partner.

➜ Lesson outcome

Say to students: *Today we looked at the past simple tense of two verbs:* be *and* can. *What's the past tense of* be? *I …?* (elicit several forms). *What's the past tense of* can? Draw students' attention to the lesson statement: *I can talk about my past.*

6C CULTURE
Tourist information

LESSON SUMMARY ● ● ● ○ ○

Reading: a leaflet about London
Listening: radio advertisements
Writing: a tourist information leaflet
Topic: travel and tourism

SHORTCUT *To do the lesson in 30 minutes, set the writing as homework.*

➡ Lead-in 2 minutes

- Before students open their books, ask them for anything they know about London. You can say: *Today, we are going to talk about London. Please think: What do you know about London? Anything you can remember about it.* Allow 20–30 seconds for students to think, then repeat the question and have a brainstorming session about London.

Exercise 1 page 60

- Ask students to look at the photos. Do they recognise any of the places? Draw their attention to the task. Remind students to use the Wordlist. Check with the whole class

KEY

1 E   2 A   3 D   4 B   5 C

CULTURE NOTE – LONDON SIGHTS

Madame Tussauds /mædəm tuːsɔːdz/ was started by a French wax sculptor, Madame Marie Tussaud (1761–1850). It contains wax figures of famous people from past and present. There are now Madame Tussauds museums in New York, Amsterdam, Las Vegas, Shanghai and Hong Kong.

The **Tate Modern** is situated on the River Thames. It has been extremely popular since it opened in 2000, partly because of the building, a disused power station. It shows modern art, i.e. since 1900.

The **London Eye** opened in March 2000 as part of the Millennium celebrations and is the world's tallest observation wheel, offering passengers a 25-mile view in every direction. It is Britain's most popular paid-for attraction.

The **National Gallery** in Trafalgar Square, London, contains the largest collections of international paintings in Britain, with paintings dating from the 14th to the early 20th century. More modern paintings are held at **Tate Britain** and **Tate Modern.**

The **British Museum** in Bloomsbury, London, has one of the world's finest collections of art and ancient objects including the Elgin marbles and the Rosetta Stone.

The **Tower of London,** built in the 11th–13th century, is best known for its use as a prison in which many people accused of crimes against the king and queen were kept. These included Mary Queen of Scots and Anne Boleyn.

St Paul's Cathedral was designed by Sir Christopher Wren and completed in 1710. It has a large dome, inside which is the *Whispering Gallery,* where if a person whispers close to the wall on one side of the gallery they can be heard by another person on the other side of the gallery 32 metres away. The Cathedral contains the graves of many famous people including Lord Nelson and the Duke of Wellington.

Harrods is a large, fashionable and expensive department store that claims to supply any article or service. It began in 1861 as a small shop selling food. It is now owned by Mohamed Al-Fayed, the father of Dodi Al-Fayed who was killed in a car accident in Paris with Diana, Princess of Wales in 1997.

Exercise 2 page 60

- Students now read the text more carefully and answer the questions individually. Do the first sentence as a class and remind them to include the preposition in the answer, e.g. *Where can you relax and walk? – In Hyde Park.* Go over answers with the whole class.

KEY

1 In Hyde Park	5 At Wimbledon
2 At Stamford Bridge	6 In the West End
3 At Madame Tussauds	7 In street markets
4 At the Tate Modern	8 From the London Eye

Exercise 3 page 60

- Students do the vocabulary exercise individually. Check with the whole class. When checking, ask students to say what the adjective describes in the text: *What does the text say is exciting?* (exciting things to do in the evening).

KEY

boring – exciting	expensive – cheap
dangerous – safe	old – modern
dirty – clean	terrible – fantastic

Exercise 4 page 60   🎧 2.24

- Tell students they are going to hear five radio advertisements for attractions in London. Ask them to read the instructions and list of places in the book. Tell them they will hear the recording twice. Play it through without stopping first, then pause after each advertisement and check answers.

KEY

St Paul's Cathedral – 5	The Science Museum – 2
The National Gallery – 1	Harrods department store – 4
The Apollo Cinema – 3	

Transcript 2.24

1 We have some beautiful paintings and drawings by famous artists like Rembrandt and Van Gogh. We're open every day from 10 until 5.

2 Are you interested in science? Then come and see our exhibitions on the planets and moons of the solar system. The exhibition starts on 1st June and finishes on 30th September.

3 Don't miss the new Julia Roberts film at the Apollo Cinema. A great evening for all the family! The film starts at three o'clock and again at half past seven.

4 The best shop in London, and probably the most famous shop in the world. Open 10 until 7 Monday to Saturday and 12 until 6 on Sundays.

5 London's most famous church is open every day. It's nearly 350 years old. Climb to the top for wonderful views over London. Adults £9. Children £3.50.

Exercise 5 page 60   🎧 2.25

- Play the first advertisement and ask how many people have got the answers. If they have, check them; if they haven't, play it again. Repeat the procedure with all five advertisements. As students read the answers, make sure they say the times and prices correctly (*Three pounds fifty* etc.).

KEY

1 10, 5	4 10, 7 and 12, 6
2 1st of June, 30th of September	5 £9, £3.50
3 3 o'clock, half past 7	

Exercise 6 page 60

- Set up the writing activity. Remind students that the first thing is always to think about what they are going to write. In this case, the steps would be:
  1 Choose the town or city.
  2 Make a list of the attractions you want to mention.
  3 Decide in what order you are going to describe the attractions.
  4 Decide what you want to say at the beginning and end.
  5 Look up the necessary words. Use your coursebook as a language resource. For example, in this lesson you have the phrases in the box and the text shows you how they are used.
  6 Write. Ask a friend to check.
  7 Make a clean copy of your leaflet with a clear layout.
- Students can now write – in class or at home. If they write in class, they can also do it in pairs. You can display all or some of the leaflets on the wall/ notice board.

OPTIONAL ACTIVITY

This can be done individually or in pairs. Students prepare radio advertisements like the ones in exercise 4 for attractions in their own town/city or a town/city they like. If they have already done the writing task in exercise 6, they can use the information and some of the vocabulary from their leaflets, but now they are going to present it in oral form. Allow 5 minutes for preparation. Each person should 'advertise' one attraction to the class. Remind students to speak loudly, clearly, not too fast and not too slowly.

➜ Lesson outcome

Ask students: *What have we talked about today?* Elicit: *London/ cities.* Ask students if they learned anything new about London. Elicit some of the vocabulary from the lesson. Draw students' attention to the lesson statement: *I can understand and write a tourist information leaflet.*

6D GRAMMAR
Past simple: affirmative (regular verbs)

LESSON SUMMARY ● ● ● ○ ○ ○

Grammar: past simple affirmative (regular verbs)
Reading: a short text with past forms
Speaking: talking about past activities

SHORTCUT *To do the lesson in 30 minutes, set the Grammar Builder for homework.*

➜ Lead-in 2 minutes

- Remind the class that they recently studied the past tense of *be* and *can*. Ask a few students: *Where were you yesterday evening? on Saturday afternoon? Last August?* Tell them that today they are going to learn more past tense forms, so they will be able to say more about what happened. Elicit or explain the meaning of these words: *decide, agree, jog, arrive, hurry, reply.*

Exercise 1 page 61

- Explain that in this text a boy named Joe tells the story of what happened last Saturday when he and his friend Laura wanted to go to the cinema. Ask students to read first the task and then the text. As this is almost the first encounter with the past tense, you may decide to have stronger and weaker students sitting together in case help is needed. Check answers with the whole class.

KEY

1 T   2 F   3 T   4 F

Exercise 2 page 61

- With a **weaker class**, read the verbs aloud. The answer to the question *What is the ending?* may be either –*d* or –*ed.* Accept either and use it to move on to the next exercise, which deals with the rules in more detail.

Exercise 3 page 61

- Students work individually or in pairs. Check answers by asking students to come to the board and write the verbs in the four groups, as they appear in the key.

KEY

1 wanted, waited, asked, answered, walked
2 decided, agreed, arrived, phoned
3 hurried
4 jogged

Exercise 4 page 61 🎧 2.25

- Apart from the difference highlighted in the book (/d/ or /t/ versus /ɪd/), it is also important to point out the difference between /d/ after voiced consonants (as in *phoned, arrived*) and /t/ after voiceless consonants (as in *asked*).

Exercise 5 page 61 🎧 2.26

- As in exercise 4, it makes sense to emphasise also the distinction between a final /d/ and /t/.

KEY

a liked 1 /t/	d agreed 1 /d/	g shouted 2
b wanted 2	e decided 2	h jogged 1 /d/
c watched 1 /t/	f hurried 1 /d/	

Exercise 6 page 61

- Make sure students understand what *most recent* means. Check the answer by asking a student to write it on the board and asking the rest of the class if they think it is correct.
- NB: The order below will usually be the answer. However, note that in January and February 'last year' may in a sense be more recent than 'three months ago', and in the first week of a new month some people may treat 'last week' and 'last month' as equally recent, depending on which part of 'last month' they have in mind. On a date like January 3, Thursday, some students might even insist that that 'last year' is more recent than 'last week'!

KEY

last night – yesterday evening – yesterday afternoon – the day before yesterday – last week – last month – three months ago – last year – two years ago

Exercise 7 page 61

- Students work individually. **Fast finishers** may help weaker classmates or write one or two sentences of their own. Check with the whole class. For sentences 1–5, you can ask the person who is reading if the sentence is true for them!

KEY

1	visited	4	parked	7	stopped
2	watched	5	decided	8	arrived
3	hurried	6	asked		

For further practice of past simple: affirmative (regular verbs), go to:

Grammar Builder 6D: Student's Book page 118

KEY

4
1	phoned	5	studied	9	travelled
2	answered	6	missed	10	spotted
3	listened	7	stopped		
4	hurried	8	visited		

5
1	hurried	4	answered	7	missed
2	studied	5	visited	8	phoned
3	listened	6	stopped		

6
1 I walked to school every day.
2 They agreed to meet at six o'clock.
3 Kevin jogged in the park before breakfast.
4 She studied maths at school.
5 The bus stopped near the school.
6 We arrived at school at quarter to nine.
7 Jim watched television after dinner.
8 Sally phoned her boyfriend on her mobile.
9 Fred helped his mum with the washing up.
10 The football match started at seven o'clock.
11 We lived in London.
12 My dad worked in Manchester.

Exercise 8 page 61

- Before students do the exercise, explain *interest* (on a loan). Depending on the age of your students, you may need to explain the concept, not just the word.
- To check, ask a different student to read each paragraph aloud. Choose students whose reading is rather good, who can be relied on to make some attempt at dramatising the narrative. Pay attention to the correct pronunciation of the past tense forms.

KEY

1	walked	4	agreed	7	asked
2	wanted	5	parked	8	continued
3	replied	6	returned	9	answered

Exercise 9 page 61

- For an activity like this, it is good to have the students sitting in a semi-circle or a similar seating arrangement, so that they can clearly see whose turn it is and always see the person who is speaking. You may set the additional rule that students are not allowed to repeat the same verb or the same phrase (e.g. *I watched TV* a second time would be unacceptable, but *I watched some old DVDs* would be OK).

→ Lesson outcome

Ask students: *What have we talked about today?* Try to elicit: *the past tense* or *past simple* or a translation. Remind students that this is the past of regular verbs and elicit the rules for forming it. Draw students' attention to the lesson statement: *I can talk about past events.*

Notes for Photocopiable activity 6.1

The Goldilocks Burglar

Pairwork

Language: past simple affirmative (regular verbs)
Materials: one cut up copy of the worksheet per pair of students (Teacher's Book page 133)

- The story is in the correct order on the page. All copies will have to be cut up in advance of the lesson, so that the students do not see the correct order before they start.
- Write on the board *The Goldilocks Burglar*. Tell students that they are going to look at a story about a burglar from Milwaukee, USA, called *The Goldilocks Burglar*. Check students are familiar with the story of *Goldilocks and the three bears*. Ask if they can guess why the burglar was given this name. (He helped himself to food and left the dirty plates out.) Be careful not to give away too many details at this stage.
- Write the first two sentences of the story on the board: *A burglar entered a house last night in Milwaukee, USA. He decided to take a television and a mobile phone.*
- Divide students into pairs and give each pair a jumbled set of cards. Tell them to find the first two sentences and then put the rest in order. Check the answers and then ask students to highlight all the examples of the past simple. Practise the pronunciation of the verbs.
- Students retell the story in pairs. One student holds the cards so that the other person can't see them. The other student tries to remember the story. The first student helps where necessary. They change roles at the end of the story.

6E READING
Out on the town

LESSON SUMMARY ● ● ● ●

Reading: a story; reading for detail
Vocabulary: verb + noun collocations, sequencing words, prepositions
Speaking: retelling a story
Topic: home

SHORTCUT *To do the lesson in 30 minutes, set the reading as homework beforehand.*

→ Lead-in 2-3 minutes

- Ask students: *Do you sometimes feel bored? What do you do when you feel bored? Did you ever do anything stupid because you were bored?* Explain that they are going to read a story about two brothers and what they did when they were bored one evening.

Exercise 1 page 63

- Ask students to look at the pictures and guess what happened. Accept all guesses and don't reveal the true story. After students have read the story and put the pictures in order, ask them to compare answers with a partner, then check with the whole class. Ask: *So, were you right about what happened?*

KEY

1 E	2 A	3 G	4 B	5 D	6 I
7 C	8 F	9 H			

Exercise 2 page 63

- Students answer the questions individually and compare answers in pairs. Check with the whole class. If there is some disagreement or uncertainty about an answer, ask someone to read the relevant passage from the text aloud and discuss reasons behind the correct answer.

KEY

1 F	2 T	3 F	4 F	5 T	6 T	7 T

Exercise 3 page 63

- Verb + noun collocations are an important key to communication and fluency, as they allow learners to build natural-sounding sentences. Before students start doing it, make sure they understand they can find all the collocations in the text. Students work individually.
- As you prepare to check answers with the whole class, say: *These words often go together.* Whenever someone reads out a collocation, reinforce it by asking a simple question, e.g.: *Can you park a car? When did you last order a pizza?* If there is time, you can ask everyone to write 2 or 3 sentences using the collocations from the exercise.

KEY

1 car	4 nightclub	7 situation
2 film	5 something	8 dent
3 pizza	6 garage	

Exercise 4 page 63

- Explain that the idea is to try and do the exercise without looking back at the text at first, to see if they can recall some of the prepositions. After that students check with the text. Ask them to read the answers aloud and again ask a few questions to reinforce the new lexis, e.g.: *Do you come to school on your own? Did you study for a long time last night? Do you like sitting at the back of the class?*

KEY

1 at	3 for	5 at the back of
2 on	4 with	6 at

Exercise 5 page 63

- Point out to students that these words will be useful to them whenever they want to tell a story. Students work on the translation in pairs, but this time without dictionaries at first – they have to try and think of translations themselves. After that, allow them to look the words up in dictionaries and discuss answers with the whole class.

KEY

Answers in students' own language.

Exercise 6 page 63

- In groups of three, students decide who is A, B and C. Allow a minute for preparation. Students should retell the story looking at the pictures, not at the text! Circulate and monitor. Then ask for the story to be retold one more time to the whole class, picking students A, B and C from different groups.

➜ Lesson outcome

Ask students: *What did we do / talk about today?* Try to elicit: *reading and telling a story*, but accept any relevant answers. Go over some of the vocabulary from the lesson: sequencing words, verb + noun collocations, prepositions. Draw students' attention to the lesson statement: *I can understand and retell a story with help.*

6F EVERYDAY ENGLISH

On the phone

LESSON SUMMARY ● ● ● ● ○

Functional English: telephoning phrases
Listening: phone calls
Grammar: *I'll* for offers
Speaking: telephone conversations
Topic: family life and relationships

SHORTCUT *To do the lesson in 30 minutes, set the Grammar Builder as homework and have fewer pairs act out their dialogues in exercise 9.*

➜ Lead-in 2 minutes

- Have a conversation about telephoning with your class. You can ask such questions as: *How often do you use your phone? Your mobile phone? Who do you usually phone? Who phones you? What do you do when the friend you're phoning is not at home? Do you prefer talking on the phone or sending text messages?*

Exercise 1 page 64 🎧 2.27

- Draw students' attention to the photographs and the dialogue. Play the recording once for students to do the task. Then play it again, pausing to explain any language your students may not have understood (e.g. ask for the translation of *speaking* as used in this dialogue), and to practise the intonation in: *Can I speak to Penny, please?* and *Do you want to leave a message?*

KEY

1 Is that Mrs Jones?	4 She isn't here.
2 Can I speak to Penny, please?	5 Bye then.
3 Just a moment.	

Exercise 2 page 64

- Read the example in the *Learn this!* box aloud. Students go over the dialogue again. When they have identified the two offers, practise pronouncing them. Have students read the whole dialogue in pairs. Ask one pair who are doing really well to read it to the whole class.

KEY

I'll see if she's here.   I'll tell her you called.

Exercise 3 page 64

- Do the exercise with the whole class, paying attention to pronunciation: *I'll* may be a difficult combination of sounds for some students, and they might try to get around it by saying *I will*. Do not accept that. Also, each sentence should be pronounced fluently, as one tone unit.

KEY

a I'll help you.	**d** I'll pay for your ticket	
b I'll give him the message	**e** I'll wait for you.	
c I'll phone again later	**f** I'll give you her number	

For further practice of I'll *for offers, go to:*

Grammar Builder 6F: Student's Book page 118

KEY

7 1 I'll open 3 I'll buy 5 I'll send
  2 I'll carry 4 I'll make 6 I'll answer

Exercise 4 page 64 🎧 2.28

- Tell students they are going to hear two more phone conversations. Ask them to read the four sentences. Make sure everyone understands the meaning of *He is in/out*. Play the recording, stopping after the first call to ask students if they need to hear it again and to check answers. Play the second call using the same procedure.

KEY

1 out	3 out
2 leaves	4 doesn't leave

Transcript 2.28

1

Mr Black	Hello.
Susan	Oh, hello, Mr Black. This is Susan. Can I speak to Mark, please?
Mr Black	I'm sorry, Susan. He isn't here at the moment.
Susan	Oh.
Mr Black	I can take a message.
Susan	Oh, thanks. Tell him that Susan called.
Mr Black	OK. What's your number?
Susan	668402.
Mr Black	That's 668402.
Susan	Thank you very much.
Mr Black	Not at all. Goodbye Susan.
Susan	Goodbye, Mr Black.

2

Mrs White	Hello.
Jack	Oh, hi. Is that Mrs White?
Mrs White	Yes, it is.
Jack	This is Jack. Can I speak to Anna, please?
Mrs White	I don't think she's in. Wait a moment, I'll look in her room.
...	
Mrs White	Hello, Jack. Sorry, Anna isn't here. She's probably in town.
Jack	Oh, OK.
Mrs White	Do you want to leave a message?
Jack	No, it's OK. I'll try her mobile.
Mrs White	Have you got her number?
Jack	I think so. Just a moment. Is it 07975 29753?
Mrs White	Yes, that's right.
Jack	Great! Thanks for your help. Bye.
Mrs White	Bye, Jack.

Exercise 5 page 64 🎧 2.29

- Students work individually. Tell them they do not have to recall all the answers, as they will have a chance to listen again. For this exercise, try to get them not to work in pairs, so that if someone cannot remember a phrase, they have to listen attentively to the recording again. Play the recording as many times as necessary for everyone to get the answers. Go over the answers with the whole class, paying attention to pronunciation.

KEY

1 sorry	4 number	7 number
2 take	5 in	8 help
3 called	6 mobile	

Exercise 6 page 64 🎧 2.30

- Read the *Learn this!* box aloud. Point out that in English we read phone numbers digit by digit, but we do pause after three or four digits, because it makes the number much easier to follow and write down: *five six three – four six five*.
- Play the recording through for students to listen; then play it again pausing after each number and asking students to repeat them chorally or in pairs.

Transcript 2.30

1 four double two four oh eight
2 three nine one nine oh two
3 five seven four eight double eight
4 double three four six double one

LANGUAGE NOTE – NUMBERS

When we say phone numbers 0 is pronounced *oh* in British English and *zero* in American English. However, *zero* has now become common in British English too. 0 is pronounced *nought* in numbers with decimal points, e.g. 0.5 is *nought point five*.

Exercise 7 page 64

- With a **weaker class**, you might start by dictating a few numbers to the whole class yourself, to provide a model of clear enunciation, good pacing and pausing; then ask two or three students to do the same, and only after that move on to the pair work. With a **stronger class**, circulate and monitor, insisting that if someone hasn't managed to write down a number correctly, their partner must repeat it, taking care to speak clearly and pause in the right places.

Exercise 8 page 64

- Depending on the level of your class and how much you think they can absorb, you may wish to pre-teach any or all of the following:
  I'm afraid he's out.
  Could you please tell him I called?
  Would you like to give me your phone number?
  Shall I read that back to you? (the number)

Exercise 9 page 64

- Have some of the pairs act out their dialogues to the whole class. Give feedback: praise good performance, correct a few mistakes (recurring ones or those concerning the language from this lesson).

➡ Lesson outcome

Ask students: *What have we talked about today?* Elicit: *telephoning / telephones.* Ask: *Can you tell me some of the things you can say on the phone?* Elicit any of the phrases from the lesson. Draw students' attention to the lesson statement: *I can make a phone call and leave a message.*

Notes for Photocopiable activity 6.2

4 Telephone Role Plays

Role play in pairs
Language: telephone English
Materials: one cut up copy of the worksheet per pair of students (Teacher's Book page 134)
- Pre-teach: *secretary, manager.*

- Divide students into A and B pairs. Give Students A and B their cut up role cards in the correct order, so that when they are placed face down role card 1 will be at the top.
- Ask students to sit back to back in order to simulate the conditions of a phone call. Students turn over the first card. Give them time to read the situation and then have the telephone conversation. Remind them to use the language in lesson 6F. If any students finish earlier than others, ask them to swap roles.

6G WRITING
A message

LESSON SUMMARY ● ● ● ● ●
Writing: a phone message
Reading: telephone messages
Listening: telephone conversations
Topic: family life and relationships

SHORTCUT *To do the lesson in 30 minutes, set the writing as homework.*

→ Lead-in 2 minutes
- Ask the class to remember when they last answered the phone for someone else. What did the caller want? Did they write the message down? Did they remember to pass it on? Say: *Today we are going to work on phone messages.*

Exercise 1 page 65
- Put students in pairs and encourage them to describe the photo in some detail. Ask for ideas regarding what the person is saying. Accept anything that makes sense, but try to elicit: *Do you want to leave a message?* or, *I can take a message.*

Exercise 2 page 65
- Students read individually and do the task. After checking the answers, write the following words and phrases on the board. Ask students to read again and try to work out what they mean from context. Explain that the numbers refer to the texts.
  1 urgent   3 he missed a train
  2 for ages   4 garage
- With a **weaker class**, do it as a matching exercise: put definitions and translations on the board.

KEY
1 police station   3 London
2 park   4 garage

LANGUAGE NOTE – NEGATIVE QUESTIONS
Message 2 contains the question: *Haven't you got a football match this morning?* It is not a real question. It is quite similar to a question tag: *You've got a football match this morning, haven't you?* where the speaker is making a statement and asking for confirmation. Negative questions are sometimes used to 'challenge' and express slight annoyance.

Exercise 3 page 65
- Students go through the four texts one more time. When checking with the whole class, point out the use of the preposition *on* with phones and phone numbers.

KEY
1 can, on   3 you, at
2 Please, on   4 call

Exercise 4 page 65 🎧 2.31
- Tell students they are going to hear two phone conversations and that they are the person who answers the phone and takes a message. Ask them to read the two incomplete messages. Ask: *In the first conversation, who calls and who answers the phone?* (a boy, Mandy's mother) *So you are Mandy's mother and you're taking this message for Mandy.* Play the recording of the first call twice. Students check answers in pairs; then check with the whole class.
- Repeat the procedure for conversation 2.

KEY
1 Tom   4 06588 49327   7 afternoon
2 café   5 garage   8 five
3 two   6 ready   9 243055

Transcript 2.31
1

Mrs Brown	Hello.
Tom	Oh, hello, is that Mrs Brown?
Mrs Brown	Yes, speaking.
Tom	Hello, this is Tom. Can I speak to Mandy, please?
Mrs Brown	She isn't here at the moment. Can I take a message?
Tom	Yes, please. I'm going to the café with Steve this afternoon. I wanted to invite Mandy.
Mrs Brown	OK. What time are you going to the café?
Tom	At two o'clock.
Mrs Brown	OK, I'll give her the message.
Tom	Thanks. Can you ask her to phone me on my mobile?
Mrs Brown	Yes, of course. What's your number?
Tom	06588 49327.
Mrs Brown	That's 06588 49327.
Tom	Thanks, Mrs Brown.
Mrs Brown	You're welcome Tom. Goodbye.
Tom	Goodbye.

2

Sarah	Hello.
Mechanic	Hello, this is Peter Grey from Grey's Garage. Can I speak to Mr Simpson, please?
Sarah	I'm sorry. He isn't here at the moment.
Mechanic	Can I leave a message, please?
Sarah	Yes, of course.
Mechanic	Can you tell him that his car is ready? He can pick it up this afternoon. The garage closes at five.
Sarah	OK, I've got that. I'll give him your message. Can you give me your phone number, please?
Mechanic	Yes, it's 243055.
Sarah	243055. OK.
Mechanic	Thanks very much.
Sarah	Goodbye.
Mechanic	Goodbye.

Exercise 5 page 65
- Set up the writing task. Tell students to decide who the message is for and who they are in relation to that person as well as the information in the bullet points. Encourage them to use the six messages on the page as models. If the writing is done in class, **fast finishers** can get together in a group and read each other's messages.

ALTERNATIVE WRITING TASK

You are in Britain. You are staying in a friend's house. You answer the phone. Your friend's friend is calling to say he/she cannot meet him/her as agreed. He/she suggests a different time and place. Write a message to your friend. Information to include:

- Who called
- The information that he/she cannot come
- The proposed new time and place
- How to contact the friend who called.

➡ Lesson outcome

Ask students: *What did we practise today?* Elicit: *writing phone messages,* or *messages.* Elicit useful phrases for talking on the telephone. Draw students' attention to the lesson statement: *I can write a phone message.*

LANGUAGE REVIEW 5–6

1 1 mountains
2 rivers
3 islands
4 beaches
5 deserts
6 seas
7 oceans
8 lakes

2 2 At the theatre.
3 At the bus station.
4 At the park.
5 At the post office.
6 At the art gallery.
7 At the library.
8 At the car park.
9 At the railway station.

3 2 Prague is further north than London.
3 The Mediterranean sea is bigger than the Baltic sea.
4 Waikiki beach is longer than Bondi beach.
5 Mount Everest is more famous than Mount Kenya.
6 Africa is hotter than Europe.
7 The Amazon is wider than the Danube.

4 2 The funniest actor in Hollywood is Jim Carrey.
3 The best football team in the world is Manchester United.
4 The most important things in life are free.
5 The easiest language to learn is English.
6 The most difficult subject at school is maths.

5 1 were
2 was
3 wasn't
4 was
5 couldn't

6 1 arrived
2 waited
3 cleaned
4 phoned
5 tried
6 replied
7 walked
8 asked
9 returned
10 shouted

7 1 information
2 help
3 time
4 entry
5 welcome

8 1 Can
2 if
3 leave

SKILLS ROUND-UP 1–6

1 1 b
2 e
3 a
4 d
5 c

2 1 T
2 F Dave and Penny are staying at a hotel.
3 F Dave and Penny arrived late because they couldn't find the hotel.
4 F Derwent Water is a large lake in the valley of Borrowdale.
5 T
6 T
7 F Penny prefers the countryside.
8 F The rent in the countryside is cheaper.

3 Open answers

Transcript 2.32

Anna	Hello?
Dave	Oh, hello. Is that Anna?
Anna	Yes, speaking.
Dave	Hi, Anna. This is Dave – you know, Márton's friend from the hotel.
Anna	Oh, hi! How are you?
Dave	Fine thanks. I'm on holiday in the Lake District! And I've got some news for Márton.
Anna	OK. I'll see if he's here.

...

Anna	I'm sorry, Dave. He isn't here. Do you want to leave a message?
Dave	No, it's OK, thanks.
Anna	Well, I'll tell him you called.
Dave	Thanks. Bye!
Anna	Goodbye.

...

Narrator	Dave is back from his holiday, and back at work.
Dave	Hi, Márton!
Márton	Hi, Dave! How are you? How was your holiday?
Dave	It was great. But I want a longer holiday next time!
Márton	Yes, a week isn't very long.
Dave	Anyway, I've got some news for you – you know I applied for that job at the hotel in the Lake District?
Márton	Yes?
Dave	Oh, wait a moment. One of our guests is coming ... Good morning. Can I help you?
Guest	Hi. I'd like some information about the Friday night party.
Dave	Certainly. How can I help you?
Guest	How much does it cost to get in?
Dave	It's £12 – but you're staying at the hotel, is that right?
Guest	Yes. I'm in room 32.
Dave	Well, it's free for hotel guests.
Guest	Really? That's great! And what time does it start?
Dave	About 8 o'clock.
Guest	OK. Thanks for your help.
Dave	You're welcome.
Márton	So? What's your news?
Dave	Well – they interviewed me on the last day of my holiday, and they offered me the job!
Márton	And you accepted, of course.
Dave	Yes.
Márton	Congratulations! When do you start?
Dave	Next month.
Márton	That's great!

4 He got the job in the Lake District.

5 1 b   2 c   3 c   4 a   5 c   6 a

6 Open answers

EXAM For further exam tasks and practice, go to Workbook page 60. Procedural notes, transcripts and keys for the Workbook can be found on the *Solutions* Teacher's Website at www.oup.com/elt/teacher/solutions

THIS UNIT INCLUDES ● ● ● ●
Vocabulary • countries • nationalities • *make, do, have* and *take* • events in life • free-time activities • phrases for reacting with sympathy
Grammar • past simple: irregular verbs • past simple: negative and interrogative
Speaking • talking about famous people • talking about your weekend
Writing • describing a hero • an e-mail message
WORKBOOK pages 62–68

A VOCABULARY AND LISTENING
On the map

LESSON SUMMARY ● ● ● ● ●
Vocabulary: countries and nationalities, jobs
Listening: short biographies of four famous people
Speaking: game; asking and answering questions about famous people
Topic: people

SHORTCUT *To do the lesson in 30 minutes, set Vocabulary Builder exercises 4–7 as homework.*

➡ Lead-in 2 minutes
- If possible, bring in a big map of the world for this lesson and put it on the wall. With or without a map, ask students if they can name any countries in English. Point to the countries on the map if there is one. Then say: *Today, we are going to talk about countries and nationalities.*

Exercise 1 page 68
- Ask students to look at the map. Can they name any of the countries on it in English? Can they find where they live?

Exercise 2 page 68
- Encourage students to refer to the map when doing the exercise. Work on pronunciation: Make sure that the final sound in *Czech* is /k/. Pay attention to all the reduced vowels (the final vowel in *Lithuania, Slovakia, Russia*; the middle syllable in *Germany*).

KEY
Answers will vary – check the answers for your class.

Exercise 3 page 68 🎧 2.33
- Students do the exercise individually or in pairs. Play the recording once for them to check, then a second time to work on pronunciation. Make sure the stress in *Japan* is on the last syllable.

Transcript 2.33

1	Austria	Austrian	13 Japan	Japanese
2	Belarus	Belarusian	14 Latvia	Latvian
3	Brazil	Brazilian	15 Lithuania	Lithuanian
4	Britain	British	16 Poland	Polish
5	China	Chinese	17 Romania	Romanian
6	Croatia	Croatian	18 Russia	Russian
7	the Czech Republic	Czech	19 Slovakia	Slovakian
8	Estonia	Estonian	20 Slovenia	Slovenian
9	France	French	21 Spain	Spanish
10	Germany	German	22 Ukraine	Ukrainian
11	Hungary	Hungarian	23 the USA	American
12	Italy	Italian		

Exercise 4 page 68
- In a class where the level of general knowledge is good, students should have fun doing this. In a generally weak class, make sure a map of Europe is available. Check with the whole class, paying attention to pronunciation.

KEY

1	Russia	6	Poland
2	Latvia	7	Ukraine
3	Lithuania	8	the Czech Republic
4	Britain	9	Slovakia
5	Germany	10	France
11	Hungary		
12	Italy		
13	Croatia		
14	Spain		

For further practice of countries and nationalities, go to:

Vocabulary Builder (part 1): Student's Book page 134

KEY
1 1 Where's New York? It's in the USA.
   2 Where's Beijing? It's in China.
   3 Where's Tokyo? It's in Japan.
   4 Where's Rio de Janeiro? It's in Brazil.
   5 Where's Sydney? It's in Australia.

2 2 Italy   5 Spain   8 Germany
   3 Sweden   6 Ukraine
   4 France   7 the Czech Republic

3 Open answers

4 1 **-an:** American, Australian, Belarusian, Brazilian, German, Italian, Lithuanian, Russian, Slovakian, Ukrainian
   2 **-ish:** British, Polish, Spanish, Swedish
   3 **-ese:** Chinese, Japanese
   4 **other:** Czech, French

5 2 Rafael Nadal is Spanish.   5 Thierry Henry is French.
   3 Brad Pitt is American.   6 Gary Kasparov is Russian.
   4 Lech Wałęsa is Polish.

Exercise 5 page 68
- Draw students' attention to the photos. With a **stronger class**, ask not only who the people are and what nationality they are/were, but also if students know something about them. Don't confirm answers before playing the recording.

KEY
Pablo Picasso was Spanish.   Zsa Zsa is Hungarian.
Marilyn Monroe was American.   Pele is Brazilian.

Exercise 6 page 68 🎧 2.34
- Play the recording once for students to check their answers.

Transcript 2.34
Pablo Picasso was a Spanish artist. He was born in 1881 in Malaga, Spain. His father was a painter and an art teacher. Picasso studied art at school. In 1904 he moved to Paris and he lived in France for the rest of his life. Picasso painted over 13000 pictures. He died in 1973.

Zsa Zsa Gabor is a Hungarian actress. She now lives in Hollywood. She was born in Budapest in 1917 and she studied at a school in Switzerland. In 1941 she moved to the USA, and decided to become an actress. She appeared in over forty films, and many TV programmes. Her most famous film is Moulin Rouge. Zsa Zsa Gabor is most famous for her marriages. She married nine times.

Norma Jean Baker was a famous film star. She was born in Los Angeles in 1926. She wanted to be an actress and a singer, so she changed her name to Marilyn Monroe. She was soon one of the most famous and richest film stars in Hollywood. She appeared in 30 films. Marilyn Monroe died in 1962, at the age of 36.

Pele is probably the most famous footballer in the world. He was born in Brazil in 1940. He played for two football clubs – Santos and New York Cosmos. He played 92 times for Brazil and appeared in four World Cups. He scored 77 goals in international matches. He stopped playing football in 1977.

Exercise 7 page 68 🎧 2.34

- Students read the task. Make sure everyone understands the true/false sentences. Some students may be able to answer some of them already – encourage them to try. Play the recording once and ask if they need to hear it again. **Fast finishers** can write corrected versions of the false statements. Check answers with the whole class.

KEY

1 F	2 F	3 T	4 F	5 T	6 F	7 F	8 F

Exercise 8 page 68

- Allow students a minute to think of a person. Make sure everyone understands how to play *20 Questions*. Play the first one or two rounds with one student sitting in front of the class and the whole class asking him questions. After that, with a **stronger class**, you can let students play in groups of 4–5, which will generate more student talking time.

For work on collocations with make, do, have *and* take, *go to:*

> **Vocabulary Builder (part 2):** Student's Book page 134

KEY

6	1	have	3	do
	2	take	4	make

7	1	phone call	4	take	7	have
	2	do	5	exam	8	friends
	3	dinner / breakfast	6	homework / housework		

➡ Lesson outcome

Ask students: *What have we talked about today?* Elicit: *countries* and *nationalities.* Ask: *Can you give me some names of countries?* For each country mentioned, ask another student to give the nationality. Draw students' attention to the lesson statement: *I can label the countries of the world and describe a famous person.*

B GRAMMAR
Past simple: irregular verbs

LESSON SUMMARY ●●○○○
Grammar: past simple of irregular verbs
Speaking: talking about past activities

SHORTCUT *To do the lesson in 30 minutes, set the Grammar Builder as homework.*

➡ Lead-in 2 minutes

- Say a few very simple sentences about yourself in the past tense, with clear expressions of past time, e.g.: *I was born in ... I went to study ... in ... I came to (your town or city) in ... I got a job in this school in ...* or any sentences using some of the verbs which will appear in the lesson. Say: *Today, we are going to study the past tense of irregular verbs.*

Exercise 1 page 69

- Focus students' attention on the photo. Discuss what they know about Václav Havel, the man on the right.

Exercise 2 page 69

- Students read the text and check their answers to exercise 1.
- They complete the task individually and compare answers in pairs.

KEY

was born, came, had, left, was, got, went, started, wrote, opposed, spent, became, won
Regular verbs: started, opposed

Exercise 3 page 69

- Students do the exercise individually or in pairs. Check with the whole class. With a **weaker class**, write the answers on the board or have students write them.

KEY

1	was/were	4	went	7	spent
2	became	5	won	8	had
3	got	6	wrote	9	came

Exercise 4 page 69

- Students work on the exercise in pairs. Check answers with the whole class. Ask students: *Which of these people do you know?* With a **stronger class**, try to elicit a few more bits of information about the people.

KEY

1	spent, became	3	was, came, won	5	had
2	went, got	4	wrote		

Exercise 5 page 69

- Read the *Look out!* box aloud. Do the first sentence as a class. Students continue to work individually, using the list of irregular verbs. You may want to allow them to compare answers in pairs, especially in a **weaker class**. Explain that *Native Americans* is a politically correct (and also more accurate) term for 'American Indians'.

KEY

1	brought, c	3	taught, a	5	fought, b
2	thought, f	4	bought, e	6	caught, d

For further practice of past simple irregular verbs, go to:

> **Grammar Builder 7B:** Student's Book page 120

1
1	I – won	4	R – lived	7	I – came
2	I – got	5	R – worked	8	R – started
3	R – studied	6	I – took		

2
1	e	3	g	5	f	7	c
2	h	4	a	6	b	8	d

3
1	ran	5	saw	9	began
2	gave	6	were	10	caught
3	made	7	said		
4	went	8	broke		

Exercise 6 page 69   🎧 2.35

- Play the recording through once for students to check their answers. Then play it again pausing after each sentence and asking students to repeat both chorally and individually. Pay particular attention to the pronunciation of past tense forms.

Transcript 2.35

1 The Spanish brought potatoes to Europe from South America.
2 Before Copernicus, people thought the sun went round the earth.
3 Marie Skłodowska-Curie taught physics at the Sorbonne University.
4 In 1626 Peter Minuit bought Manhattan Island for $24 from Native Americans.
5 Rosa Parks fought for the rights of black Americans.
6 King Henry VIII caught malaria when he was 35.

Exercise 7 page 69   🎧 2.36

- Allow some time for students to look up the past tense forms. If you don't think your students will be able to put the verbs in rhyming pairs without hearing them, play the recording before they start doing it. Allow some time for students to write, then play the recording for them to check. Have some students repeat the rhyming pairs. The most surprising one will be *saw – wore*; it may be worth pointing out that both the *w* in *saw* and the *r* in *wore* are silent.

Transcript 2.36

began – ran   broke – spoke   bought – caught   went – sent
made – paid   read – said   saw – wore

Exercise 8 page 69

- Read the example. Ask a few strong students to say a sentence each about themselves. Point out that the time expression will always come at the end of the sentence. (You may choose to add that it can also come at the beginning: *Yesterday afternoon I did some housework.*) All students write sentences about themselves. Circulate and help. Allow the work to continue until most students have got nine or ten sentences and everyone's got at least six. **Fast finishers** may write 2–3 additional sentences.

> **LANGUAGE NOTE – COLLOCATION**
>
> Encourage students to notice which verbs are used with which nouns and to record and learn them, especially **do** *homework,* **make** *a phone call,* **tell** *a lie* and **take** *an exam.*

Exercise 9 page 69

- As students talk in pairs, circulate and monitor. Correct the pronunciation of past tense forms if necessary. At the end give some feedback on common mistakes.

➡ Lesson outcome

Say to students: *Today we studied the past simple tense of irregular verbs. What's the past tense of become?* (Try to elicit past tense forms of all the verbs that appeared in the lesson). Draw the students' attention to the lesson statement: *I can talk about past events.*

Notes for Photocopiable activity 7.1

Keep talking!

A group board game
Language: past simple affirmative (regular and irregular)
Materials: one copy of the board, enlarged to A3 if possible, per group of three to four students. (Teacher's Book page 135) Dice and counters.

- Make sure students are familiar with the language for playing a board game: *Throw the dice. It's my/your turn. Whose turn is it? Go forward. Go back.*
- Divide students into groups of three or four. Hand out a copy of the board and a set of dice and counters to each group. (If you do not have dice students can use a coin instead. For heads they move forward one square, for tails they move forward three). Explain that students are going to talk about things that they have done in the past. Choose one of the topics from the board and give a demonstration, asking a student to time you.
- Ask students to appoint a time-keeper for each group. (Someone who has a second hand on their watch.) Students take it in turns to throw the dice and move along the squares. When they land on a square they talk about the topic for fifteen seconds without stopping. If they can't do it they move back to their previous square. In a **weaker class** they can have fifteen seconds' thinking time before they speak. The winner is the first student to reach *Finish*.
- Go around listening and helping with vocabulary and checking for correct pronunciation.

CULTURE
An American hero

LESSON SUMMARY ● ● ○ ○ ○

Reading: a text about Martin Luther King
Listening: four people talking about their heroes
Writing and Speaking: a famous person from the past
Topic: society

SHORTCUT *To do the lesson in 30 minutes, set the reading and exercise 3 (and potentially 4) as homework in advance.*

➡ Lead-in 2 minutes

- Before students open their books, write on the board *human rights.* Ask if anyone can guess what it means. Agree a translation with the class. Ask if students can name any famous people who fought for human rights. If Martin Luther King is mentioned, use that as a lead-in to the lesson. If he is not, mention him yourself.

Exercise 1 page 70

- Draw students' attention to the photo. Ask: *What is he doing?* Students may be able to answer: *speaking,* or *speaking to people,* but probably not *making a speech.* In that case introduce the phrase yourself by saying: *He is making a speech,* and possibly miming the gestures of a public speaker.
- Students answer the question individually.

KEY

2

Exercise 2 page 70

- Students read the text quickly. Ask them if their answer to exercise 1 was right.

Exercise 3 page 70

- Some words in the text may be new: *priest, to judge (someone), the content of their character, the law, to continue*. With a **weaker class**, pre-teach them. With a **stronger class**, encourage the use of dictionaries. Students read the text in more detail and answer the questions. Check answers with the whole class.

KEY

1 F – MLK Day is an American national holiday.
2 F – He was born in Georgia.
3 T
4 T
5 T
6 F – In the end they won, and Alabama changed the law.
7 F – He won the Nobel Peace Prize in 1964.
8 F – All four of his children continued his work.

Exercise 4 page 70

- Students go through the text again and underline or highlight past tense forms. When checking, ask for the sentence in which the word appears in the text, e.g. *Martin studied at college*.

KEY

1	was/were	5	decided	9	shot
2	studied	6	won	10	had
3	got	7	made		
4	wanted	8	hated		

Exercise 5 page 70

- Students do the vocabulary task in pairs. When checking with the whole class, ask also for translations of the words (*equal, enemy, nation*, etc.) To some learners it may appear surprising that *country* and *nation* are treated as synonyms; explain that in English they can be treated as more or less synonymous (as in: *... live in a nation where they will be judged not by the colour of their skin ...*). Point out that when we talk of two countries being at war it is really the people that are fighting.

KEY

1	equal	3	nation	5	holiday
2	enemies	4	hero		

Exercise 6 page 70

- If students find the questions too easy, ask them to give some more information about each of the four people (in English).

KEY

1 b   2 b   3 b   4 b   5 a   6 b

Exercise 7 page 70 🎧 2.37

- Play the recording once for students to check their answers. With a **stronger class**, play it again once or twice (depending on how students feel about it) and ask everyone to write down one fact that they didn't know before. Check with the whole class.

Transcript 2.37

Girl My hero is a sportsperson. He's American, and he's from Texas. He was born in 1971. In 1996, he was very ill and doctors said that he had cancer. But he got better, and he won the Tour de France seven times! Now that he has stopped cycling, he has a charity which helps people with cancer. I think he's very kind and very brave.

Boy My hero is a politician. He's South African and he was born in 1918. He was the first black president of South Africa – he was president from 1994 to 1999. But before that he fought for the rights of black Africans in South Africa and he spent 27 years in prison. He's a very brave and honest man, and he's a hero for millions of people around the world.

Girl My hero is a political leader. He was born in India in 1869 and he died in 1948. At that time, India was ruled by the British. For more than 30 years, he worked hard to get the British to leave India. I think he is one of the most important people in history. He was very intelligent and brave.

Exercise 8 page 70

- Make sure students know that the others will have to guess the identity of the person from the sentences they write. Encourage them to use not only the phrases from the box, but also some of the irregular verbs from Lesson 7B.

Exercise 9 page 70

- All or some students (depending on time) read their sentences to the whole class, who guess the identity of the person. Give feedback. Praise well-composed and interesting sentences, and correct errors in the use of past tenses or past time expressions.

➡ Lesson outcome

Ask students: *What have we talked about today?* Accept all relevant answers: *Martin Luther King, heroes*, etc. Ask everyone to say one new fact or new word they learned from the lesson. Draw students' attention to the lesson statement: *I can write about famous people and their achievements.*

7D GRAMMAR
Past simple: negative and interrogative

LESSON SUMMARY ● ● ● ○ ○ ○

Grammar: past simple negative and interrogative
Speaking: asking and answering questions about past activities

SHORTCUT *To do the lesson in 30 minutes, do exercises 5 and 6 with the whole class and set the Grammar Builder for homework.*

➡ Lead-in 2 minutes

- Quickly revise past simple forms: *be, can*; a few regular verbs with different-sounding endings (e.g. *help, watch, agree, phone, want, wait*); a few irregular verbs (e.g. *come, go, spend, buy, make*).

- Ask a student: *Do you watch much TV nowadays?* (If the student answers just *Yes* or *No*, remind them to say: *Yes, I do./ No, I don't.*) Then ask: *And what about when you were young, did you watch much TV when you were a little boy/ girl?* Accept *Yes* or *No* as an answer to this.
- Ask another student: *Do you like … ?* (*football, coffee, reading* – whatever you think will be of interest to the student). When they answer, ask: *Did you like … when you were younger?* Explain to students they are going to learn to ask and answer questions about the past.

Exercise 1 page 71

- Students describe the photo in pairs. Circulate and listen. Ask two students who had interesting things to say to describe the photo to the whole class.

CULTURE NOTE – LIVE 8

Live8 was the name of a series of charity concerts which took place simultaneously in the G8 countries and South Africa in July 2005. They were timed to take place just before a G8 summit meeting in order to put pressure on leaders to drop the debts of the world's poorest countries and increase aid. At the summit the world leaders promised to double aid to these countries by 2010.

Exercise 2 page 71 🎧 2.38

- Words which may need explaining: *band, charity, amazing.* With a **weaker class**, pre-teach them. For *band*, some students may know the synonym *rock/pop group*. With a **stronger class**, let students use dictionaries, but let individual students decide themselves if they're going to use them or try to guess from context. After playing the dialogue (once or twice, depending on what the students need) and making sure everyone has got the answers, check if they understand the words mentioned above.

KEY

1 photo	3 Africa	5 speech
2 London	4 bands	

Exercise 3 page 71

- Read the table aloud. When students have finished doing the task, go over answers with the whole class or write them on the board

KEY

Negative: I didn't take it. I didn't go. I didn't know that.
Interrogative: Did a lot of bands play? Yes, they did.

Exercise 4 page 71

- Allow students a moment to work out the answers. Ask someone – possibly a weaker student with clear, neat handwriting – to write the forms on the board.

KEY

1 didn't   2 Did

Exercise 5 page 71

- Read the example aloud or ask a student to read it. Do the first one or two sentences as a class. When checking the answers, have one student read the question (e.g. *Did Molly take the photo?*) and another one the reply (*Yes, she did.*) to make it sound like a natural exchange.

KEY

1 Did Suzie take the photo? No, she didn't.
2 Did Molly take the photo? Yes, she did.
3 Did Molly go to the Live 8 concert? Yes, she did.
4 Did Suzie go to the Live 8 concert? No, she didn't.
5 Did Suzie watch the concert on TV? Yes, she did.
6 Did Jack watch the concert on TV? No, he didn't.
7 Did Bill Gates make a speech at the concert? Yes, he did.

Exercise 6 page 71

- Do the first one or two sentences as a class.

KEY

1 I didn't watch Live 8 on television.
2 We didn't go on holiday last year.
3 It didn't rain last weekend.
4 I didn't have breakfast this morning.
5 My sister didn't break my mobile phone.
6 England didn't win the World Cup in 2006.
7 Joe didn't buy a CD.

For further practice of past simple (negative and questions), go to:

Grammar Builder 7D: Student's Book page 120

KEY

4 1 They didn't watch TV last night.
  2 He didn't win a Nobel Prize.
  3 I didn't see you at the party.
  4 Harry didn't tidy his room yesterday evening.
  5 I didn't forget your birthday.
  6 We didn't go to school yesterday.
  7 She didn't study music at university.
  8 You didn't buy a new sweatshirt.

5 2 didn't take   7 didn't have
  3 didn't do   8 didn't write
  4 didn't send   9 didn't become
  5 didn't win   10 didn't spend
  6 didn't work   11 didn't finish

6 2 What time did you get up?
  3 Did you go to school?
  4 Did it rain in the morning?
  5 Where did you have lunch?
  6 Did you watch television?
  7 What time did you go to bed?

7 Open answers

8 2 Who did you go with?
  3 What was the weather like?
  4 Did you go to / spend any time in Berlin?
  5 How did you travel / get there?
  6 How long did you spend in Germany?
  7 What was the food like? / Was the food good?
  8 Did you learn any German (expressions)?

Exercise 7 page 71

- Make sure everyone understands the phrases in the chart and knows what they have to do at this stage (put ticks in the second column, ignore the third for the time being). Students work individually.

Exercise 8 page 71
- Elicit the first 2–3 questions from the class. With a **weaker class**, write them on the board. Ask students to repeat them chorally and individually to practise intonation. Model the rising tone for them. As students talk in pairs, circulate, monitor and help.

Exercise 9 page 71
- Depending on the size of the class and the time, have some or all of the students report back to the class, saying 3–8 sentences about their partner's weekend.

➡ Lesson outcome
Ask students: *What have we talked about today?* Try to elicit: *questions (and answers) in the past tense* or an equivalent. Ask students to tell you the rules: *How does a question in the simple past tense begin? How can you answer it?* Draw the students' attention to the lesson statement: *I can say what I did and didn't do last weekend.*

Notes for Photocopiable activity 7.2

World Famous People Quiz
Pair work
Language: past simple questions
Materials: one copy of the worksheet per pair of students (Teacher's Book page 136)
- Divide the students into pairs of A and B and give out copies of worksheet A to students A and worksheet B to students B. Explain that students have different questions from their partners and that they have to write the questions to ask their partners. Students work individually to write the questions. Monitor to make sure they are forming the questions correctly.
- Student A reads out his/her questions. Student B answers and gets a mark for each correct answer. Then Student B asks his/her questions. At the end find out which student has the highest score in the class.

E READING
Discoveries

LESSON SUMMARY ● ● ● ● ●
Reading: an article about two great inventors; reading for detail
Vocabulary: discoveries; major life events
Speaking: asking and answering questions about famous scientists
Topic: science and technology

SHORTCUT *To do the lesson in 30 minutes, ask students to read the text for the first time at home and do exercise 5 orally with the whole class.*

➡ Lead-in 2–3 minutes
- Ask students if they can name any Nobel Prize winners for science. What did they do? Say: *Today we are going to read about some famous scientists.*

Exercise 1 page 72
- This task will stimulate some discussion. Some people get married while at university, some have children before getting married, etc. Help with questions: *So, do you know someone who did something different? Who is it? What did he/she do?* Help students build sentences, e.g. *My aunt/ cousin had a child before she got married.*

KEY

Possible order: be born – go to school – go to university – get a job – get married – have children – retire – die

Exercise 2 page 72
- Exercise 1 should provide a smooth transition to this task. After a few students have spoken about their family members, ask everyone to write sentences about theirs. Ask students to share what they have written in groups.

Exercise 3 page 72
- Look at the two photos which accompany the reading text. Discuss student's ideas with the class.

KEY

See exercise 4

Exercise 4 page 72
- Students read the text. Check answers to the questions from exercise 3 with the class.

KEY

Photo 1: The Biro, invented by László Biró, Hungarian
Photo 2: The Rubik's Cube, invented by Ernő Rubik, Hungarian

Exercise 5 page 72
- Ask students to complete the task. Check with the whole class.

KEY

1 B   2 D   3 F   4 C   5 E   6 A

Exercise 6 page 72
- The students have not done an exercise like this yet. Make sure they understand the questions must be formed so that they can be answered with the exact words of the given reply. Students work individually and compare answers in pairs. Finally check with the whole class.

KEY

2 What did he study?
3 What was his mother?
4 When did he move to Paris?
5 How many cubes are there in the world?
6 Where did he die?

Exercise 7 page 73
- Before doing this exercise, look at the photos and ask how many students can name any of the inventors.
- Students complete the task in pairs.

KEY

1 c   2 e   3 d   4 a   5 b

John Logie Baird (1888–1946) was born in Scotland in 1888. He is credited with being the inventor of the television. He gave the first demonstration in January 1926. He sent pictures via telephone lines from London to Glasgow in 1927, and, using radio waves, across the Atlantic to New York in 1928. However, an American system devised by Marconi and EMI replaced a lot of Baird's work.

Alexander Graham Bell (1847–1922) was born in Scotland, but moved to America. He is famous for inventing the telephone. In April 1875, he created the 'harmonic telegraph' which sent sounds along electric telegraph wires.

Bell worked with Thomas Augustus Watson to develop the harmonic telegraph into a way of sending speech down wires. Bell's telephone was built by March 1876. Within three years there were 30,000 telephones in use around the world.

Thomas Edison (1847–1931) developed his first invention at the age of 16: an 'automatic repeater' which allowed people to translate code easily and accurately. He went on to invent the first electric light bulb, and in 1882 he designed the first power station to supply electricity to New York.

Edison developed his other ideas for alkaline storage batteries, recorded music and motion pictures. They were sold all over the world. At the time of his death, he had 1,093 patents in his name.

Marie Curie (1867–1934) was born in Warsaw, Poland. At that time women were not allowed to go to university in Poland, so she moved to France and studied at the Sorbonne. In 1906 she became the first woman to teach there. In 1895 she married Pierre Curie. They discovered radium and polonium and won a Nobel Prize for Physics in 1903. Marie also won a Nobel Prize for Chemistry in 1911. Marie's work made her ill, and she died of cancer in 1934.

Ada Lovelace (1815–1852) was the daughter of the Romantic poet, Lord Byron. From 1842–43 she worked with Charles Babbage on a machine of his called the Analytical Engine. She wrote a set of notes explaining how to calculate Bernoulli numbers with the Engine. These calculations are recognised by historians as the world's first computer programme.

Exercise 8 page 73

- This can be done in open pairs with the whole class: ask student A the first question, A answers and asks B the next question, B answers and asks C, etc.

This activity involves an Internet search. It can be done in class if you can have the lesson in a computer room. Otherwise the search has to be homework.

1 Individually or in pairs, students choose a scientist and look for information about him/her on the Internet.

2 They prepare a mini presentation about the scientist. Useful language:

X was born in …   He/she studied at … in …
He/ she discovered … / invented … / developed …
He/ she wrote …   He/She worked …
He/she won …   He/ she died in …

3 Students practise saying their presentations in pairs. Go round and help them, especially with pronunciation.

4 Students deliver the presentations. They can be treated as a guessing game – the speakers do not say the name of the scientist and the audience has to guess it.

→ Lesson outcome

Ask students: *What did we do/ about today?* Elicit: *read about famous scientists* or another relevant answer. Ask everyone to tell you one thing they learned from the lesson, e.g. a fact or a new word. Draw students' attention to the lesson statement: *I can understand a biographical text.*

F EVERYDAY ENGLISH
Talking about your weekend

LESSON SUMMARY ● ● ● ○ ○

Functional English: social English; talking about your weekend
Listening: listening to friends discussing their weekend
Vocabulary: verb + noun collocations: free-time activities; phrases for reacting with sympathy
Speaking: talking about your weekend
Topic: people

SHORTCUT *To do the lesson in 30 minutes, do exercise 2 quickly with the whole class and have only a few pairs act out their dialogues in exercise 10.*

→ Lead-in 2 minutes

- It would be ideal to do this lesson on a Monday or Tuesday, when it's natural to chat about the weekend. Before the lesson, put these sentences on the board:
  It was great.   It was OK.   It was awful.
- Start by asking: *How was your weekend?* You can point to the phrases on the board to help. When a student answers, ask: *What did you do (at the weekend)?* You can also tell students about your weekend.
- Finally, announce: *Today we are all going to talk about our last weekend.*

Exercise 1 page 74 🎧 2.39

- Ask students to look at the verbs in the box. Ask: *Do you remember what they mean? Do you remember the past tense forms?* Students do the task using the list of irregular verbs if necessary. Play the dialogue once or twice for them to check. Ask why the form in item 2 is *go*, but in item 3 it is *went*.

KEY

1 was	4 see	7 watched
2 go	5 saw	8 made
3 went	6 stayed	

LANGUAGE NOTE – FILMS

It is possible to say *see a film* or *watch a film*.

Exercise 2 page 74

- Students do the exercise and compare answers in pairs.

KEY

go to the cinema   watch TV   make phone calls

Exercise 3 page 74

- Play the dialogue one more time, asking students to focus on pronunciation. Practise the pronunciation of the sentence *How was your weekend?* and the collocations: *We saw a film, I stayed in, watched TV, made some phone calls.* Students then read the dialogue in pairs. Ask two students who were not a pair to read it aloud to the whole class.

Exercise 4 page 74 🎧 2.40

- Tell students they are going to hear another conversation about the weekend. Ask them to read the task.

KEY

a

Transcript 2.40

Naomi Hi, Jack. How was your weekend?
Jack It was terrible – really bad!
Naomi Oh dear. Why was it so bad?
Jack Everything I did went wrong. On Saturday morning, I went shopping to buy a present for my dad. I bought a DVD for him, but when I got home, I didn't have it.
Naomi Oh no! How did you lose it?
Jack I'm not sure. I think I left it on the bus.
Naomi Oh well …
Jack Then on Saturday night, I met some friends in town and we had dinner at a café.
Naomi That sounds good.
Jack It wasn't. The food was terrible. I couldn't eat it.
Naomi That's a shame. What about Sunday?
Jack On Sunday, I wrote a really long e-mail to my friend in Canada. But there was a problem with the computer and I lost the e-mail before I sent it!
Naomi Poor you! You had a really bad weekend.
Jack And that's not all. On Sunday evening, I rented a DVD – *Troy* with Brad Pitt. But when I started to watch it, it was a different film. The wrong DVD was in the box.
Naomi What a disaster! So what did you watch?
Jack It was a Hungarian film about workers' rights.
Naomi Was it good?
Jack I don't know. I fell asleep. Anyway, how was your weekend?
Naomi Oh, it was OK.
Jack Good.

Exercise 5 page 74

- Students do the task individually. Go over the answers with the whole class, paying attention to the pronunciation of the collocations as single tone units: *went'shopping*, *,metsome'friends*, etc.

KEY

1 went	3 had	5 rented
2 met	4 wrote	

Exercise 6 page 74 🎧 2.40

- Ask the students to read the questions. Can they answer any of them already? Play the recording once or twice as necessary. Check answers with the whole class.

KEY

1 b 2 b 3 a 4 b 5 a

Exercise 7 page 74 🎧 2.41

- Play the recording. Students practise the sympathetic responses. Try to get them to speak 'with feeling'.

LANGUAGE NOTE – *OH WELL*

Oh well has a different meaning from the other expressions. It is similar to *Never mind* and is used to show that you accept that things can't change. It can be used in response to somebody else's news or after one's own statement, e.g. *We lost again… Oh well.*

Exercise 8 page 74

- Do the exercise as a class in open pairs: say line 1 to student A, A responds and says the next line to B, B responds and addresses C, etc. Insist on students saying both the complaint and the response 'with feeling'. Model the intonation for them if necessary. You may support it with exaggerated facial expressions if you feel comfortable doing that.

Exercise 9 page 74

- As students work on the activity in pairs, circulate and monitor, helping especially with pronunciation. Students may also need some help with responses to good news – they practised the sympathetic phrases in exercises 7 and 8, but what if their partner had a great weekend? Suggest a few simple phrases: *Cool! Sounds super! Oh, fantastic!* etc.

Exercise 10 page 74

- Depending on time and on students' patience, have 3–5 pairs act out their dialogues in front of the class. Give feedback: praise good performance, correct a few mistakes (recurring ones or those concerning the language from this lesson).

OPTIONAL ACTIVITY

Work in pairs. You are both on a summer language course in England. You are from different countries, so you speak English.

A Ask B about his / her weekend.

B Tell A about one thing you did alone and one thing you did with your friends. Ask A about his / her weekend

A Tell B about one thing you did alone and one thing you did with your friends. Say what the best part of the weekend was.

B Say what the best part of the weekend was.

➡ Lesson outcome

Ask students: *What have we talked about today?* Elicit: *weekend/ how was our weekend.* Ask: *Can you tell me some of the things you can do during the weekend?* Elicit any of the collocations from the lesson. Draw students' attention to the lesson statement: *I can talk about what happened at the weekend.*

G WRITING
An e-mail message

LESSON SUMMARY ● ● ● ●

Writing: an e-mail
Reading: e-mails
Vocabulary: useful phrases for e-mails
Topic: people

SHORTCUT *To do the lesson in 30 minutes, set the writing as homework.*

➡ Lead-in 2 minutes

- Have a chat with your class about e-mailing. Ask any of these questions: *How often do you send e-mails? How many e-mails do you send a day/ a week? How many did you send last weekend? Who do you write e-mails to? How long are your e-mails? Did you ever write or receive an e-mail in English? In another language?*

Exercise 1 page 75

- Students read the e-mails and decide who had a better weekend. Ask: *Why?* You may also ask: *Who do you think Jack is?*

> ### LANGUAGE NOTE – E-MAILS
> Point out that *Hi* can be used to begin e-mails but not letters. Other ways of signing off e-mails include *All the best* and *Bye for now.*

Exercise 2 page 75

- Students read and do the task individually. Check answers with the whole class. Try to get students to produce sentences, e.g. *Lauren went to bed early* rather than *go to bed early – Lauren.* Work on the pronunciation of the collocations as single tone units.

KEY

activity	Gail	Lauren
do homework	✓	
go to bed early		✓
read a book		
go to the cinema		✓
go shopping	✓	
have a barbecue		✓
have lunch in a cafe	✓	
go to a disco		
play tennis	✓	
play volleyball		✓
watch a basketball match	✓	
watch a DVD	✓	

Exercise 3 page 75

- Students go through the two texts one more time. Check answers with the whole class.

KEY

1 two new T-shirts
2 Yes (it was exciting).
3 No, she didn't.
4 No, they lost.
5 It was boring.
6 Because she didn't feel well.

Exercise 4 page 75

- Students read the writing tip box and find the phrases in the two e-mails. Encourage them to remember to refer to this box later when writing.

KEY

Great to hear from you! L
How was your weekend? G
I hope you're well. G
(Jack) sends his love. L
Say hi to Jack. G
Speak to you soon. L

Exercise 5 page 75

- Remind students they can use the chart in exercise 5 and also the lists of activities in exercises 2 and 5 on page 74 (lesson 7F). If they want to mention other activities, help with the necessary vocabulary.

Exercise 6 page 75

- Set up the writing task. Tell students to decide who they are writing to. Encourage them to use all available resources: their notes, the writing tip, the two e-mails in exercise 1. If the writing is done in class, **fast finishers** can get together in a group and read each other's e-mails.

> ### ADDITIONAL WRITING TASK
> This is a exam-type task. You can photocopy it and distribute it to students to do at home. Emphasise that it is important to include *all* the information listed as bullet points.
>
> - Write an e-mail to a friend that you met on your holidays abroad. Tell him/her about your last weekend.
> - Write what plans for the weekend you had.
> - Describe one plan that did not work out and give a reason.
> - Tell him/her about one plan which worked out very well.
> - Ask about your friend's weekend.

➡ Lesson outcome

Ask students: *What did we work on today?* Elicit: *e-mails,* or *writing e-mails.* Elicit any of the useful phrases from the lesson. Draw students' attention to the lesson statement: *I can write an e-mail message to a friend describing my weekend.*

Get ready for your EXAM 7

TOPIC ● ● ○ ○
Travel and tourism

→ Lead-in 2–3 minutes

- Tell students in this lesson they are going to do a listening and matching task. Ask if they remember anything about this type of task – the structure, any tips, etc. (e.g. there is an odd element that doesn't fit anywhere; you should read all the questions or sentences before you listen, etc.).
- Ask students to recall (individually) as many words connected with the theme *cities* as they can in 30 seconds. Then ask everyone to say one word.

Exercise 1 page 76

- Read the listening tip as a class. Students do the exercise individually or in pairs. Compare ideas as a class.

KEY

A unfriendly	C fast	E big
B wet and cold	D cars	F dirty

Exercise 2 page 76 🎧 2.42

E Listening: matching statements to speakers

- Remind students to read all the statements before they listen. Remind them also there is one extra statement that won't match any of the speakers.
- Play the recording through once, then again stopping after each speaker to check the answers. Finally, ask which the odd statement was.

Transcript 2.42

1 Well, New York is fantastic, of course. It's where they make all the films. Every street, every shop, every restaurant looks like a Hollywood film or American TV programme. It's all so exciting – it's noisy and dirty with lots of yellow taxis – and I love it. But there's one thing I don't like. Everybody talks very fast. Everybody is running in a hurry. I know cities are like that, but it's worse here. People don't have time to stop and talk to you.

2 I think London is great. It's got everything: great history, great shops, great nightclubs. There is something for everyone here. It even has big beautiful parks. Here you can feel that you are in the country. In fact I like going to the parks a lot, even when it's cold. This is because I think that a lot of London is quite dirty. The tourist attractions are clean. But the shopping streets aren't. It's a small thing, but I don't like it.

3 The best thing about this city is the art and architecture. The buildings in Paris are all so beautiful, and so are the churches. And there are so many wonderful art galleries where you can see so many famous paintings. I love all that. But the worst thing about this city is that the people are quite cold and unfriendly. I don't think that people here like tourists very much. Maybe it's because I don't speak French very well!

4 Edinburgh is amazing. It is such a beautiful city. It is unusual, too, with the castle in the middle of the city. I love all the different architecture. The people seem friendly, too. It's got lovely shops, houses, restaurants. I could live in a place like this, except for one thing. It's freezing cold! I have to wear a big coat, hat and gloves. And it's spring!

5 I think Rome is incredible – it's busy, hot and dirty. It's got everything: fantastic art, fantastic shops, fantastic food. The people here are so lively, warm and friendly. Everything is open all the time, and everybody stays up late. There are always lots of people in the streets. Unfortunately, there are always lots of cars as well. It's so noisy, and there are traffic jams all the time. It's a pity.

KEY

A 3	B 4	C 1	D 5	E –	F 2

Exercise 3 page 76

- Students study the words with a dictionary and choose the ones they associate with the photos in exercise 7. Ask them to compare their choices in pairs.

Exercise 4 page 76

- Explain that making notes in this way will prepare students for the speaking task in exercise 7. Students think about what the photos show, what is similar and what is different about them.
- Ask one or two students to read out their sentences, and discuss ideas as a class.

Exercise 5 page 76

- Explain to students that the phrases describing activities in this exercises are *collocations* – words that often go together. Point out that collocations, especially verb + noun collocations, are extremely useful, because they allow you to build correct, natural-sounding sentences more easily.
- Students do the exercise individually or in pairs, then choose the activities they like and tell each other about them.

KEY

1 admire	4 go to	7 eat
2 go on	5 buy	8 go
3 visit	6 stay	9 wander

Exercise 6 page 76

- Students work in pairs and make notes on one of the photos in exercise 7. You may ask them to tell another pair about their city.

Exercise 7

E Speaking: picture-based discussion

- Refer students back to the useful phrases for comparing and contrasting photos on page 56 of the Student's book.
- Read the exam task as a class and check understanding.
- Allow students two or three minutes to prepare. In pairs, students take it in turns to speak about the photos for 1–2 minutes. Their partner listens.
- When all the students have had a chance to discuss the photos, ask for ideas from the class about each of the questions. Which city would most students prefer to visit?
- In a stronger class, try to generate a discussion about the photos and about cities in your own country.

OPTIONAL ACTIVITY

Speaking: situational role-play

- Ask students to work in pairs. They each choose a picture and make notes about their reasons for wanting to visit it. Remind them to use the adjectives and activities from the lesson in their reasons.

- In pairs, students discuss their reasons for wanting to visit the city they have chosen.

→ Lesson outcome

Ask students: *What did we do today?* Elicit: *listening, speaking, negotiating.* Ask students if they remember any of the good advice about doing listening tasks. Elicit some of the words and collocations from the lesson.

TOPIC ● ● ● ●
Society

➜ Lead-in 2 minutes

• Ask students if any of them read magazines about celebrities. What sort of information can be found in such magazines? Do they think it is interesting to read such information? Why?/ Why not? How about biographies of famous writers or scientists – are those interesting to read? Why/ Why not?

Exercise 1 page 77

• Before students start reading, ask them if they remember what the tips in previous *Get Ready for your exam* lessons (2 and 4) advised them to do first when doing a reading task. (Read through it quickly to find out what it is about in general.) Ask them to read the instructions and do exercise 1.

KEY

1 Paris Hilton was born.
2 She started to work.
3 She finished her first album.

Exercise 2 page 77

E Reading: true/false sentences

• Look at the reading tip with the class. Explain that they can use this technique to answer detailed questions about a text.
• Allow students two or three minutes to read and understand sentences 1–8.
• Students read the text and do the task. Ask them to underline the parts of the text where they found each answer. Check the answers with the whole class.

KEY

1	F	3	T	5	NG	7	NG
2	F	4	T	6	T	8	F

Exercise 3 page 77 🎧 2.43

• Ask students to read the exam task in exercise 7. Tell them they are going to hear two students doing the task. Play the recording and check the answers.

KEY

1	health	2 friends and family	3	money

Transcript 2.43

Boy   I think money is very important.
Girl   Really? Why do you think that?
Boy   Well, if you don't have money, you can't buy clothes, or food, or a house, or a car.
Girl   That's true. But I don't think money is the most important thing in life.
Boy   Poor people are often unhappy. Rich people are usually happy.
Girl   I don't agree. Lots of rich people are unhappy. They are often unhappy because all they think about is money.
Boy   Maybe you're right. So, which do you think is the most important?
Girl   Well, I think friends and family are more important than money.
Boy   More important than health?
Girl   Hmm, perhaps not. If you aren't healthy, it's difficult to be happy.

Boy   Yes, I see your point. Let's say health is the most important then.
Girl   OK. Next is friends and family.
Boy   Yes, OK, I agree. And finally, money.
Girl   Yes.

Exercise 4 page 77 🎧 2.43

• Ask students to read sentences 1–5 carefully.
• Play the recording again. Students listen for sentences 1–5 and write the answers individually. Then they compare answers in pairs.

KEY

1	B	2	G	3	B	4	B	5	G

Exercise 5 page 77

• Students work in pairs. Ask them to say if they agree or disagree with the statements, and if they can, to give reasons.
• Circulate and monitor. At the end, ask the class for their ideas about the sentences.

Exercise 6 page 77

• Students read the phrases and complete the task.
• Check answers as a class.

KEY

1	Why	3	agree	5	point
2	true	4	right		

Exercise 7 page 77

E Speaking: topic-based discussion

• Read the task as a class. Tell students that this conversation should last for 3–5 minutes, so they will need to talk about their ideas in some detail.
• Give students two or three minutes to plan their ideas.
• As students are talking, go around and listen. Make a note of any persistent errors and correct these as a class at the end of the task.
• At the end, ask the class, *How many agreed with their partners? How many had different ideas?*

OPTIONAL ACTIVITY
Speaking: situational role-play

• Students work in pairs. One of them is a famous celebrity, and the other is a journalist.

• Students make notes about their character. The celebrity has to argue that their money makes them happy, and the journalist must try to persuade them of the other point of view: that family and friends are more important. Brainstorm ideas about what could make the celebrity happy. Examples could include:
holidays   clothes   cars   eating in restaurants
Examples of the other point of view could include:
being with friends   relaxing   spending time with family

• Allow students time to prepare and then let them perform their conversations in pairs.

➜ Lesson outcome

Ask students: *What did we do today?* Elicit: *reading, speaking, listening.* Ask students if they remember any of the phrases for agreeing or disagreeing.

8 On the menu

THIS UNIT INCLUDES ● ● ○ ○
Vocabulary • food and drink • countable and uncountable nouns
• partitives (*cup of coffee, slice of pizza*, etc.)
Grammar • quantity: *some* and *any, How much / many?*
• Articles (definite and indefinite)
Speaking • talking about traditional food • ordering food in a café
Writing • a formal letter
WORKBOOK pages 70–76

A VOCABULARY AND LISTENING
Breakfast

LESSON SUMMARY ● ● ● ○ ○
Vocabulary: breakfast food
Listening: short dialogues
Grammar: countable and uncountable nouns
Speaking: talking about food
Topic: food and drink

SHORTCUT *To do the lesson in 30 minutes, set Vocabulary Builder (part 1) as homework.*

➜ Lead-in 2 minutes
• Before students open their books, ask them: *What do you like eating? What kind of food do you like? What other names of food do you know in English?* If possible, elicit one food word from every student. (There are so many international names that it should be possible! *Pizza, spaghetti, paella, tortilla, sushi,* etc. are all acceptable answers.) Tell the class: *Today we start a unit about food.*

Exercise 1 page 78
• This exercise may not need checking with the whole class. Encourage students to check answers with each other and with the Wordlist if they are not sure; watch weaker students while they are working and help them.

KEY

1	apples	7	cheese	13	sausages
2	bread	8	tea	14	jam
3	bananas	9	eggs	15	toast
4	cereal	10	milk	16	orange juice
5	bacon	11	ham	17	water
6	coffee	12	hot chocolate	18	tomatoes

Exercise 2 page 78
• Read the *Learn this* box with the whole class. Read the instructions and do the first few words as examples, to make sure everyone understands the difference.

KEY
Countable: apples, bananas, eggs, sausages, tomatoes
Uncountable: bacon, bread, cereal, cheese, ham, jam, toast, coffee, hot chocolate, milk, orange juice, tea, water

Exercise 3 page 78 🎧 2.44
• Play the recording once without stopping for students to check their answers. Play it a second time pausing after each item to work on pronunciation. Ask students to repeat individually and chorally.

Exercise 4 page 78
• Write *There is ... There are ...* on the board. With a **stronger class**, do the first few examples as a class; with a **weaker class**, do the whole exercise with the whole class to ensure accurate production.

For further practice of breakfast food vocabulary, go to:

Vocabulary Builder (part 1): Student's Book page 135

KEY
1 1   3   2   1   3   4

2 sausages, tomatoes, tea, toast, jam

3 Open answers

Exercise 5 page 78 🎧 2.45
• Tell students they are going to hear three hotel guests phoning room service. Explain what *room service* is. Ask students to read the menu. Play the recording through once. You may invite students to comment on the surly attitude of the room service operator: *Is he very polite?*
• Play the recording again, stopping after each call. Allow students to compare answers in pairs, then check with the whole class.

KEY
Caller 1: room 101, cereal, sausages, eggs, toast, orange juice, hot chocolate
Caller 2: room 257, sausages, banana, toast, jam, tea
Caller 3: room 569, cereal, eggs, banana, water, coffee

Transcript 2.45

RS	Hello, room service.
Man	Oh, hello. I want to order breakfast, please.
RS	Room number?
Man	It's 101.
RS	One hundred and one. OK. (SILENCE) Yes? I'm ready.
Man	Oh. Well, I'd like a bowl of cereal, please.
RS	OK. Anything to drink – tea, coffee?
Man	Wait a moment! I want sausages and eggs, too.
RS	Oh, right. Sausages and eggs. And do you want bread or toast with that?
Man	Toast, please. Two slices of toast.
RS	And to drink?
Man	I'd like a glass of orange juice. And a cup of hot chocolate, too.
RS	Orange juice and hot chocolate. OK. Ten minutes.
Man	Thank you.
...	
RS	Hello, room service.
Man	Oh, hello. Can I order some breakfast, please?
RS	Room number?
Man	It's 257.
RS	Two ... five ... seven. (SILENCE) Yes? I'm ready.
Man	I'd like sausages, please.
RS	Sausages ... and eggs?
Man	No, thanks. I don't like eggs.
RS	You don't like eggs. OK. Toast?
Man	Yes, please. And jam.
RS	Toast and jam. Any cereal, fruit?
Man	Can I have a banana, please?
RS	Yes.
Man	Thank you.

RS	To drink?
Man	A cup of tea, please.
RS	Is that all?
Man	That's all, thank you.
RS	OK. Ten minutes.
...	
RS	Hello, room service.
Man	Oh, hello. I want to order some food – for breakfast.
RS	Room number?
Man	Er ... it's 569.
RS	Five ... six ...
Man	I'd like cereal, please.
RS	Just a moment, please. Five ... six ... nine. OK. I'm ready.
Man	A bowl of cereal, please.
RS	Cereal. Anything else?
Man	Yes, please. I want eggs and a banana.
RS	Eggs and a ... banana. Any bread or toast?
Man	No thanks.
RS	To drink?
Man	A cup of coffee, please. And a bottle of water.
RS	Coffee. And a bottle of water.
Man	Yes, please.
RS	OK. Five minutes.
Man	Thank you.

Exercise 6 page 78 🎧 2.46

- Students match the expressions. Play the recording once for them to check their answers. Practise pronunciation: model the expressions for the students to repeat, taking care that they be produced as single tone units.

KEY

1 d   2 a   3 c   4 b   5 e

Exercise 7 page 78

- Students talk about their breakfasts. When they've finished, you can ask the whole class: *Who has a very small breakfast? Who has a big breakfast? Who has the biggest breakfast?*

For work on food categories, go to:

> Vocabulary Builder (part 2): Student's Book page 135

KEY

4 1 salmon, sardines, lobster
    2 beef, chicken, lamb,
    3 cream, cheese
    4 carrots, cabbage, onions, peas, potatoes
    5 lemons, oranges, pears

5 🎧 3.10
    Students listen and check

6 2 ham, bacon, sausages
    3 milk, eggs
    5 banana, tomatoes, apple

7 Open answers

➡ Lesson outcome

Ask students: *What have we talked about today?* Elicit: *food/ breakfast.* Ask: *Can you give me some names of food?* Accept all answers, but praise especially the students who come up with phrases (*a slice of toast,* etc.). Draw students' attention to the lesson statement: *I can describe what I have for breakfast.*

8B GRAMMAR
some and *any,* How much/many?

LESSON SUMMARY ● ● ● ● ●

Grammar: *some* and *any, How much/many?*
Vocabulary: food
Speaking: talking about quantity

SHORTCUT *To do the lesson in 30 minutes, do exercise 8 with the whole class and set the Grammar Builder as homework.*

➡ Lead-in 2 minutes

- Write on the board: *some, any, How much? How many?* Say a few sentences about what there is in your classroom, e.g. *We've got some plants/flowers in this room, but we haven't got any goldfish. Have we got any chalk? How many desks have we got?* Explain: *Today we are going to talk about how these words are used.*

Exercise 1 page 79 🎧 3.01

- Tell students they are going to hear a dialogue between a young couple who are at home and would like to have some lunch. Ask them to read the task. Play the recording.

KEY

bread ✗	cheese ✓	pizzas ✗
butter ✓	ham ✓	

Exercise 2 page 79

- Students analyse the dialogue. Ask a few students to read the examples they found aloud. They should read whole sentences. Students go on to fill in the *Learn this!* box and compare answers with their partners. Check as a class.

KEY

In the dialogue: some lunch, any pizzas, some cheese, some ham, any butter, any bread
Learn this: some   any   any

LANGUAGE NOTE – *SOME* AND *ANY*

The rules in the box do not, of course, give the full picture. (e.g. *any* is used in positive sentences such as *He'll eat any food.*) However, it is helpful as a general rule for elementary students.

It is common to use *some* in offers and requests, e.g. *Do you want … ?, Would you like … ?* and *Can I have …?* Students may want to use these in Everyday English p84.

Exercise 3 page 79

- Say something like: *Hannah and Oliver still want some lunch. They are looking for some food.* Ask students to do the exercise, using the information in the *Learn this!* box. Check whether everyone knows what *pasta* is.

KEY

1 any	3 any	5 some
2 some	4 any	6 some

Exercise 4 page 79 🎧 3.02

- Play the recording for students to check their answers. Ask if they need to hear it again. Explain the British meaning of *chips* – students might be more familiar with the American meaning of potato crisps.

OPTIONAL ACTIVITY

Students work in pairs. Ask them to read the whole dialogue between Oliver and Hannah, change some of the names of foods, and practise reading the changed version aloud. Circulate and monitor. Pick one or two pairs to read their versions to the whole class.

For further practice on quantity, go to:

Grammar Builder 8B: Student's Book page 122

KEY

1
1	u	4	u	7	tomatoes
2	u	5	sausages	8	carrots
3	apples	6	u		

2
1	some	4	some	7	some
2	any	5	any	8	any
3	any	6	any		

3
1	some	4	any	7	any
2	any	5	any	8	any
3	some	6	any		

4
1	How many	3	How many	5	How much
2	How much	4	How much	6	How many

5 Open answers

Exercise 5 page 79

- Students read the text quickly. Check answers with the whole class. Ask: *Would you like to have a pizza like this? Would you like to have it with your family or your friends?*

KEY

Name: The Big One   Price: $99

Exercise 6 page 79

- Read the *Learn this!* box aloud. Check that everybody understands the two phrases *How much* and *How many*. Use translations if necessary. Read the example and do sentence 2 with the whole class to make sure everyone knows how to build the questions. Explain *dough*. After students have finished, check with the whole class.

KEY

1 How much money does the Big One cost? ($99)
2 How much pizza dough is there in the pizza? (9 kg)
3 How many slices are there in the pizza? (150)
4 How much cheese is there in the pizza? (7 kg)
5 How many minutes does it take to cook? (40)
6 How many Big Ones do they sell a year? (300)

Exercise 7 page 79

- With a **weaker class**, do this exercise in open pairs, to monitor how well students cope with saying the numbers.

Exercise 8 page 79

- Let students compare answers in pairs, then check with the whole class. If an error has been made, discuss it: ask students to consider the noun – can it be counted? Is it plural or singular? Go over the rule for *how much/ how* many again if necessary. Try to make sure everyone writes down the correctly built questions, as they are going to need them in the next exercise.

KEY

1	How much	4	How much	7	How many
2	How much	5	How many	8	How much
3	How many	6	How many		

Exercise 9 page 79

- As students ask and answer in pairs, circulate and monitor, helping especially with numbers.

OPTIONAL ACTIVITY

In this lesson and elsewhere in the unit, there is food vocabulary throughout the lessons. You could ask students to look back through lessons A and B and start compiling a list of all the food as it comes up. They might want to organise it in categories, as in Vocabulary Builder (part 2) or you could ask students to start to build up a mind map that they can keep adding to as the unit progresses.

➡ Lesson outcome

Ask: *What did we talk about today?* Elicit: *some and any, how much and how many.* Ask: *Can you tell me when* any *is used? What about* some? *And what is the difference between* How many *and* How much? Elicit the rules. (If students look for the rules in the book, don't stop them – they haven't had the time to learn them yet, and knowing where to find the rule is also a skill.) Draw students' attention to the lesson statement: *I can talk about quantities.*

8C CULTURE
Traditional dishes

LESSON SUMMARY ● ● ● ○ ○

Reading: British food
Listening: descriptions of traditional dishes
Speaking: speaking about food
Topic: culture

SHORTCUT *To do the lesson in 30 minutes, ask students to read the text for the first time at home.*

➡ Lead-in 2 minutes

- Before students open their books, ask them if they know any traditional British food. If they cannot come up with much, ask them about traditional foods from other countries (it will provide an opportunity to revise names of countries, too). You may want to give the names of countries as prompts (e.g. *What kind of food comes from Japan? – Sushi.*), or the other way round (e.g. *Where does sushi come from? – Japan*).

Exercise 1 page 80

- Students look at the photos and discuss the foods in pairs. Ask question 3 of the whole class.

KEY

roast beef, fish and chips, cooked breakfast

Exercise 2 page 80

- Ask students if they have heard any opinions about British food. Do not agree or disagree with what they say, but invite them to read the text.

KEY

The text says good things about British restaurant food.

CULTURE NOTES – FOOD
British food

For many years British food has suffered from a negative image. In recent years, however, there has been a food revolution. There has been a major revival of interest in cooking and eating both British and international food. Celebrity chefs have become an important part of the culture and have influenced people to cook more varied and healthy food.

Pubs

Many pubs in Britain serve food. Pubs have become more 'family friendly' in recent years. By law under 16s can go into pubs (if the management allows it) but they must be accompanied by an adult. To buy or drink alcohol you must be 18 or over. 16 and 17 year olds can drink alcohol (but not spirits) with food.

Traditional pub food includes fish and chips, steak pie, hamburgers, curry and jacket potatoes. There is also a large number of pubs nowadays which serve food of a similar standard to an expensive restaurant. These are known as *gastropubs*.

Exercise 3 page 80

- Students read the text in more detail. They can compare answers in pairs, then check with the whole class.

KEY

1 No, they don't
2 more than 8,600
3 bacon, eggs, sausages, tomatoes and toast
4 £27
5 about 8,000
6 chicken curry

Exercise 4 page 80

- Students go over the text again. Check answers with the whole class. If you wish to share your own impressions of British food with your class, this is a good time to do it – after all the work with the text has been done.

KEY

1 eating out	3 microwave	5 pubs
2 snacks	4 dish	6 traditional

Exercise 5 page 80 🎧 3.03

- Play the recording once and see if most students have got the answers. If not, play it again. Check answers. It would be good to have a map of Britain available to point out Wales, Scotland, Lancashire and Cornwall.

KEY

1 Wales	3 the north of England
2 Scotland	4 south-west England

Transcript 3.03

1

Int. Are there any traditional dishes where you come from?
Man Yes, there are. There's a kind of soup – a thick soup –its name is 'cawl'.
Int. And is cawl only popular in Wales?
Man Yes, I think so.
Int. What are the ingredients?
Man Well, there's lamb and potatoes. And carrots, too. And other vegetables, maybe – I'm not sure.

2

Int. Are you from Wales too?
Woman No, I'm not. I'm from Scotland.
Int. Can you give me an example of a traditional Scottish dish?
Woman Yes, I can. It's a vegetable dish called colcannon.
Int. Colcannon?
Woman That's right. It's made with potatoes and cabbage.
Int. Are there any other ingredients?
Woman It's got onion in it too. It's nice!

3

Int. Which part of the UK are you from?
Man I'm from Lancashire.
Int. That's in the north of England, isn't it?
Man Yes, it is.
Int. And are there any traditional dishes where you live?
Man Lancashire hotpot.
Int. Ah, yes. Hotpot. What is it, exactly?
Man It's made with lamb and onions.
Int. Lamb and onions.
Man Yes, and it's got slices of potato on the top.
Int. Mmm. Sounds good.

4

Int. What part of the UK are you from?
Woman I'm from Cornwall – south-west England.
Int. Oh, right. Are there any traditional dishes from the south-west of England?
Woman There's stargazey pie.
Int. Stargazey pie?
Woman Yes. It's a strange dish. It's a pie made with small fish – for example, sardines – and eggs. And there's pastry on top, of course.
Int. Right. So why is it strange?
Woman Because the heads of the fish come up through the pastry.
Int. So they're looking at you when you eat them.
Woman In a way … yes.
Int. Hmm.

Exercise 6 page 80 🎧 3.03

- Explain *ingredients*. Make sure everyone reads the instructions and the table. If students need to check the meaning of the ingredients, talk through them with the class, to see if anyone knows them, or encourage students to refer to page 135. Play the recording again, once or twice depending on students' needs. Students compare answers in pairs; then check with the whole class.

KEY

Cawl: carrots, lamb, potatoes
Colcannon: cabbage, onions, potatoes
Lancashire hotpot: lamb, onions, potatoes
Stargazey pie: eggs, pastry, sardines

Exercise 7 page 80

- You may wish to photocopy transcript 3.03, so that students can read it (if there is time) and have a better idea of whether they would like each of the dishes or not.

Exercise 8 page 80

- Students discuss the questions in groups of 3–4. At the end, share ideas as a class.

OPTIONAL ACTIVITY

Ask everyone to think about a fairly simple dish that they like, and that they can name most of the ingredients of in English. First, they have to list the ingredients. Then, using their list and language from the lesson (including the photocopied transcript 3.03) they write a description of the dish in a few sentences. They can then share their descriptions in groups of three.

➡ Lesson outcome

Ask students: *What have we talked about today?* Elicit: *food/ British food/ traditional food.* Ask students what they learned about British food. Accept any accurate bits of information from the lesson. Draw students' attention to the lesson statement: *I can understand descriptions of traditional food.*

Notes for Photocopiable activity 8.1

School lunches around the world

An individual reading comprehension text
Language: language related to food and meals
Materials: one copy of the worksheet per student (Teacher's Book page 137)

- Students work in pairs or small groups to discuss the first two questions.
- Exercise 3 can be done as a straight, individual reading comprehension exercise.
- Alternatively, you might want to set it up as a race. Introduce your students to the concept of 'scanning' – reading quickly to find a specific piece of information – and ask them to answer the questions as quickly as possible.

KEY

1 F	3 S	5 S	7 F	9 K
2 J	4 N	6 S	8 J/K	10 F

8D GRAMMAR Articles

LESSON SUMMARY ● ● ● ● ◌

Grammar: articles
Reading : short texts about restaurants

SHORTCUT *To do the lesson in 30 minutes, do exercise 6 as a class and set the Grammar Builder for homework.*

➡ Lead-in 2 minutes

- You may wish to ask students (probably in their own language) if they have observed the little words which appear before nouns in English and don't seem to mean anything. What are they? (Elicit *a, the,* possibly *an.*) Say these words are called *articles* and tell the class that they are going to learn more about them today, but they are also going to talk about restaurants. Ask a few students: *Do you like eating in restaurants? Is there a good restaurant near your house? Why is it good? Which is your favourite restaurant in our town/city? Why is it good?*

Exercise 1 page 81

- Draw students' attention to the photos. Tell them they are going to read what someone called Jack thinks about the restaurants near his house. Students read the instructions and the text. Ask: *So, which restaurant is Jack's favourite, do you think? Why?*

KEY

The Italian restaurant because it's cheap and the food is good.

LANGUAGE NOTE – *THE*

The is not normally used when talking about streets. *The High Street* is an exception.

Exercise 2 page 81

- Ask students to read the instructions and look at the *Learn this!* box. Elicit what *countable* and *uncountable* nouns are.
- Ask for the first one or two examples of *a, an, the* together with the nouns that follow. This is important, because some students may think the article goes with the adjective it precedes ('*a Chinese*').
- Students do the task and compare answers in pairs. Check with the whole class. Emphasise that they have now learned the first important fact about articles: that *a* and *an* can only be used with singular, countable nouns, while *the* can be used with uncountable and countable, singular and plural nouns. Say something like this: *This means a singular, countable noun can sometimes be preceded by* a *or* an *and sometimes by* the. *Why? When is it* a, *when* an, *and when* the? *This is what we will find out next.*

KEY

the High Street	an Indian restaurant
a Chinese restaurant	the Indian restaurant
an Italian restaurant	the food
the Chinese restaurant	
the Italian restaurant	*a/an:* singular countable nouns
the pizzas	*the:* all three groups of nouns

Exercise 3 page 81 🎧 3.04

- Ask students to look at the words in the book and listen. Play the recording through once. Play it again, stopping after each word and asking students to repeat. Then ask if anyone sees why it is sometimes *a* and sometimes *an*. They can answer in their own language. Emphasise that the difference between *a* and *an* has to do with pronunciation only, not with meaning.

Exercise 4 page 81

- Ask students to do the exercise according to the rule they have just discovered. Check with the whole class. Insist on clear but fluent pronunciation (each article + noun is pronounced 'like one word').
- Students may be more likely to make mistakes in example 8. Ask a few of them to repeat the word *young* and ask everyone what the first *sound* is (not the first letter). Explain that *a/an* are used depending on the sound, not the spelling. You can give the example of *an hour* (silent *h* – the spoken word starts with a vowel sound.)

KEY

1	a	4	an	7	an
2	an	5	a	8	a
3	an	6	an		

Exercise 5 page 81

- Tell students that they are now going to look at the difference between *a/an* and *the*, and that the difference has to do with meaning.
- Students do the exercise individually and compare answers in pairs. Check with the whole class. Point to the examples in the text in exercise 1: *There's a Chinese restaurant and an Italian restaurant* – mentioned for the first time. *The Chinese restaurant is good, but it's expensive* – mentioned again.

KEY

a   the

For further practice on articles, go to:

Grammar Builder 8D: Student's Book page 122

KEY

5	1	an	4	a	7	an
	2	a	5	an	8	an
	3	a	6	a		

6 1 a, a, the, the
  2 a, a
  3 a, an, The, the, the, the
  4 a, a, The, the
  5 the, a
  6 a, a, The, the, an
  7 an, the
  8 a, a, The

7	1	–	5	–, the, –	9	a
	2	the	6	–	10	–
	3	the	7	the, the		
	4	a	8	–		

Exercise 6 page 81

- Ask students to read through the text first. Do the first one or two sentences as a class. Students continue on their own. Check with the whole class.

KEY

1	a	5	a	9	an
2	a	6	the	10	the
3	the	7	the	11	the
4	the	8	The		

Exercise 7 page 81

- Read the *Learn this!* box as a class. Students do the exercise individually. Check with the whole class.

KEY

1	✓	5	the	9	the
2	the	6	the	10	✓
3	✓	7	a	11	✓
4	✓	8	✓		

OPTIONAL ACTIVITY

Ask students to write a paragraph similar to the one in exercise 1 about places in their neighbourhood or in your town/city. The places could be restaurants / cafés/ clubs / shops/ cinemas / Internet cafés / discos, or any kind of place a student wishes to write about. Tell them to use the text about three restaurants as a model, changing whatever they need to change e.g. *There are* **two cinemas** *near my house* ... In groups of 3–4, students read one another's texts. You may also wish to ask 2–3 people to read their paragraphs to the whole class.

➡ Lesson outcome

Ask students: *What have we talked about today?* Try to elicit: *articles* or *a, an and the,* and *restaurants*. Ask students to tell you the rules: *When do we use* a/an? (Please note that the complete rule: *Before singular countable nouns when mentioning something for the first time* was not formulated in class. If someone manages to formulate it, they deserve to be praised.) *When is it* a *and when* an? *When do we use* the? Elicit answers. Draw students' attention to the lesson statement: *I can correctly use* a/an *and the* with nouns.

8E READING
Healthy eating

LESSON SUMMARY ● ● ● ● ●

Reading: an interview; reading for detail
Vocabulary: food and food groups
Listening: a song: *Junk food junkie*
Topic: health and fitness

SHORTCUT *To do the lesson in 30 minutes, ask students to read the text for the first time at home.*

➡ Lead-in 2 minutes

- Ask students what they consider to be healthy food and healthy eating habits. You can help with questions: *What should you eat? How often should you eat? At what time? How much?* Brainstorm ideas with the whole class. Help students express their ideas if they're struggling for words. You may wish to write the ideas on the board.

Exercise 1 page 82

- Talk about the diagram with the whole class, explaining any unfamiliar vocabulary (*dairy protein*). You may need to explain what *cereal* is used to mean in this context – not only breakfast cereal, but any kind of grain.

Exercise 2 page 82

- Everyone makes a list for themselves. You may ask students to share their thoughts in pairs if you think everyone will feel comfortable discussing their eating habits. (If so, they should be allowed to do it with partners of their own choice.) Ask students why they think the diagram is in the form of a pyramid. What does it suggest about the proportions of different foods in our diets?

Exercise 3 page 82

- Do the first example together as a class. Students continue the matching in pairs. Discuss answers with the whole class.

KEY

1 chicken curry: cereal and rice / protein
2 strawberries and cream: fruit and vegetables / fat and sugar
3 cheesecake: fruit and vegetables / fat and sugar
4 hot dog: cereal and rice / protein
5 baked beans on toast: cereal and rice / fruit and vegetables

Exercise 4 page 82

- Ask a student to read the reading tip aloud. Invite students to look at the photo and the title and consider the question in exercise 4. Get a few students to say something about the photo.
- Ask students which answers they have chosen and why, but do not reveal the right answer.

Exercise 5 page 82

- Ask students to read the text. Ask what the answer to exercise 4 is. Students will probably wish to make some comments on the content of the text. Allow them to do this, helping them to express their thoughts in English.

KEY

d

CULTURE NOTE – COMPETITIVE EATING

Competitive eating is a 'sport' which involves the consumption of large quantities of food, usually fast food or desserts, in a short time. It is most popular in the USA, where eating competitions were traditionally held at county fairs. Like Sonya Thomas, the top competitors tend to be slim. This allows the stomach to stretch as it is not constricted by fat.

Exercise 6 page 83

- Explain to students that you are asking them to do the exercise without using dictionaries or the Wordlist, because it is the context that will tell them what the words mean. Students work individually. Check with the whole class. You may wish to check understanding by eliciting translations.

KEY

1	healthy	3	thin	5	nickname
2	natural	4	spider	6	take part

Exercise 7 page 83

- Check answers with the whole class. Ask students if they agree with Sonya that eating competitions are a real sport. Why/ Why not?

KEY

1	c	2	c	3	a	4	a	5	b

Exercise 8 page 83 🎧 3.05

- Tell students they are going to hear a song about a junk food addict. Ask them to read the glossary first. Play the song once without stopping, then again pausing after each gap to check.

KEY

1	microwave	4	know	7	arithmetic
2	junk food	5	slow	8	classroom
3	bad	6	stressed		

CULTURE NOTE – *JUNK FOOD JUNKIE*

Highlight the play on words in the song's title, *Junk food junkie*. *Junk food* is food that is not healthy because it contains a lot of fat, salt and sugar and a *junkie* (informal) is an addict. The song is by a 1970s British punk band called X-RAY SPEX.

Exercise 9 page 83

- With a **weaker class**, you may have to accept *yes* / *no* as answers to the question *Do you agree?* With a **stronger class**, ask: *Why?*

KEY

c

ADDITIONAL SPEAKING ACTIVITY

Students work in pairs. One of them is a doctor, the other a TV journalist who's going to interview him/her about healthy eating and a healthy lifestyle. The interview is intended for a programme for teenagers.

Put these jumbled questions on the board:
- mean/ What / 'healthy eating' / does ?
- it / to be a vegetarian / a good idea / Is ?
- food / for young people / is good / who do / What kind of / a lot of sports ?
- do you / fast food / about / What / think ?
- good and bad / staying slim / What are / ways of ?
- to stay healthy / can / we / do / What else ?

The first stage is to unscramble the questions. Allow 1–2 minutes for that, then check with the whole class. Tell students they can add their own questions if they wish. In the second stage pairs prepare their interviews. Allow about 5 minutes for preparation, more if students ask for it. Circulate and help. Students act out their interviews in front of the class.

➡ Lesson outcome

Ask students: *What did we do today?* Elicit: *read about healthy eating* or *eating competitions* or another relevant answer. Ask everyone to tell you one thing they learned from the lesson, e.g. a fact or a new word. Draw students' attention to the lesson statement: *I can understand an interview in a magazine.*

8F EVERYDAY ENGLISH
In a café

LESSON SUMMARY ● ● ● ● ● ○
Functional English: ordering food, saying prices
Listening: short dialogue
Vocabulary: food
Speaking: ordering food
Topic: shopping and services

SHORTCUT *To do the lesson in 30 minutes, have fewer groups act out their dialogues in exercise 9.*

➡ Lead-in 2 minutes
- Have a conversation about eating out with your class. You can ask such questions as: *How often do you eat out? Do you have a favourite restaurant? What do you like about your favourite restaurant? Do you always order the same favourite dishes or something new every time? What do you order?*

Exercise 1 page 84
- Ask students to describe the photo in pairs, answering the questions in the exercise. Share ideas as a class.

Exercise 2 page 84 🎧 3.06
- Ask students to read the menu first and decide what they would order. Then read the instructions for exercise 2 as a class and point out the waitress' notes. Play the dialogue once. Check with the whole class.

KEY
1	cheese sandwich	3	ham	5	a Coke
2	pizza	4	coffee		

CULTURE NOTE – ENJOY YOUR MEAL
Enjoy your meal is used by waiters in restaurants. However, the British do not have the custom, common in many other countries, of saying it to other family members at the table.

Exercise 3 page 84
- Play the dialogue again, asking students to underline the expressions. Ask different students to read the expressions, paying attention to pronunciation.

KEY
1 Could I have…, please?   Can I have…, please?
   I'd like…
2 Sure. No problem.

Exercise 4 page 84 🎧 3.07
- Read the *Learn this* box aloud, then ask students to say the prices, playing the appropriate bit of the recording after a student has read a price.

Transcript 3.07
1 six pounds
2 two pounds fifty / two fifty
3 ten pounds
4 one pound twenty-five / one twenty-five
5 six pounds ninety-nine / six ninety-nine
6 eight pounds twenty / eight twenty
7 one pound fifty / one fifty
8 three pounds

Exercise 5 page 84
- Tell students in a moment they are going to read the dialogue aloud, but first ask them to listen to it one more time, paying attention to pronunciation. Play the recording for students to repeat individually and chorally.
- Put students in groups of three. With a **weaker class**, you might ask them to read the dialogue as it is first. Allow a minute for students to decide who is who and look at the menu to decide what they are going to order. Students read the dialogue in groups. Circulate and help with pronunciation.

Exercise 6 page 84 🎧 3.08
- Students read the instructions and the exam tip. Play the recording once. Allow students to compare answers in pairs, but don't check with the whole class yet.

Transcript 3.08
Waitress Hi. What would you like?
Woman Fish and chips, please.
Waitress Anything to drink?
Woman Yes, please. A bottle of water.
Waitress No problem. What can I get for you?
Man Could I have tomato soup, please?
Waitress Of course. Anything else?
Man Yes, chicken curry.
Waitress OK. Would you like a drink?
Man Tea, please.
Waitress Is that all?
Man Yes, thanks.
Waitress That's £17.05, please.
Woman Here you are.
Waitress £20. Thank you. Here's your change. I'll bring the food to your table.

Exercise 7 page 84 🎧 3.08
- Play the recording again and check answers with the whole class.

KEY
woman: fish and chips, a bottle of water
man: tomato soup, chicken curry, tea

Exercise 8 page 84
- Remind students that they can use this lesson and other lessons in the unit as a resource when preparing their dialogues.

Exercise 9 page 84
- Have some of the groups act out their dialogues to the whole class. Give feedback: praise good performance, correct a few mistakes (recurring ones or those concerning the language from this lesson).

OPTIONAL ACTIVITY

Students work in pairs. Tell them they are opening a café, a snack bar or a small restaurant. They need to decide what kind of place it is, what kind of food it serves, and then write a short menu. Give some suggestions for different menus: for example, it could be just cakes, desserts and drinks, or just pizzas with different toppings, etc. Each pair has to write two copies of their menu. When the menus are ready, students get into new pairs. They read each other's menus and order meals from each other.

➡ Lesson outcome

Ask students: *What have we talked about today?* Elicit: *restaurants* or *ordering food in a restaurant.* Ask: *Can you tell me some of the things you say in a restaurant?* Elicit any of the phrases from the lesson. Draw students' attention to the lesson statement: *I can order food and drink in a café.*

Notes for Photocopiable activity 8.2

A meal at the White Horse Pub

A group role play
Language: food vocabulary; ordering food
Materials: one copy of the menu per student. One set of role cards, cut up, per group of four students. (Teacher's Book page 138)

- Pre-teach *burned*
- Hand out a copy of the menu to each student. Students work in pairs to complete the menu with words from the box. Check the answers.
- Explain that students are going to practise ordering food in a pub. Divide students into groups of four. Explain that one student is the waiter. Hand out the waiter role cards and put customer role cards face down on the desk.
- Ask the waiters to greet the customers, hand out the menus and take the orders for food and drink. When the food and drink arrives the customers take it in turns to take a customer role card and tell the waiter what's wrong. The waiter has to deal with the problem. At the end they ask for the bill.
- When they have finished they can change roles and repeat the role play.

KEY

1	soup	4	curry	7	hot
2	beef	5	chips	8	apple
3	peas	6	sauce	9	water

WRITING
8G A formal letter

LESSON SUMMARY ● ● ○ ○ ○

Writing: a formal letter requesting information
Reading: a formal letter requesting information
Topic: shopping and services

SHORTCUT *To do the lesson in 30 minutes, set the writing as homework.*

➡ Lead-in 2–3 minutes

- Explain the term 'formal letter'. Ask students around the class for their ideas about when you would write a formal letter. Answers might include *job applications, when you are complaining about something, when you want information about something.* Students can use their own language if necessary.
- Compare these to informal letters. Ask *Who do you write informal letters to?* (*friends, penfriends,* or *people you email* for example)
- Tell students that this lesson is about formal letters requesting information.

Exercise 1 page 85

- Students read the advertisement and the letter. They complete the task individually then compare answers in pairs.
- Check answers as a class.

KEY

1 ... could you please tell me if there is a good choice of vegetarian dishes...
2 ... could you please let me know how much the set menu costs?
3 Could you please let me know if that is possible?

Exercise 2 page 85

- Read the rubric and the sentences with the students, then let them complete the sentences.
- With a **stronger** class, ask individual students for their answers. With a **weaker** class, allow them time to compare their answers before asking for ideas.

KEY

1	Indian	3	seven
2	ten	4	vegetarian

Exercise 3 page 85

- Students look at the text again and compare the phrases. Check the answers with the class.

KEY

1 let; know   2 could; tell

Exercise 4 page 85

- Explain that students will now use the phrases from exercise 3 to make new requests. Do the first item as a class, then ask them to complete the rest in pairs. Remind them that the phrases have the same meanings, and that they should try to use both of them in their requests.
- Check answers around the class. As students give their answers, point out that the auxiliary verb *do* is no longer needed in the formal phrase (items 1,3 and 4), and that the word order changes after the formal phrase from a direct question: *are – you – open* on to that of a statement: *you – are – open* (items 2 and 5).

KEY

1 Could you please tell me if / Could you please let me know if you serve fish?
2 Could you please tell me if / Could you please let me know if you are open on Sunday evenings?
3 Could you please tell me if / Could you please let me know if you have a table for five people?
4 Could you please tell me if / Could you please let me know if the restaurant is in the town centre?

Exercise 5 page 85

- Ask students to read the writing tip. Ask if they would use the phrases in the box to write to a friend (*No*).
- When they have read and understood the box, refer them back to page 15 to compare these phrases with informal letters.

Exercise 6 page 85

- Set up the writing task. Explain that students are now going to write their own letter using the notes they have made.
- Read through the advert for Stefano's and the writing guide with the class. Remind them to include all the information in the letter, and to use the text in exercise 1 as a model.

ALTERNATIVE WRITING TASK

Tell students they are going to write another formal letter, but this one is to a tourist information office. They can use vocabulary from unit 6 to help them.

Each student has to choose a town and write a formal letter to a tourist information office requesting information.

Remind them to use appropriate phrases to start and end a formal letter. They can choose what information they would like to request, but ideas could include places to visit, cost of entry to attractions, and places to eat and drink.

➡ Lesson outcome

Ask students: *What did we do today?* Elicit: *writing formal letters*, or *ways of requesting information*. Ask students for phrases used in formal letters. Draw students' attention to the lesson statement: *I can write a letter requesting information*.

LANGUAGE REVIEW 7–8

1
1	Italian	4	Russian	7	Sweden
2	Germany	5	Chinese	8	Belarus
3	Greek	6	Czech	9	British

2
1	bananas	4	u	7	u
2	u	5	u	8	sausages
3	u	6	apples		

3
1	cereal	2	toast	3	orange juice

4
1	was	4	gave	7	became
2	went	5	spent	8	wrote
3	were	6	won		

5
1	He went out	3	He played	5	He didn't see
2	He didn't watch	4	He didn't write	6	He bought

6
1 Did he go out with friends? Yes, he did.
2 Did he watch TV? No, he didn't.
3 Did he play computer games? Yes, he did.
4 Did he write a letter? No, he didn't.
5 Did he see a film? No, he didn't.
6 Did he buy a CD? Yes, he did.

7
1	any	3	many	5	the
2	some	4	a	6	much

8
1 How was your weekend?
2 Did you go out on Saturday night?
3 Where did you go?
4 What was the food like?
5 How about Sunday?

9
1	Can	3	to
2	have	4	like

SKILLS ROUND-UP 1–8

Transcript 3.09

Narrator	It's Monday morning. Dave and Márton are both working at the hotel.
Márton	Hi, Dave. How was your weekend?
Dave	It was OK. I worked on Saturday.
Márton	How about Sunday?
Dave	I stayed at home. I phoned some friends, cleaned my flat … nothing exciting. How about you?
Márton	Well, on Saturday evening, I went to the theatre.
Dave	Really? What did you see?
Márton	I saw *Romeo and Juliet*.
Dave	Oh, right. That's Shakespeare, isn't it?
Márton	Yes, it is.
Dave	Who did you go with?
Márton	My housemate, Anna. She had two free tickets.
Dave	Really? How did she get those?
Márton	She works for a magazine. They wrote an article about Shakespeare's Globe Theatre and the theatre gave them some free tickets.
Dave	That's good. So Anna invited you.
Márton	Yes, that's right. Anyway, I really enjoyed the play. And after the play, we went for a pizza – and I saw your friend there, in the restaurant.
Dave	Which friend?
Márton	Your Italian friend – Francesca!
Dave	That's amazing! Did you speak to her?
Márton	Not really. We just said hello.
Dave	Actually, she's coming to the hotel today. I'm meeting her for lunch. Why don't you join us?
Márton	Thanks! If you don't mind …
Dave	Of course not. Anyway, what did you do on Sunday?
Márton	I went shopping.
Dave	Did you buy anything?
Márton	Only a shirt – a white shirt, for work.
Dave	Did you do anything on Sunday evening?
Márton	Not really, Anna and I watched a DVD. It was a romantic comedy – I can't remember the title Then I sent a few e-mails to friends in Hungary. I didn't go to bed until …
…	
Narrator	It's lunchtime. Dave and Márton are in the hotel restaurant.
Dave	Could I have a large Coke, please?
Waitress	Of course. And for you?
Márton	I'll just have a glass of water, please,
Waitress	Still or sparkling?
Márton	Still.
Waitress	Sure. Anything to eat?
Dave	Actually, we're waiting for a friend.

1
1	b	2	e	3	a	4	d	5	c

2 **Dave:** a large Coke
Márton: a glass of still water

3 c

4
1 In 1599.
2 about 3,000 people
3 a fire destroyed the theatre
4 in 1642
5 in the centre of London on the south side of the River Thames
6 there isn't a roof

5–6 Open answers

EXAM For further exam tasks and practice, go to Workbook page 78. Procedural notes, transcripts and keys for the Workbook can be found on the *Solutions* Teacher's Website at www.oup.com/elt/teacher/solutions

9 Journeys

THIS UNIT INCLUDES ● ● ● ●
Vocabulary • transport • prepositions (*by bike, on foot,* etc.) • phrasal verbs • weather
Grammar • present perfect affirmative • *just* • present perfect negative and interrogative • *already, yet*
Speaking • talking about how you get around • talking about living in a foreign country • buying a train ticket
Writing • an e-mail
WORKBOOK pages 80–86

A VOCABULARY AND LISTENING
Transport

LESSON SUMMARY ● ● ● ● ●
Vocabulary: means of transport
Listening: short dialogues
Speaking: talking about the way to school
Topic: travel and tourism

SHORTCUT *To do the lesson in 30 minutes, set Vocabulary Builder (part 1) exercises 1, 2 and 4 as homework.*

➡ Lead-in 2 minutes
• Write *transport* on the board. Say this is going to be today's topic. Ask students if they know any names of means of transport in English. Some of them will probably know *bike, bus, car, plane,* possibly *train* and *ship,* but they may need prompting – you may show them pictures, sketch the vehicles on the board, or mime them.

Exercise 1 page 88
• Students label the pictures in pairs. Ask them to try and do as much as they can without the Wordlist first; they can start using it after they have done as much as they can. Elicit which items are not shown in the pictures.

KEY

1	scooter	4	underground	7	tram
2	lorry	5	coach	8	helicopter
3	ship	6	van		

Not illustrated: bicycle (bike) boat bus car motorbike plane taxi train

LANGUAGE NOTE – ARTICLES
Highlight the fact that no article is needed with *go by bike, go by train, go by car,* etc. but that we do use the definite article *the* with *take,* e.g. *take the train, take the car,* etc.

Exercise 2 page 88 🎧 3.11
• Play the recording once for students to check their answers. Then play it again pausing after each item and asking them to repeat chorally and individually. Point out that the *–or* in *mot**or**bike* and the *–er* in *scoot**er*** and *und**er**ground* do not sound like they are written: they are not pronounced /ɔːr/ and /er/, but /ə/ – the reduced vowel. With a **weaker class,** ask for Polish equivalents of the words to check they understand.

Exercise 3 page 88
• Students do the exercise individually or in pairs. Check with the whole class.

KEY
land: bicycle, bus, car, coach, lorry, motorbike, scooter, taxi, train, tram, underground, van
air: helicopter, plane
sea: boat, ship

Exercise 4 page 88 🎧 3.12
• Tell students they are going to hear 5 teenagers talking about their way to school. Ask them to look at the instructions and the chart. Say they will hear the recording twice. Play it through once without stopping; the second time, stop after each dialogue and ask for answers.

KEY

		Distance	Time
1	Danny	1 km	15 mins
2	Charlotte	6 km	20-25 mins
3	Craig	200 m	2-3 mins
4	Ann	2-3 km	about 20 mins
5	Joe	4 km	20 mins

Transcript 3.12
1 Danny
Int. How far do you live from the school?
Boy About one kilometre.
Int. And how do you get to school?
Boy I usually walk to school.
Int. How long does it take?
Boy About 15 minutes.

2 Charlotte
Int. How far do you live from the school?
Girl I live in a village, about six kilometres away.
Int. How do you get to school?
Girl My dad gives me a lift in the morning. He works near the school. But he finishes work late so I go home by bus.
Int. And how long does it take?
Girl About 20 or 25 minutes.

3 Craig
Int. How far do you live from the school?
Boy I live just round the corner – about 200 metres.
Int. So do you go on foot?
Boy Yes, usually. Or sometimes I go by bike.
Int. How long does it take?
Boy Just two or three minutes.

4 Ann
Int. How far do you live from the school?
Girl I'm not sure – about two or three kilometres, I think.
Int. And how do you get to school?
Girl I take the tram. It stops right outside our block of flats.
Int. How long does it take?
Girl About twenty minutes.

5 Joe
Int. How far do you live from the school?
Boy About four kilometres.
Int. How do you get to school?
Boy I go by underground.
Int. How long does it take?
Boy It takes five minutes to walk to the station, ten minutes on the train, and another five minutes from the station to the school.

For further practice of the transport vocabulary, go to:

Vocabulary Builder (part 1): Student's Book page 136

KEY

1 1	train	4	ship	7	bus
2	plane	5	car	8	bicycle
3	motorbike	6	taxi		

2 1	coach	4	scooter	7	underground
2	helicopter	5	ship	8	van
3	lorry	6	tram		

3 🎧 3.25

1	motorbike	4	bike	7	ship
2	tram	5	plane	8	lorry
3	helicopter	6	train		

4 2 In bad weather, I go to school by bus.
   3 I always go to the station on foot.
   4 I usually cycle to school.
   5 My dad usually drives to work.
   6 Do you walk to school?
   7 My mum gives me a lift to the bus station.

Exercise 5 page 88 🎧 3.12

- Read the *Learn this* box with the whole class. Ask students to read the sentences in exercise 5. Play the recording again. Let students compare answers in pairs, then check with the whole class.

KEY

1	Craig	3	Danny	5	Charlotte
2	Ann	4	Joe		

Exercise 6 page 88

- Make sure students know how to pronounce *kilometres*, *metres* and *minutes*. It would be better if they worked in pairs with classmates they do not know very well, so that the information is new to them.

For work on phrasal verbs used with transport, go to:

Vocabulary Builder (part 2): Student's Book page 136

KEY

5 1	get out of	4	take off	7	get in
2	get on	5	get off	8	slow down
3	get back	6	break down		

6 got, took, broke

7 1	got off	4	got in	7	got on
2	took off	5	slowed down	8	got out of
3	broke down	6	got back		

OPTIONAL ACTIVITY

Students work in teams of 3–4. Tell them their task is to compare different forms of transport. Ask them to look at the means of transport in this lesson and to look back at lessons 5B and 5D on comparative and superlative adjectives. Write on the board: *fast, slow, cheap, expensive, safe, exciting, healthy* (and other adjectives you think are relevant). You can also write an example: *A car is faster than a bike.* Tell students to write as many sentences comparing different means of transport as they can in two minutes. After two minutes, they stop writing and the teams take turns to read their sentences. Each correct sentence scores a point. The team with the most points wins.

➡ Lesson outcome

Ask students: *What have we talked about today?* Elicit: *transport* or an equivalent (e.g. *Cars and trains and planes and …*). Ask: *Can you tell me some words you learned today?* Acknowledge all answers, but praise the students who come up with collocations, e.g. *to catch a bus, to drive somebody somewhere, to give somebody a lift.* Draw students' attention to the lesson statement: *I can explain how I get to school.*

9B GRAMMAR
Present perfect: affirmative

LESSON SUMMARY ● ● ● ○ ○

Grammar: present perfect: affirmative
Speaking: talking about very recent events

SHORTCUT *To do the lesson in 30 minutes, set the Grammar Builder as homework.*

➡ Lead-in 2–3 minutes

- Tell students they are going to learn a new tense. Write its name on the board: *present perfect*.

Exercise 1 page 89

- Draw students' attention to the picture. Ask them what they can see. Ask a few students to describe the picture. Then ask them to do the task.

KEY

1 Simon	2 Sam and Julie	3 Lucy

Exercise 2 page 89 🎧 3.13

- Play the recording once for students to repeat and check.

Exercise 3 page 89

- Do this task step by step, reading each bullet point aloud and asking students to complete the examples in pairs. Make sure they use the list of irregular verbs when doing the third bullet point.

KEY

have	has
dropped, dropped	missed, missed
ate, eaten	heard, heard
has lost	have eaten

Exercise 4 page 89

- Students work individually with the list of irregular verbs. Go over answers with the whole class.

KEY

written	walked	stopped
had	drunk	gone
cooked	done	

Exercise 5 page 89

- Do the first one or two sentences with the whole class to make sure everyone knows what they have to do. Students work individually and compare answers in pairs. After they have finished, check with the whole class.

KEY

1	've walked	4	've drunk	7	's gone
2	've written	5	's cooked	8	've done
3	's stopped	6	's had		

For further practice on the present perfect: affirmative, go to:

Grammar Builder 9B: Student's Book page 124

KEY

1
1	has started	4	have cycled	7	has landed
2	have decided	5	have studied		
3	has phoned	6	has cooked		

2
1 know, knew, known
2 write, wrote, written
3 sleep, slept, slept
4 sell, sold, sold
5 think, thought, thought

3
1	have seen	4	has won	7	has broken
2	has gone	5	have eaten		
3	have left	6	has done		

4
2	has stopped	5	have spoken	8	have eaten
3	have arrived	6	has finished		
4	have had	7	have missed		

5
2 I've just phoned him.
3 He's just left.
4 We've/I've just watched it.
5 I've just read it.
6 I've just written to her.
7 I've just packed it.
8 I've just booked them.

Exercise 6 page 89

- Read the *Learn this!* box with the whole class. Also read the example and do sentence b with the whole class to make sure everyone knows how to build the sentences with *just* in the right place. Students do the exercise individually or in pairs. Check answers by asking different students to read the short dialogues in open pairs.

KEY

1 'Is it a good party?'
c 'I don't know. I've just arrived.'
2 'Why are you laughing?'
a 'I've just heard a really funny story.'
3 'Is your brother wearing a new jacket?'
f 'Yes. he's just bought it.'
4 'Can I have a biscuit?'
b 'Sorry. I've just eaten them.'
5 'Is Suzie at home?'
e 'No. She's just gone out.'
6 'Why are they tired?'
d 'They have just played football'

Exercise 7 page 89

- Students read the same mini-dialogues in pairs. With a **stronger class**, ask them to think of their own responses. With a **weaker class**, if time permits, you might ask them to read the dialogues as they appear in the book first, and then read the same questions but alter the replies.

➡ Lesson outcome

Say to students: *Today we looked at the present perfect tense. How is it constructed? When is it used?* (elicit various bits of information). Draw students' attention to the lesson statement: *I can say what I have just done.*

9C CULTURE
People on the move

LESSON SUMMARY ● ● ● ● ●

Reading: a text about immigrants in Britain
Listening: people talking about life in Britain
Speaking: speaking about life in other countries
Topic: society

SHORTCUT *To do the lesson in 30 minutes, ask students to read the text for the first time at home.*

➡ Lead-in 2 minutes

- Before students open their books, ask them if they know anyone who has gone to live in Britain. *Why did they do it? Which city are they in? What are they doing there? Are they happy? Why in general do many people go to Britain these days?* Tell the class that the topic of the lesson will be immigrants in Britain.

Exercise 1 page 90

- Students describe the photos in pairs or groups of three. Share ideas as a class.

Exercise 2 page 90

- Pre-teach *former*. Students read the text individually and do the task, then compare answers in pairs. Check with the whole class.

KEY

A Introduction
B Ireland
C The former colonies
D The EU
E How have immigrants influenced British life?

Exercise 3 page 90

- Students do the vocabulary exercise individually. Check with the whole class. You may ask for translations of the more difficult words to check understanding.

KEY

1	colonies	3	settled	5	famine
2	majority	4	recently	6	immigrants

CULTURE NOTES – MULTI-CULTURAL BRITAIN

Multicultural Britain

The population of Britain is just over 60 million.

91.3% are white

4.4% are Asian/Asian British (Indian/Pakistani/Bangladeshi and other)

2.2% are Black/Black British (Caribbean/African and other)

0.4% are Chinese

0.4% are from other races

1.4% are mixed race

European Migration

At the end of 2006 there were over 600,000 migrant workers in Britain from the 8 nations that joined the European Union in 2004. This number is expected to rise steadily over the years. They help to fill the gaps in the UK's labour market, especially in administration, business and management, hospitality and catering.

Exercise 4 page 90

• Students read again more carefully and do the task. **Fast finishers** may write corrected versions of the false statements.

KEY

1 F   2 T   3 F   4 T   5 F   6 F

Exercise 5 page 90   🎧 3.14

• Play the recording once and ask for answers to the questions. In a stronger class, ask students if they can remember anything else that the speakers mentioned.

KEY

a Abdul   b Ania

Transcript 3.14

1

Woman My name's Ania Chomacka. I'm a dentist and I live in Birmingham. I came to Britain a year ago from Gdańsk in Poland. It was quite difficult at first. I was a bit homesick and I missed my family a lot. I studied English at school in Poland so I don't find it very difficult to communicate with English people, but sometimes they speak very fast. I like Birmingham – there's lots to do here – it's a very exciting city. I've made a lot of friends, both English and Polish – there's a big Polish community here in Birmingham. It's nice to meet up with people from back home and to speak my own language.

2

Man My name's Abdul Khan. I'm a student at Bradford University in the north of England. I live here in Bradford with my parents and grandparents. My grandparents came over from Pakistan in the 1960s, when my parents were young. I was born here but I speak Punjabi as well as English. In fact we all speak Punjabi at home. I'm British but I'm also Pakistani – I think it's important not to forget where you come from. Sometimes people are a bit racist but generally there's a good relationship between the Asian and white communities in Bradford.

Exercise 6 page 90   🎧 3.14

• Play the recording through again. Then play the part featuring Ania only and check answers. Play Abdul and check answers.

KEY

1 a   2 b   3 b   4 a   5 b   6 b

Exercise 7 page 90

• Students discuss the questions in small groups. Circulate and help with language. Share ideas as a class. Encourage those whom you heard saying something interesting to share it.

OPTIONAL ACTIVITY

Ask students to think back to question 3 from exercise 7. In pairs or groups of three, they make lists of things which make the life of an immigrant difficult. Share ideas as a class. You may list them on the board, on the left-hand side. Students continue working in the same pairs or groups. For each difficulty listed, ask them to write how people should behave to make immigrants' life easier. You may put an example on the board, e.g.:

Problems

It's difficult to understand when people speak very fast.

You can feel homesick.

People can be racist.

Discuss ideas with the whole class.

➜ Lesson outcome

Ask students: *What have we talked about today?* Elicit: *immigrants* or an equivalent. Ask students if they learned anything new about immigrants in Britain. Elicit some of the vocabulary from the lesson. Draw students' attention to the lesson statement: *I can talk about living in a foreign country.*

9D GRAMMAR
Present perfect: negative and interrogative

LESSON SUMMARY ● ● ● ● ○

Grammar: present perfect: negative and interrogative

Listening: dialogues about travel

Speaking: talking about what you have and haven't done today

SHORTCUT *To do the lesson in 30 minutes, do exercises 4 and 7 orally as a class and keep exercise 11 short.*

➜ Lead-in 2 minutes

• Ask a few strong students questions in the present perfect to which the likely answer is *No*, e.g.: *Have you talked to X today?* (where X is a classmate who is absent.) If the student answers *No*, say: *Oh, so you haven't talked to X. Have you had lunch yet?* (if the lesson is in the morning) *Have you ever been to New Zealand/ Indonesia?* (or any country you are fairly confident they have not been to) *Have you ever eaten frogs?* etc.

• Remind students that they recently studied the present perfect tense. Explain that now it is time to look at questions and negative sentences in that tense. You may wish to elicit some information about the present perfect: how is it formed? How is it used?

Exercise 1 page 91

• Students describe the photo in pairs. Circulate and help, then ask 2–3 students to describe it to the whole class.

Exercise 2 page 91 🎧 3.15

• Play the recording. Students do the task individually. Go over answers quickly as a class. The meanings of *guidebook* and *suitcase* may need clarifying. You may ask: *What kind of book do you need when going on holiday? It can be for example about Italy or about Paris* (as in the dialogue). *What do you need to pack when you're going on holiday? You put your clothes in it.*

KEY

Tick: book tickets, find passports, buy guidebook

Exercise 3 page 91

• Ask students to consider the task individually first, then compare answers in pairs. Check with the whole class. Point out that here again we have the ending *–s* in the third person singular. You may wish to ask for other verb forms which have this ending.

KEY

haven't	Have	haven't

Exercise 4 page 91

• With a **weaker class**, have students work on the sentences in pairs, or first individually and then compare answers in pairs, before finally checking with the whole class. With a **stronger class**, you can do the exercise quickly with the whole class.

KEY

They've booked the tickets.
They've found the passports.
They haven't changed the money.
They've bought a guidebook.
They haven't packed their suitcase.

Exercise 5 page 91

• As in exercise 4, with a **stronger class** you can do the exercise with the whole class with little or no preparation.

KEY

1 Have they booked the tickets? Yes, they have.
2 Has Sarah found the passports? Yes, she has.
3 Has Peter changed the money? No, he hasn't.
4 Has Peter bought a guidebook? Yes, he has.
5 Have they packed the suitcase? No, they haven't.

For further practice on the present perfect (negative and interrogative), go to:

Grammar Builder 9D: Student's Book page 124

KEY

6 1 Harry hasn't had breakfast.
   2 I haven't lost my personal stereo.
   3 Rachel and I haven't spent all our money.
   4 You haven't eaten the apple.
   5 Vicky hasn't taken the train to Leeds.
   6 Luke and Emily haven't visited Spain.
   7 I haven't done my homework.
   8 He hasn't gone to New York by ship.

7 2 Have you decided what to do? Yes, I have.
   3 Has Robert packed his bags? No, he hasn't.
   4 Have Kate and David written any postcards? No, they haven't.
   5 Have you bought any CDs? No, I haven't.
   6 Have you and Tony had lunch? Yes, we have.
   7 Has Sarah gone to Edinburgh? Yes, she has.

8 2 Have you had breakfast? No, I haven't (had breakfast) yet.
   3 Have you phoned Joanna? Yes, I've just phoned her.
   4 Have you bought the new Anastacia CD? Yes, I've already bought it.
   5 Have you found your keys? No, I haven't found them yet.
   6 Have you written to Ian? Yes, I've already written to him.
   7 Have you changed the holiday money? Yes, I've already changed it.
   8 Have you seen my new scooter? No, I haven't seen it yet.

Exercise 6 page 91 🎧 3.16

• Ask students to read the list of things to do in Paris. Ask which of the things they would like to do. Ask if anyone has been to Paris and done them. Play the recording twice and check answers.

KEY

Tick: climb the Eiffel Tower, see the paintings in the Louvre Museum, take a boat trip on the River Seine, have a meal in the Latin Quarter

Transcript 3.16

Tania Are you having a good time in Paris?
Sarah Yes, we arrived two days ago.
Tania What have you done so far?
Sarah We've met our friend Sam and he's shown us some of the sights.
Tania Have you climbed the Eiffel Tower yet?
Sarah Yes, we have. We went up on Saturday. The views from the top were fantastic.
Tania Have you visited Notre Dame Cathedral?
Sarah No, not yet. We're going there tomorrow. But we've seen the paintings in the Louvre Museum. They were fantastic.
Tania Have you taken a boat trip on the River Seine yet?
Sarah Yes, we have. We went last night – it was really romantic!
Tania Have you walked up the Champs Elysees?
Sarah No. We want to walk up the Champs Elysees, but we haven't had time.
Tania What's the food like? Have you eaten in any nice restaurants?
Sarah Yes, we've had a meal in the Latin Quarter. It was delicious! We're coming home next Saturday. I'll tell you all about it then …

Exercise 7 page 91

• With a **weaker class**, have students work on the sentences in pairs, or first individually and then compare answers in pairs, before finally checking with the whole class. With a **stronger class**, you can do the exercise quickly with the whole class.

KEY

They've climbed the Eiffel Tower.
They haven't visited Notre Dame cathedral yet.
They've seen the paintings in the Louvre Museum.
They've taken a boat trip on the River Seine.
They haven't walked up the Champs Elysees.
They've had a meal in the Latin Quarter.

Exercise 8 page 91

- With a **weaker class,** or just when you want more control over accuracy, this can be done in open pairs with the whole class: ask student A the first question, A answers and asks B the next question, B answers and asks C, etc.

Exercise 9 page 91

- Students answer individually. Help with any comprehension problems. With a **weaker class**, you might wish to read the whole list as a class and make sure they understand.

Exercise 10 page 91

- Before students start asking and answering in pairs, make sure they know how to build the questions. Some of the verbs in the list are irregular.
- Go over all the questions once in open pairs as in exercise 8. If anyone makes a mistake, encourage them to correct themselves; if they cannot, ask the class for help. Write the correct form of the problematic question on the board. As the students talk in pairs, circulate and help. If they're making errors in the target language, insist on self-correction.

Exercise 11 page 91

- Have a few students report back to the class on some of the things they found out.

OPTIONAL ACTIVITIES

1 Ask everyone to write 2–3 more questions of the form: *Have you... today?* Circulate and help. It is important that all the questions should be correct – you may ask students to read them aloud. When the questions are ready, ask everybody to stand up and ask everyone in the room their questions, marking the answers in two columns – 'yes' and 'no'. When they've finished, they have to write sentences reporting their findings: *8 people in our class have eaten cereal today, 6 haven't eaten cereal,* etc. Monitor and ask for all or just the most interesting findings to be read aloud to the whole class.

2 Make photocopies of transcript 3.16. In pairs, students prepare and act out a similar dialogue about a different city.

➡ Lesson outcome

Ask students: *What have we talked about today?* Try to elicit: *the present perfect, questions and negative statements* or equivalent. Go over the forms as studied in exercise 3. Draw students' attention to the lesson statement: *I can talk about recent events.*

Notes for Photocopiable activity 9.1

My day so far ...

Pairwork
Language: present perfect for recent experiences
Materials: one copy of the worksheet per student (Teacher's Book page 139)

- Give each student a copy of the worksheet. Students work individually to write their answers in the boxes in random order. Ask them to write in as many answers as possible. They might not be able to answer one or two of them.
- They should write just one word or short phrases.
- When they have finished they swap worksheets with a partner and then take it in turns to use the answers to ask questions to find out why their partner has written the words. For example, *Why have you written 'Anita'?*

The other student answers using the present perfect tense. *I haven't seen Anita today.* Encourage them to ask a follow-up question after each statement.
- At the end of the activity conduct a brief class feedback where students report some information about their partner to the class.

9E READING
Alone on the water

LESSON SUMMARY ● ● ● ● ○

Reading: an article; reading for detail
Vocabulary: weather
Speaking: an interview
Topic: people and society

SHORTCUT *To do the lesson in 30 minutes, ask students to read the text for the first time at home.*

➡ Lead-in 2–3 minutes

- Explain the word *disabled*. Write it on the board. In pairs, ask students to write down 2–3 things which disabled people can't do and 2–3 things they can do. (Sample answers: *They cannot walk, they cannot see, they cannot use their hands well. They can play sports, they can write books, they can paint.*) Explain that today the students are gong to read a text about a very special disabled person.

LANGUAGE NOTE – *DISABLED*

Nowadays **disabled** is generally the most acceptable word used to refer to people with a permanent illness or injury that makes it difficult for them to use part of their body completely easily. Other words such as *handicapped* or *invalid* should be avoided as they are considered offensive by many people because of their negative associations.

Exercise 1 page 92

- Students label the pictures. When checking, ask additional questions: *Do you like stormy weather? What kind of weather do you like? What kind of weather is good for sailing?*

KEY

1	icy, cold, foggy	5	rainy
2	sunny, warm	6	windy
3	stormy	7	foggy
4	cloudy	8	snowy

Exercise 2 page 93 🎧 3.17

- Work on pronunciation. To pronounce *weather* correctly, students may need to forget the way it's written and just listen to the sounds!

Exercise 3 page 92

- This can be done in open pairs or in closed pairs. Make sure the students understand the question: *What's the weather like?* – You may wish to ask for a translation. After going over the pictures, ask: *What's the weather like today?* (You may need to point to the window.)

Exercise 4 page 92

- Read the reading tip aloud and discuss: why is this important? What is the effect of reading in that way? (From the first paragraph you can find out what the text is about, what kind of information you can find in it, and maybe decide whether you want to read it. In an exam, it helps you prepare to read the rest of the text by predicting what might be in it.)
- Students read the first paragraph of the text. You may need to explain that *the English Channel* means *La Manche*. Discuss answers to questions 1 and 2 with the whole class.

KEY
1 She has just sailed alone across the English Channel.
2 Because she can't move her arms or legs or even her head.

CULTURE NOTE – THE CHANNEL
The *English Channel* or *the Channel* is the stretch of water that runs between southern England and northern France. At its narrowest point it is only 20 miles / 32 kilometres wide. On a clear day it is possible to see Calais from Dover.

Exercise 5 page 92

- Students read the text in more detail. Words which may need explaining: *harbour, design, controls (n.) wheelchair*. With a **strong class**, students should use dictionaries or the Wordlist. With a **weaker class**, you may choose to explain the words yourself. In both cases, you can encourage students to infer meaning from context (*The boat is going out of Portsmouth Harbour – Portsmouth is the name of the town, but what is a harbour, if boats can go out of it and into it?*) or from the form of the word (*What kind of chair does a paralyzed person have? Why is it called a wheelchair?*). Students do the task individually, compare answers in pairs, check with the whole class.

KEY
1 e	3 c	5 f	7 g
2 h	4 a	6 b	8 d

Exercise 6 page 92

- Do the first sentence together as an example. Then students continue individually. Check with the whole class.

KEY
1 sailed	3 given	5 had
2 become	4 been	6 changed

Exercise 7 page 92

- Make sure everyone understands *opposite*. Dictionaries may be needed for some of the words. Students do the task individually, then compare answers in pairs. Check with the whole class.

KEY
1 always	4 found	7 first
2 left	5 longest	8 loved
3 rare	6 alone	9 happy

Exercise 8 page 92

- Emphasise that this exercise needs to be done *with the text*. Students can use the exact phrases from the text, there's no need to try and put the ideas 'in their own words'. Don't check answers with the class, they will appear in the next exercise.

KEY (sample answers)
1 Because it makes me feel happy and free
2 A friend took me sailing and I loved it, but I didn't want to be a passenger, so I had sailing lessons.
3 With my mouth.
4 Very tired, but very happy.
5 I want to sail around Britain.

Exercise 9 page 92

- Pairs act out their interviews. This is also the time to check answers to exercise 8. If some pairs create an answer that is imaginative and makes sense, but has no foundation in the text, praise them for creativity, but emphasise that when working with a text it is essential to be able to read carefully, know exactly what the text says, and not drift away from it.

ADDITIONAL SPEAKING ACTIVITY
Below are two activities to choose from; both involve Internet searches. The search can be done in class if you can have the lesson in a computer room. Otherwise it has to be homework.

1 Students have to find out and note 3 more facts about Hilary Lister on the Internet (her website is www.hilarylister.com, but information can also be found on other sites). They then share their findings in groups of 3–4.

2 Individually or in pairs, students look for information about other disabled people who have done something special. They prepare mini presentations. Here are some questions to help them:
Who is the person?
What is his/ her health problem?
What cannot he/she do?
What has he/she done/achieved?
What special equipment did he/she need?
Who helped him/her?
How does he/she feel about it?

➡ Lesson outcome
Ask students: *What did we do/ talk about today?* Try to elicit: *Hilary Lister* or *disabled people*, or *disabled people who have done something special*. Ask students for any facts they learned today and for new vocabulary. Draw students' attention to the lesson statement: *I can understand a magazine article in detail.*

EVERYDAY ENGLISH
Buying a train ticket

LESSON SUMMARY ● ● ● ○
Functional English: buying a train ticket
Listening: short dialogues
Vocabulary: words related to rail travel; the 24-hour clock
Speaking: buying a train ticket
Topic: travel and tourism

SHORTCUT *To do the lesson in 30 minutes, have only a few pairs act out their dialogues in exercise 9.*

→ Lead-in 2 minutes

- Put these questions on the board: *Do you like travelling by train? Why?/ Why not? What was your longest train journey?*
- Ask students to discuss these questions in pairs for 1–2 minutes, then say: *Today we are going to buy train tickets.*

Exercise 1 page 94 🎧 3.18

- Play the recording once. Check answers. Can students guess what a *platform* is? If you have a map of Britain in the room, during the whole lesson point out all the cities and towns that are mentioned on the map.

KEY

She wants to go to London and to return today.

Exercise 2 page 94 🎧 3.19

- Read the *Learn this!* box aloud.
- Play the recording through once, then again, pausing after each item to check. Write the times on the board to avoid confusion.

KEY

1	12:28	4	06:00
2	09:15	5	23:55
3	18:49	6	17:17

CULTURE NOTE – 24-HOUR CLOCK

The 24-hour clock times practised in the exercise are used in official situations, on timetables, etc. You are likely to hear them spoken in e.g. railway station announcements but most people in everyday conversation would use the more standard formulation: *I'm getting the train at 5 o'clock,* rather than the military-sounding *seventeen hundred.*

Exercise 3 page 94

- With a **weaker class**, you might start by dictating a few times to the whole class yourself, to provide a model of clear enunciation and stress; then have a few students dictate times and other students write them on the board, and then move on to the pairwork. Circulate and monitor, insisting that if someone hasn't managed to write down a time correctly, their partner must repeat it, taking care to speak clearly.

Exercise 4 page 94

- Tell the students in a moment they will be asked to read the dialogue, but first they are going to hear it again to have a model of pronunciation. Play the dialogue. Ask students to read and do the task. If time allows, you may wish to ask 2–3 pairs to read their dialogues to the class.

Exercise 5 page 94 🎧 3.20

- Tell students they are going to hear two conversations at a station ticket office. Play the recording through once, then again pausing after each part to check answers. Ask if anyone remembers any additional details – when are the people travelling? When are they coming back? Do they have to change?

KEY

	destination	price	platform	time
1	Liverpool	£35	7	17.35
2	Manchester	£12.50	10	10.47

Transcript 3.20

1

Clerk	Can I help you?
Boy	Yes, can I have a return ticket to Liverpool, please?
Clerk	When are you coming back?
Boy	Next Saturday.
Clerk	That's £35, please.
Boy	Here you are … Which platform does it depart from?
Clerk	Platform 7.
Boy	When's the next train?
Clerk	At 17.35.
Boy	Do I have to change?
Clerk	No, it's a direct train.

2

Clerk	Next please.
Girl	Is there a train for Manchester at about 11 o'clock on Saturday morning?
Clerk	Yes, there's a direct train at 10:47.
Girl	OK. And how much is a return ticket?
Clerk	Are you coming back on the same day?
Girl	Yes.
Clerk	It's £12.50. Would you like a ticket?
Girl	No thanks, I'll get one on Saturday … Oh, which platform does it depart from?
Clerk	Number 10.
Girl	OK. Thanks!

Exercise 6 page 94

- Explain that all the sentences come from the dialogues students have just heard.

KEY

1	return	3	change	5	same
2	next	4	direct	6	platform

Exercise 7 page 94 🎧 3.21

- Play the recording to check the answers. Ask students to repeat the phrases, paying attention to intonation.

Exercise 8 page 94

- Read the speaking tip as a class. As students work on the activity, circulate and monitor, helping with pronunciation and any vocabulary issues.

Exercise 9 page 94

- Depending on time and on students' patience, have 3–5 pairs act out their dialogues in front of the class. Give feedback: praise good performance, correct a few mistakes (recurring ones or those concerning the language from this lesson).

OPTIONAL ACTIVITY

Ask students to imagine they are in Britain on a school exchange and need to buy tickets for the whole group. If you have a map of Britain in the room, let them look at it and choose a destination. Teach the sentence: *Is there a discount for …?* or *Can we / Do we get a discount?* In pairs, students act out the dialogue.

→ Lesson outcome

Ask students: *What have we talked about today?* Elicit: *trains/ train tickets/ buying tickets*, etc. Elicit some words and phrases from the lesson. Draw students' attention to the lesson statement: *I can buy a train ticket.*

9G WRITING — An e-mail

LESSON SUMMARY ● ● ● ● ● ●

Writing: an e-mail
Reading: e-mails
Grammar: *already* and *yet*
Topic: travel and tourism

SHORTCUT *To do the lesson in 30 minutes, set the writing as homework.*

➡ Lead-in 2–3 minutes

- Remind students that they already had a lesson on e-mail writing. Ask: *Since that lesson, has anyone written an e-mail in English? (Who did you write to? What about?)* Ask further: *Do you e-mail your friends and family when you're on holiday? How often? Where do you e-mail from? Do you think e-mails are just like letters or different?*

Exercise 1 page 95

- Ask students if they recognise the places in the photos. If they do, they'll only need to read the first sentence of one e-mail to do the matching exercise, so you may want to ask them some additional questions: *What do you think Debbie is writing about from Sydney? What do you think Chris is writing about from Moscow? What are they doing there?* Students can then read to check their guesses.

KEY

1 B 2 A

LANGUAGE NOTE – REGISTER

Highlight the use of informal language in the e-mails. In addition to the words in the greetings and endings, words such as *lovely*, *really*, and *lots of* (more informal than a lot of) are only used in informal writing.

Exercise 2 page 95

- Read the information and the examples aloud. Ask students to come up with translations of the examples.
- With a **weaker class**, you might want them to translate the examples from the text as well when checking. Point out the unexpected pronunciation of *ballet*.

KEY

We've already spent a lot of time on the beach.
I haven't visited the opera house yet.
Have you booked your holiday yet?
We've already seen a lot of sights.
We haven't seen a ballet yet.

Exercise 3 page 95

- Students go through the two texts one more time. Check answers with the whole class.

KEY

| 1 F | 3 F | 5 T | 7 T |
| 2 T | 4 F | 6 F | 8 F |

Exercise 4 page 95

- Students read the writing tip. For e-mail openings, refer them to Lesson 1G – say they can use the same openings as for informal letters.

KEY

Love   Best wishes

Exercise 5 page 95

- Students work individually. **Fast finishers** can add one or two more ideas. They can use the information about London in Lesson 6C.

Exercise 6 page 95

- Encourage students to use other parts of the unit as a resource – e.g. the weather vocabulary in lesson 9E.

ALTERNATIVE WRITING TASK

Students write similar e-mails from other cities of their choice. They then get together in groups of 3–4 and read each other's work.

➡ Lesson outcome

Ask students: *What did we do today?* Elicit *write e-mails* or an equivalent. Elicit various ways of beginning and ending an e-mail. Draw students' attention to the lesson statement: *I can write an e-mail about my holiday.*

Notes for Photocopiable activity 9.2

Travel Interview

Pairwork
Language: language related to travel
Materials: one copy of the worksheet per student (Teacher's Book page 140)

- Pre-teach *MP3 player*, *can of drink*, *packet of crisps*, and *immediately*.
- Give each student a copy of the worksheet. Ask students to work individually to match the interview questions with their answers and then compare answers with a partner.
- Tell students that they are going to ask their partner the questions from the interview. Give them time to think about their answers on their own and make notes. Then, in pairs, the students take it in turns to ask and answer the questions.

KEY

| 1 d | 3 b | 5 h | 7 f | 9 g |
| 2 c | 4 a | 6 e | 8 i | |

TOPIC ● ● ● ○ ○
Travel and tourism

➡ Lead-in 2 minutes
- Ask students to write down as many names of foods as they can in one minute. Then ask everybody to give one word; if they cannot or if they repeat a word that has already been mentioned, they are out.

Exercise 1 page 96
- Tell students they are going to prepare some vocabulary before they listen. Ask them to do the matching exercise.
- Check answers as a class.

KEY

1 passenger	3 depart	5 buffet car
2 midnight	4 inspection	6 apologise

Exercise 2 page 96 3.22
E Listening: true/false statements

- Read the listening tip as a class. Students read the task and the statements. Play the recording twice. Check answers with the whole class.

KEY

1 T	3 T	5 T	7 F
2 F	4 T	6 F	

Transcript 3.22

1
The train now arriving at platform 4 is the 12.52 service from London Paddington. We apologise for the late arrival of this train. This was due to problems on the line at Oxford.

2
The Manchester train departs shortly from platform 10, not from platform 2. All passengers for Manchester, please go immediately to platform 10.

3
The train now at platform 6 is the 13.45 service to Edinburgh. It stops at York, Darlington, Berwick-Upon-Tweed and Edinburgh.

4
It is now 11.45, and the ticket office is closing in 15 minutes. All passengers who want to buy tickets, please come to the ticket office before midnight.

5
This train is for Swansea. The next stop is Bristol. All passengers for Exeter and Plymouth, please get off at Bristol and change trains. This is the Swansea train; all passengers for Exeter and Plymouth please change at Bristol.

6
Welcome to the 10.35 service to Liverpool, calling at Crewe and Chester. Please have your tickets ready for inspection.

7
The buffet car is now open, serving hot and cold drinks, sandwiches and light snacks. The buffet car is in carriage number 2, near the front of the train.

Exercise 3 page 96
- Tell students they are going to prepare some vocabulary which will help them do the exam task. Students sort the words. Write the categories on the board as column headings and ask four students to come and write the foods and drinks underneath.

KEY

Meals	Snacks	Hot drinks	Cold drinks
pasta with mushroom sauce	a sandwich	coffee	lemonade
fish and chips	biscuits	tea	orange juice
hamburger			

Exercise 4 page 96
- Students discuss eating in restaurants versus eating at home in pairs or groups of three. Circulate and monitor. If some pairs come up with good ideas of their own, ask them to tell these to the whole class.

Exercise 5 page 96
E Speaking: picture-based discussion

- As revision, quickly brainstorm useful expressions for describing a photo and giving opinions (e.g. *In the first photo there is … / I can see …, I think …, In my opinion …*).
- Read the exam task as a class and check understanding.
- Allow students two or three minutes to prepare. In pairs, students take it in turns to speak about the photos for 1–2 minutes. Their partner listens.
- At the end, ask students for their ideas. Ask, *Which of these restaurants would you like to eat in? Which of them is the healthiest?*

OPTIONAL ACTIVITY
Speaking: situational role-play

Ask students to work in pairs. They have to decide on a place to go for lunch. They each think about what kind of place they would like to eat in, and try to persuade their partner to go.

Encourage them to think of as many different types of restaurants as they can. Brainstorm ideas and give examples:
pizza restaurant   café   Italian food   hamburger restaurant vegetarian restaurant

Students can use the phrases from exercise 4 to help them justify their choices and try to persuade their partner.

➡ Lesson outcome
Ask students: *What did we do today?* Elicit: *listening, speaking, describing photos*. Elicit some of the vocabulary from the lesson.

TOPIC ●●●○○
Travel and tourism

➡ Lead-in 3 minutes

- Put these words on the board:
  film director plane crash jungle died survived
- Elicit the meanings of the words from the class. If there is a word nobody knows, ask students to look it up in a dictionary. Then tell students they are going to read a story in which these words will appear. Ask them to imagine what may happen in the story. Accept all ideas without revealing what really happens in the story.

Exercise 1 page 97

- Remind students it is good to read through a text quickly for general understanding before doing any tasks. Ask them to read the three summaries (explain *summary*), then read the text and choose the one that contains the same information. Check the answer with the whole class.

KEY
b

Exercise 2 page 97

E Reading: missing sentences

- Read the reading tip as a class. In a **stronger class** students do the task individually, then compare answers in pairs.
- With a **weaker class**, read the sentences as a class, checking that students understand them. Point out some of the links: e.g. if the sentence begins with *Her,* the sentence before must be about a woman; if a sentence says 'after ten days, *they* decided...' they previous sentence will have a plural noun in it. Students continue to work on the task individually, then compare answers in pairs.
- Check answers with the whole class. Ask students to justify their answers by pointing out links.

KEY
1 B   2 F   3 A   4 G   5 D   6 E

C does not belong anywhere and does not agree with the rest of the text, which indicates that she was able to walk.

Exercise 3 page 97   🎧 3.23

- Ask students to read the instructions for the Speaking exam task in exercise 5. Tell them they are going to hear two candidates doing the task.
- Play the recording. Students do the task. Check answers as a class.

KEY
1 Paris   2 train

Transcript 3.23

Boy	Where would you like to go, Sally?
Girl	Hmm, I'm not sure. What about Rome? I've never been to Italy.
Boy	I have. I went there last year with my mum and dad. I think I'd like to go somewhere different. How about Stockholm or Helsinki?
Girl	Too cold! I think we should go somewhere warmer.
Boy	OK ... what about Paris? Have you ever been to Paris?
Girl	No, I haven't. OK. Let's agree on Paris. Do you want to fly there?
Boy	No, I don't want to go by plane. I think we should go by train.
Girl	But that would take ages!
Boy	I disagree. You can get a direct train from London to Paris. You don't have to change.
Girl	How long does it take?
Boy	About two and a half hours.
Girl	OK – I agree. Let's go by train.

Exercise 4 page 96   🎧 3.23

- Read the phrases as a class. Students listen and tick the ones they use. Play the recording again to check.

KEY
I think we should ...
I agree.
Let's agree on ...
I disagree.

Exercise 5

E Speaking: situational role-play

- Read the exam task and tell students that they will work in pairs. Explain that they need to agree on both a city to visit and how they will travel. The discussion should last for about three minutes, so they shouldn't reach agreement immediately.
- Give them three minutes to plan the general outline of the dialogue and to consider individually what they will say.
- Students do the task. Circulate and monitor. If there are stronger pairs, you could ask them to perform their dialogues at the end.

OPTIONAL ACTIVITY

Speaking: topic-based discussion

Ask students to think of a journey they went on recently. They should make notes about the type of transport they used, whether they liked it, and whether the journey was good or bad.

They can then discuss their journey with a partner.

➡ Lesson outcome

Ask students: *What did we do today?* Elicit: *reading, speaking, agreeing and disagreeing.* Elicit some of the reading tips and some vocabulary from the lesson.

10
Just the job

THIS UNIT INCLUDES ● ● ● ●
Vocabulary • jobs • suffixes *-er/-or* and *-ist* • places of work
Grammar • *going to* • *will* • *should/shouldn't*
Speaking • talking about your plans • giving opinions • giving advice
Writing • a letter of application
WORKBOOK pages 88–94

A VOCABULARY AND LISTENING
Jobs and work

LESSON SUMMARY ● ● ● ● ●
Vocabulary: jobs
Listening: four people talking about their jobs
Speaking: discussing the best and worst jobs
Topic: work

SHORTCUT *To do the lesson in 30 minutes, set Vocabulary Builder (part 1) exercises 1 and 2 as homework.*

➡ Lead-in 2 minutes
• Inform the class of the lesson topic. Ask students if they know any names of jobs in English.

LANGUAGE NOTE – UNIT TITLE
Just the job is an idiomatic expression meaning 'exactly what is needed in a particular situation', e.g. *I need something smart to wear for Sue's wedding. This dress will be/do **just the job**.*

Exercise 1 page 98
• Students label the pictures. Some of the words will already have been mentioned; for others use dictionaries or the Wordlist.

KEY

1 chef	3 computer programmer	5 factory worker
2 bus driver	4 shop assistant	6 nurse

Not illustrated: actor artist builder cleaner doctor engineer farmer hairdresser mechanic politician secretary teacher writer

Exercise 2 page 98 🎧 3.25
• Play the first part of the recording once for students to check their answers, then play the whole recording, pausing after each word for students to repeat. Pay attention to reduced vowels, and point out that the endings *–or* and *–er* are pronounced exactly the same, as /ə/.

LANGUAGE NOTES – JOBS AND WORK
Job and *work* mean the same but *job* is countable and *work* is uncountable. They also collocate with different words, e.g. *a temporary job, job interview, work experience, go to work.*

Engineer has two meanings: 1) a person who designs engines, machines, roads, bridges, etc. and 2) a person who is trained to fix machines and electrical equipment. E.g. *They're sending an engineer to fix the phone.*

Actor usually refers to a man (feminine = actress) but many women prefer to be called *actors* too. The same is true for *manager*. Few women nowadays like to be called *manageress*. The word *waiter*, however, can only refer to a man. (Feminine = *waitress*).

Exercise 3 page 98
• Read the *Look out!* box aloud. As students write about their family members, they may need help with job names not listed in the box. Ask students to read their sentences in groups of 3.

For further practice of the jobs and work vocabulary, go to:

Vocabulary Builder (part 1): Student's Book page 137

KEY

1
1 scientist	4 artist	7 builder
2 priest	5 computer programmer	8 politician
3 mechanic	6 cleaner	9 waiter

2
1 chef	4 hairdresser	7 doctor
2 farmer	5 teacher	8 engineer
3 shop assistant	6 actor	

3 Open answers

Exercise 4 page 98
• Read the listening tip aloud. Students work individually. **Fast finishers** should add their own ideas. Some students may assign the words differently from what is in the key – accept their answers if they can justify them.

KEY

1 dish, kitchen, customers, *soup, vegetables, fresh, cook, prepare …*
2 clothes, department store, customers, *jacket, change, shoes …*
3 animals, countryside, outside, weather, *field, cereal, chicken …*

Exercise 5 page 98 🎧 3.26
• Ask students to read the instructions. Play the recording through once, then play it again stopping after each speaker to check the answer with the class. Ask which of the key words (or other words related to the jobs) students heard.

KEY

1 farmer	3 chef	
2 nurse	4 shop assistant	

Transcript 3.26

Int.	Where do you work?
Farmer	I work in the countryside. I've got 2,000 hectares in the north of England.
Int.	Do you enjoy your job?
Farmer	Yes, I do.
Int.	Why do you like it?
Farmer	I like working outside. The scenery is beautiful. And I like working with animals. We've got pigs and cows. I prefer animals to humans, I think!
Int.	Is there anything you don't like about it?
Farmer	The weather isn't very good in the winter – but I still have to work outside, in snow, rain – everything. That's difficult sometimes.

Int.	Where do you work?
Nurse	At St Mary's in the town centre.
Int.	Do you enjoy your job?
Nurse	Yes, I do. I don't earn a lot of money. But I like helping my patients.
Int.	What else do you like?
Nurse	I work as part of a team. I enjoy that. For example, we work with the doctors at the hospital.
Int.	Is there anything you don't like about it?
Nurse	I have to work with the general public. That's sometimes difficult. People are sometimes angry or upset when they come to hospital.

Int.	Where do you work?
Chef	At the Bombay House restaurant.
Int.	Do you enjoy your job?
Chef	Hmm … it's OK. I like some of it!
Int.	What do you like?
Chef	I enjoy working with my hands. And I like making new dishes. For example, my special chicken curry with rice is a really popular dish.
Int.	And what don't you like about your job?
Chef	I'm on my feet all day. So I'm always very tired when I finish work. And it's always so hot in the kitchen!

Int.	Where do you work?
S.A.	At Wright's Department Store.
Int.	Do you enjoy your job?
S.A.	Hmm … well, no, not really.
Int.	Why don't you like it?
S.A.	Well, a few years ago we didn't use computers. But now I have to use them. I don't like using a computer. I hate computers! And another problem is, I don't earn very much money. I'd like to earn more!
Int.	Anything else?
S.A.	I'm on my feet all day, so I get very tired. And I have to work with customers. They can be really difficult people!

Exercise 6 page 98 🎧 3.27

- Students do the task individually, then listen, then compare answers in pairs. With a **weaker class,** go over the answers with the whole class; with a **stronger class,** just ask if everyone is sure or if they've got any questions.

KEY

1	outside	4	public	7	computer
2	money	5	hands	8	customers
3	team	6	feet		

Exercise 7 page 98

- As students write down their reasons, circulate and help with vocabulary and structures.

Exercise 8 page 98

- If you can, put students in pairs/ groups of three with classmates they will not agree with for this task. At the end, you may ask pairs/groups to report briefly on their views to the whole class (*He thinks … is the best job and I think …*)

For work on the suffixes -er, -or and -ist, go to:

Vocabulary Builder (part 2): Student's Book page 137

KEY

4 –er: builder, cleaner, computer programmer, factory worker, farmer, hairdresser, teacher, waiter
–or: actor, doctor,
–ist: artist

5	1	footballer	3	translator	5	dancer
	2	guitarist	4	tourist	6	receptionist

6	1	receptionist	4	tourist	7	director
	2	guitarist	5	dancer	8	footballer
	3	translator	6	journalist		

➡ Lesson outcome

Ask students: *What have we talked about today?* Elicit: *jobs.* Ask: *Can you give me some names of jobs, and any other words connected with work?* Praise the students who come up with the more sophisticated ones, such as *politician* or *factory worker.* Draw students' attention to the lesson statement: *I can describe different jobs.*

10 B GRAMMAR *going to*

LESSON SUMMARY ● ● ● ● ○

Grammar: *going to*
Speaking: talking about plans

SHORTCUT *To do the lesson in 30 minutes, do exercise 4 as a class, set the Grammar builder as homework, and keep exercise 8 short.*

➡ Lead-in 1 minute

- Say to the students: *I'll tell you something about my plans for tonight, this weekend and the next holidays. Tonight I'm going to (prepare lessons for tomorrow and read a book by Graham Greene). This weekend, I'm going to (mark your writing and watch a new DVD I got for my birthday). During the next holidays I'm going to (cycle 500 kilometres around Mazury), etc.* Write *plans* on the board and say: *After today's lesson, you will also be able to tell me about your plans using this form: 'I'm going to …'* Write one of your sentences on the board and explain that the 'going to' form doesn't necessarily refer to going anywhere, but is used to speak about future plans.

Exercise 1 page 99

- Ask students to describe what they see in the photo. You may ask: *Do you ever spend your holidays like this? Would you like to do it? Why?/Why not?* Ask the class to read the instructions and the text.

KEY

Two or more countries

Exercise 2 page 99

- Read the first line of the box and the first example with the whole class. Explain that in this form the word *going* does not have its usual meaning of walking, moving or travelling; it is a grammatical word, used to show that we are talking about a future activity, a plan for the future. 'Going to' is not exactly a future tense, but it is a form used for speaking about the future.
- Students study the rest of the information in the box and the text and find the relevant forms. Check with the whole class.

KEY

affirmative: are going to start **interrogative:** are we going to go
negative: aren't going to stay

For further practice of going to, *go to:*

Grammar Builder 10B: Student's Book page 126

KEY

1 2 We're going to play tennis next Saturday.
3 I'm going to surf the Internet this evening.
4 They're going to visit their grandparents next month.
5 You're going to meet me at the café.
6 We're going to see a film this evening.
7 Pete and Sue are going to study maths at university.
8 I'm going to watch TV this evening.

2 2 We aren't going to play tennis next Saturday.
3 I'm not going to surf the Internet this evening.
4 They aren't going to visit their grandparents next month.
5 You aren't going to meet me at the café.
6 We aren't going to see a film this evening.
7 Pete and Sue aren't going to study maths at university.
8 I'm not going to watch TV this evening.

3 1 What film are you going to see?
2 Who are you going to go with?
3 How are you going to get there?
4 What are you going to do after the film?
5 What time are you going to arrive home?

4 Open answers

Exercise 3 page 99

- Students do the exercise individually or in pairs. Check with the whole class. With a **stronger class**, you could do the exercise quickly with the whole class.

KEY

2 aren't going to work
3 are going to stay
4 is going to work
5 isn't going to have
6 is going to save
7 is going to have
8 isn't going to see
9 is going to study

Exercise 4 page 99

- With a **weaker class**, have students work on the sentences in pairs before finally checking with the whole class. With a **stronger class**, you can do the exercise quickly with the whole class.

KEY

1 Where is Paula going to go with her friends?
2 Are they going to work?
3 Where are they going to stay?
4 Where is Carl going to work?
5 Is Carl going to have a holiday?
6 What is he going to do with money?

7 Where is Victoria going to have lessons?
8 Is Victoria going to see her friends?
9 What is she going to study?

Exercise 5 page 99

- With a **weaker class,** or just when you want more control over accuracy, this can be done in open pairs with the whole class: ask student A the first question, A answers and asks B the next question, B answers and asks C, etc.

Exercise 6 page 99

- Ask students to read through the list of activities first to make sure they understand. *Stay up late* may need explaining. Students answer the questions about themselves.

Exercise 7 page 99

- Before students start asking and answering in pairs, make sure they know how to build the questions. Go over the first two or three questions in open pairs. If anyone makes a mistake, encourage them to correct themselves; if they cannot, ask the class for help. With a **weaker class**, write *Are you going to …?* on the board. As students talk in pairs, circulate and monitor, paying attention to pronunciation.

Exercise 8 page 99

- Have a few students report back to the class on some of the things they found out about their partners.

➡ Lesson outcome

Ask students: *What have we talked about today?* Try to elicit: *plans with going to*, but accept any answer that refers to the content of the lesson. Briefly revise the forms of *going to* future. Draw students' attention to the lesson statement: *I can talk about my plans for the future.*

10C CULTURE
Jobs for teenagers

LESSON SUMMARY ●●●○○

Reading: jobs for teenagers in the UK
Listening: teenagers talking about part-time jobs
Speaking: talking about part-time jobs
Vocabulary: phrases for agreeing and disagreeing
Topic: work, society

SHORTCUT *To do the lesson in 30 minutes, ask students to read the text for the first time at home.*

➡ Lead-in 2 minutes

- Before students open their books, ask them if they have ever done a part-time job. Have their brothers, sisters or friends done it? What were the jobs? Were they satisfied? Why? Why not? Do they think it was useful? Inform the class of the topic of the lesson.

Exercise 1 page 100

- Students look at the photos and discuss the questions in pairs. If there are any problems with vocabulary, refer students to the Wordlist or their dictionaries. Ask question 3 of the whole class.

Exercise 2 page 100

- Tell students they are going to read a text about teenagers and jobs in the UK. Ask them to read through the questions first. It would be good to have dictionaries when reading. *Paper round* may need explaining.

KEY

1 About half of them	4 12 hours	7 £3.30
2 babysitting	5 Yes	8 There isn't one
3 paper rounds	6 To earn some money	

> **LANGUAGE NOTE**
>
> A *paper round* is the job of delivering newspapers to houses, if it's done by a teenager or young person.
>
> A *wage* is a regular amount of money that you earn, usually every week. *Salary* refers to the money that is paid, usually monthly, to professional people, or people who work in an office.

Exercise 3 page 100

- Students work on the task individually and compare answers in pairs before checking with the whole class.

KEY

1 babysitting	3 part-time jobs	5 not allowed
2 earn	4 minimum wage	6 paper rounds

> **CULTURE NOTE – WORK EXPERIENCE**
>
> Work experience is offered to 15/16 year old students in the UK as part of the National Curriculum. The placements are either organised by their school or by the pupils themselves. It is not compulsory but schools gain credit for taking part in the scheme. The recommended minimum period for work experience is 10 days.

Exercise 4 page 100 🎧 3.28

- Ask students to read the instructions and the four opinions. Point out that one opinion will not be expressed by anyone. Play the recording through once, then again pausing after each speaker to check answers. Ask your class which speaker they agree with.

KEY

1 a	2 d	3 b

Transcript 3.28

Jack I think it's a good idea for teenagers to do part-time work. Part-time jobs give you good experience of working. It's important to find out what kind of job you want to do – before you leave school. The other advantage of a part time job is that you can earn some money. When you're 16, it's better to have your own money – not ask your parents for money! Anyway, my parents haven't got much money, so they definitely can't afford to give money to me. That's fine. I'm happy to earn it.

Ryan A lot of my friends have got part-time jobs. Part-time jobs are a good way of meeting people. You can make some really good friends. The problem is, you spend all your time working – working at school or working in your job – and you're always tired. Sometimes, part-time jobs make teenagers too tired to study! But they're still a good way to earn some money and meet people, so they aren't a bad thing, really.

Lauren I don't have time to do a part-time job – and I don't really need one either. My mum and dad give me money. The most important thing for teenagers is to get a good education. Then they can get good jobs in the future. Teenagers can only get part-time jobs that are badly paid – £3.00 an hour, or perhaps £3.50. You can't earn much money like that. Parents have to give teenagers more money so that that they don't have to do these jobs. That's my opinion.

Exercise 5 page 100 🎧 3.29

- Ask students to read the instructions, the words in the box and the six opinions. You may ask them to see if they can complete some of the sentences without listening again. Play the recording once and see if most students have got the answers. If not, play it again. Check answers and explain any unfamiliar words.

KEY

1 experience	3 meeting	5 education
2 advantage	4 tired	6 paid

Exercise 6 page 100

- Ask students to read the expressions in the box. (You might consider supplying them with some stronger ones, such as *Absolutely!* or *That's complete nonsense!* as long as they are aware that the latter is not always appropriate.) Students discuss their views in pairs. As they might want to express more than they have language for, it is important to circulate and help.

➡ Lesson outcome

Ask students: *What have we talked about today?* Elicit: *jobs/teenagers and jobs*. Ask everyone to say one word or phrase related to work that they learned. Draw the students' attention to the lesson statement: *I can give an opinion on part-time jobs*.

10 D GRAMMAR *will*

LESSON SUMMARY ● ● ● ● ⋯

Grammar: *will* for future
Reading: short texts about entrepreneurs
Speaking: predictions about the future

SHORTCUT *To do the lesson in 30 minutes, set the Grammar Builder for homework.*

➡ Lead-in 2 minutes

- Write *your future* on the board. Ask your class: *What is important in your future?* Elicit some ideas, e.g. *work, family, money, children*. Remind students they have already studied a structure used to talk about future *plans*. Elicit what it was. Tell students now they are going to learn another structure used to speak about the future.

Exercise 1 page 101

- Ask students to look at the title and the photo. What do they think the 'million dollar idea' was? They read the text quickly to see if their guesses were right.

KEY

b

Exercise 2 page 101

- Students study the information box and the text and find the relevant forms. Check with the whole class. Work on the pronunciation of *I'll* – do not let students avoid it by saying *I will* and *won't* (make it clear that it doesn't sound the same as *want*).

KEY

I'll invent a new kind of webpage	What will he do?
He'll need money	I'll save some
he won't need	I'll spend some

LANGUAGE NOTE – SHORT FORMS *'LL* AND *WON'T*

As with other short forms, it is important to emphasise that they should be used after pronouns. If the full forms are used, e.g. *I will go, I will not go* it sounds over-emphatic and unnatural. After nouns, however, it is more common to use the full forms.

For further practice of will, *go to:*

Grammar Builder 10D: Student's Book page 126

KEY

5
1 won't   4 won't   7 will
2 will   5 won't   8 will
3 will   6 will

6 (Answers will vary)
2 Who will you live with?
3 Where will you work?
4 What job will you do?
5 How many children will you have?
6 What car will you drive?
7 Will you have any pets?

Exercise 3 page 101

- Students work individually or in pairs. Check with the whole class.

KEY

1 will make	4 will take	7 Will (the company) make
2 will fly	5 will be	8 will be
3 won't carry	6 won't get	

Exercise 4 page 101

- With a **stronger class**, you can do this exercise quickly with the whole class.

KEY

1 will, make	3 will, fly	5 will, take
2 will, fly	4 Will, carry	6 Will, get

Exercise 5 page 101

- Ask a few students: *Do you think you'll make a lot of money some day?* Draw their attention to the exercise. Tell them if they want the statements to sound less categorical, they can begin with *I think: I think I'll make a lot of money.* To be more definite, they can say *I'm sure: I'm sure I won't live in this town.*

Exercise 6 page 101

- Do a few examples in open pairs with the whole class, then let students continue in closed pairs.

OPTIONAL ACTIVITY

Explain the words *fortune-teller* and *to tell someone's fortune*. Tell students they are going to tell each other's fortunes. Allow them a minute to think of ideas. You might demonstrate by asking a student who you know is imaginative, eloquent and good at English to tell your fortune. You might help with questions, e.g.: *Will I be rich and famous? Will I marry a millionaire? How many children will I have? How many grandchildren? Will I star in a film? Will I win any awards? Will I travel to all the continents? Will I have a house in the mountains? Will I die young?* (or any other nonsense). Students work in pairs, look at each other's palms (or whatever other ritual pleases them) and tell each other's fortunes. Circulate, monitor and help. Pick a few students who had their fortunes told particularly creatively and ask them to report to the class. Ask: *What will happen to you?*

➡ Lesson outcome

Ask students: *What have we talked about today?* Elicit: *will* or *the future.* Briefly revise the forms of *will* future. Draw students' attention to the lesson statement: *I can make predictions about my future.*

Notes for Photocopiable activity 10.1

Review Board Game

Board game

Language: *going to, will*, jobs vocabulary
Materials: one copy of the board, enlarged to A3 if possible, per group of three to four students. (Teacher's Book page 141) Dice and counters.

- Divide the class into groups of three or four students. Give each group a copy of the worksheet, dice and counters.
- Look at the board game with the class. Explain that there are three types of task: correct the mistake, complete the sentence and talk about a topic for 20 seconds.
- Explain the rules of the game. Students throw a dice and move around the board doing the task for the square they land on. If the task is completed successfully, the student continues from that square in the next round. If not, they go to the square they have just come from. Go round monitoring and acting as a referee.
- Students play the game in groups. The game finishes when the first student reaches the *Finish* square.

10 E READING
A year abroad

LESSON SUMMARY ● ● ● ● ○
Reading: a magazine article; reading for detail
Vocabulary: places of work, verb collocations
Listening: a song
Topic: work

SHORTCUT *To do the lesson in 30 minutes, ask students to read the text for the first time and do task 2 at home.*

→ **Lead-in** 5 minutes
- Write on the board: *What are you going to do after you finish school?* Ask students to stand up, ask everybody in the room this question and note their answers (you can also limit the number of people to 10 or 5). When everyone has finished, ask them to sit down and write a report like this:
  __ *people are going to study.*
  __ *people are going to find jobs.*
  __ *people are going to ... (something else?)*
- Explain that the topic of the lesson will be people who do 'something else'.

CULTURE NOTE – GAP YEARS IN BRITAIN
It has become very common for students in Britain to take a 'gap year' between finishing school and starting university. This year is often used as an opportunity to travel and to gain interesting experiences such as those described in the texts. Many students use their gap year to raise money for charity and do charity work experience in developing countries.

Since the introduction of fees for university, many students now also use their gap year as a time to work and save money for their time at university. Many universities regard gap years as a positive thing, as students come to their studies more mature.

Exercise 1 page 102
- Students talk about the photos in pairs, then share ideas as a class.

Exercise 2 page 102
- Students read the reading tip and the instructions, then go through the text quickly and do the task. Check answers and ask students if they have noticed any other words in the text which are explained by the photos. They might come up with *animal rescue centre* and *restore*.

KEY
1 A   2 C   3 B

Exercise 3 page 103
- Students work individually or in pairs, taking notes on the three people. Alternatively, the reading could be done as a jigsaw activity: in groups of three, each student reads in detail about one person, answers the questions about him/her, and then communicates the information to the others. Check with the whole class. You might need to explain what an *animal rescue centre* is if it hasn't been worked out when doing exercise 2.

KEY
Jacqui:
1 She's going to study physics.
2 To Thailand.
3 She'll work at an animal rescue centre.
4 Nine months.

Oliver:
1 He's going to start his first job at a sports centre.
2 To Ghana in Africa.
3 He'll teach basketball to schoolchildren and help with other lessons.
4 Six months.

Darren:
1 He's going to work in a bank.
2 To the west of France.
3 He'll help restore an old castle.
4 Seven months.

Exercise 4 page 103
- Students do the exercise individually. Check with the whole class. Practise the collocations by asking students questions: *Would you like to take a break between school and university? Would you like to live abroad? Is it easy for you to make new friends? Do you like learning about other cultures? Do you think you can learn more about other cultures from books or by spending time abroad? Have you ever had to show a visitor around the school? Or around some other place?* In a stronger class, you might ask students to write 2–3 sentences each using some of the collocations.

KEY
1 c   2 a   3 d   4 g   5 b   6 f   7 e

Exercise 5 page 103
- As students check the meanings of the words, ask them to tick the places where they would like to work and put a cross next to the places where they would never want to work.
- They can then tell it to their partners:
  I would like to work in/at a ...
  I would never want to work in/at a ...

KEY
sports centre   school   bank   office

Exercise 6 page 103
- Students list jobs in pairs. Share ideas with the whole class. You may wish to ask: *So which is the most universally useful job?* (It looks as if it's the cleaner!)

KEY – Sample answers
bank – manager, cashier, computer programmer, cleaner
building site – builder, engineer
café – waiter, cleaner
factory – factory worker
garage – mechanic
hair salon – hairdresser, cleaner
hospital – doctor, nurse, cleaner
office – secretary, politician, cleaner
school – teacher, nurse, cleaner
shop – shop assistant, cleaner
sports centre – coach, nurse, cleaner
theme park – computer programmer, engineer

Exercise 7 page 103 🎧 3.30

- Tell students they are going to hear a song about working at a car wash. Can they guess what *car wash* means? Ask them to read the words in the box first. Play the song once without stopping, then again pausing after each gap to check.

KEY

1	rich	3	hard	5	cars	7	pay
2	star	4	star	6	home		

CULTURE AND LANGUAGE NOTE – *CAR WASH*

Car Wash was originally sung by Rose Royce in 1976. Christina Aguilera and Missy Elliot released a cover version in 2004.

Highlight the use of the ungrammatical *ain't* /eɪnt/ (meaning *am not*, *aren't* or *isn't*) and *the boss don't mind*. This kind of ungrammatical language is common in song lyrics.

Exercise 8 page 103

- When checking, ask students to quote specific passages from the text to support their answers.

KEY

Good things: b, c   Bad things: d, e

ADDITIONAL SPEAKING ACTIVITY

This activity is a role play. Students work in groups of three. Assign (or let them choose) the following roles (you can print the descriptions as they appear here and distribute them on slips of paper, or display them all using an OHP):

A You are the son/daughter. You want to take a gap year between high school and university.
   - *Before you speak:* decide what exactly you want to do (and tell your partners so they can also work on ideas!).
   - Tell your parents what you want to do.
   - Defend your plan when they disagree with it – explain why it is a good idea!

B You are the father. You think your son's/ daughter's plan is good in general, but may need some changes.
   - *Before you speak:* decide what is good and what is bad about the plan, in your opinion.
   - Defend your son's / daughter's idea when your wife criticises it.
   - Propose a compromise.

C You are the mother. You think your son's /daughter's idea is complete nonsense.
   - *Before you speak:* decide why you think the plan is bad (Dangerous? Waste of time? ...)
   - Criticise your son's /daughter's plan when he/ she tells you about it.
   - Agree to the compromise – or not!

Allow 3–4 minutes for students to work on ideas and language (more if they ask for it). Remind them to use language from the lesson (e.g. Students A will need some of the collocations from exercise 4). Students hold the conversations in their groups of three. Person A begins. At the end, if it goes well, you may ask two or three groups to act out their conversations in front of the others. Choose those who speak loudly, clearly and with some feeling.

→ Lesson outcome

Ask students: *What did we do today?* Elicit: *We read about a gap year* or another relevant answer. Ask everyone to give one new word or phrase they learned from the lesson. Draw students' attention to the lesson statement. *I can understand a magazine article.*

10 F EVERYDAY ENGLISH
Giving advice

LESSON SUMMARY ● ● ● ● ●
Functional English: giving advice
Listening: short dialogues
Grammar: *should*
Speaking: giving advice
Topic: work

SHORTCUT *To do the lesson in 30 minutes, have only a few pairs act out their dialogues in exercise 9.*

→ Lead-in 2 minutes

- Write *job interview* on the board and try to elicit the meaning or a translation. Ask students to think of any words they associate with a job interview. (*When you think 'job interview', what else does that make you think of?*) Write all ideas on the board. If students are stuck for ideas, use these prompts: *Think about people … feelings … places … clothes …*

Exercise 1 page 104

- Students discuss the question in pairs. You may encourage them to use the vocabulary from lesson 4A (about clothes).

Exercise 2 page 104 🎧 3.31

- Ask students to read the dialogue and the words in the box. Can they try and complete the dialogue before they listen? Play the recording once. Ask what they think, *you should* means. Elicit a translation or provide one. Ask if they agree with Judy's advice. Does it depend on the job Rowan is applying for?

KEY

1	jacket	3	jeans
2	tie	4	T-shirt

Exercise 3 page 104

- Before students read the dialogue, you may wish to play it one more time for them to listen to the pronunciation. Model the intonation of, *Do you think so?* Ask a few students to repeat. Do the same with, *You're probably right.* and, *You're welcome.*

Exercise 4 page 104

- Read the *Learn this!* box aloud. Students work on the task individually. Go over answers with the whole class.

KEY

You should wear a jacket and tie.
You shouldn't wear jeans and a T-shirt.

For further practice of advice with should *and* shouldn't, *go to:*

Grammar Builder 10F: Student's Book page 126

KEY

7 1 shouldn't   3 should   5 shouldn't
    2 should   4 shouldn't

Exercise 5 page 104   🎧 3.32

- Tell students they are going to hear two dialogues. In each of them someone tells a friend about a problem they've got. Ask them to read the four problems a–d. The task is to match the people to two of the problems; the other two are not mentioned. Play the recording through once, then again pausing after each part to check answers.

KEY

Keith **b**   Sonia **d**

Transcript 3.32

Keith	Hi, Mary.
Mary	Hi, Keith. How are you?
Keith	Terrible! I feel really ill this morning.
Mary	Yes, you look bad.
Keith	Thanks. (SNIFF)
Mary	Why are you at the bus stop?
Keith	I'm going to school, of course.
Mary	You shouldn't go to school!
Keith	Really?
Mary	Of course not! You should go home and call the doctor.
Keith	Maybe you're right. I do feel really bad.
Mary	I hope you feel better soon.
Keith	Thanks.
Sonia	Hi, Tom.
Tom	Hi, Sonia. What are you doing?
Sonia	I'm looking for a website.
Tom	What kind of website?
Sonia	I want to find a biology essay. I don't understand my homework – and I have to finish it tonight.
Tom	So, are you going to copy it from the Internet?
Sonia	Yup.
Tom	You shouldn't do that! You'll get into trouble.
Sonia	So what should I do?
Tom	You should talk to your teacher.
Sonia	Do you think so?
Tom	Definitely. Explain that you're having problems with the homework.
Sonia	OK. Thanks for your advice. (CLICK) Ah, found it. And … download.

Exercise 6 page 104

- Students can complete the sentences individually, using the prompts. Check as a class.

KEY

a shouldn't	d should	g shouldn't
b should	e should	h shouldn't
c shouldn't	f should	

Exercise 7 page 104   🎧 3.32

- Play the recording again for students to focus on the advice that is offered.

KEY

Keith's friend says: d, g   Sonia's friend says: a, f

Exercise 8 page 104

- Encourage students to use the book as a resource. Remind them that in Lesson 7F (exercise 7) there is a list of expressions to use when you hear someone's bad news. Students work on their dialogues. Circulate and monitor.

Exercise 9 page 104

- Depending on time and on students' patience, have 3–5 pairs act out their dialogues in front of the class. Choose those whose dialogues either show very good use of language or are interesting and imaginative, or both. Give feedback: praise good performance, correct a few mistakes (recurring ones or those concerning the language from this lesson).

OPTIONAL ACTIVITY

Put the following statements on the board:

I am bored.

I don't know what to buy my parents for Christmas.

My neighbours play awful music very loud.

I'm in love with someone who doesn't love me.

I think you should …

You shouldn't …

No, I can't do that.

No, I don't want to do that.

That's a good idea. Thanks.

You're probably right. Thanks.

In pairs or groups of three, each student chooses a different problem (or two) he/she is going to talk about. Each student in turn says what their problem is and the other(s) have to give him/her advice. He/she can decide whether he/she likes the advice or not.

➡ Lesson outcome

Ask students: *What have we talked about today?* Elicit: *advice* or *should and shouldn't.* Elicit some examples of how *should* is used to give advice. Draw students' attention to the lesson statement: *I can give someone advice.*

10G WRITING
An application letter

LESSON SUMMARY ● ● ○ ○ ○

Writing: an application letter
Reading: an application letter
Topic: work

SHORTCUT *To do the lesson in 30 minutes, set the writing as homework.*

➡ Lead-in 2–3 minutes

- Remind students that they recently talked about job interviews. Ask: *What do you have to do before you can have a job interview?* They will probably be able to answer in their own language, but not in English. Tell them the kind of letter you have to write when looking for a job is called a *letter of application* or an *application letter,* and that it is the topic of this lesson. Ask: *What kind of things should you write in an application letter?* Elicit ideas.

Exercise 1 page 105

- Ask students to try and answer the question as quickly as possible. If they manage to do it really fast, say: *Why was it possible for you to answer this question in (15 seconds)?* Elicit or explain that Emily stated the purpose of her letter in the first sentence, and that this is very important, as it allows the person who is reading the letter to find out very quickly what the letter is about and, for example, who should be dealing with it.

Exercise 2 page 105

- Now ask students to analyse the letter in more detail. When checking, discuss the relevance of each item: *Why does she write about this? Why is it important?* (e.g. where she saw the advert – the employer will know exactly which job she means; experience – shows that she is good for the job, etc.) You may mention that in a real job application one would give the names, addresses, phone numbers, etc. of the referees.

KEY

Paragraph 1
- the job she is applying for
- where she saw the advert

Paragraph 2
- her work experience

Paragraph 3
- her personal qualities
- who can give references
- when she can start work

Exercise 3 page 105

- Students go through the text one more time. Check answers with the whole class.

KEY

1 From an advertisement in the *Coventry Daily News*.
2 In her local pet shop.
3 For six weeks.
4 She says she is honest, reliable and hardworking.
5 Two.
6 On 2nd July

Exercise 4 page 105

- Students work individually or in pairs. Check answers with the whole class. Point out that the sentence openings, 1–5, are typical phrases used in this kind of letter, so it is well worth learning them.

KEY

1 c I am writing to apply for a summer job at W.A.R.C.
2 a I saw the advertisement in the Coventry Daily News.
3 e I have experience of working with animals.
4 d I worked for six weeks as a shop assistant.
5 b I can send you a reference from the manager of the pet shop.

Exercise 5 page 105

- Read the writing tip as a class. Discuss the differences between formal and informal letters.

Exercise 6 page 105

- Ask students to read the advert and consider the question in exercise 6. What other experience would be useful for a job like this? Brainstorm ideas and note them on the board.

Exercise 7 page 105

- Before they write, tell students to prepare all the information they are going to include using the plan in exercise 2. Where did they find the ad? What is their experience? What qualities are they going to say they have? (*Reliable* and *hardworking* are an obvious choice, as they are mentioned in the ad, but maybe they could add something else that is also relevant.) Help with vocabulary and note useful words on the board, especially if they are new. Who are they going to quote as a referee?
- Remind them that a formal letter must have a date (top right or top left), the appropriate opening and ending as described in the writing tip, and clear paragraphs.

ALTERNATIVE WRITING TASK

Put the following names of part-time or holiday jobs on the board (plus any others you think are relevant):

waiter

babysitter

assistant at a video rental shop

pizza delivery man/woman

cleaner

Each student has to choose a job and write a letter of application for it. Remind them to:

- think what experience, personal qualities, referees, etc. they are going to quote
- organise their letter clearly
- use appropriate openings and endings

➜ Lesson outcome

Ask students: *What did we today?* Elicit *Write application letters.* or an equivalent. Elicit various ways of beginning and ending a formal letter. Tell students: *Today, you have practised the second, more difficult written exam task.* Draw students' attention to the lesson statement: *I can write a letter applying for a job.*

Notes for Photocopiable activity 10.2

Alphabet Race

Class race

Language: vocabulary from Units 1 to 10
Materials: one copy of the worksheet per pair of students (Teacher's Book page 142)

- Divide students into pairs and hand out a copy of the worksheet to each pair. Explain that students are going to do a race in which they revise vocabulary from *Solutions* Units 1 to 10.
- Give a time limit and asks students to work with a partner to complete the sentences with a word beginning with the given letter. Insist on correct spelling and remind students that some words are in the plural form.
- The pair who come up with the most correct answers within the time allotted are the winners.
- If necessary, to avoid cheating, ask students to swap worksheets with another pair for marking.

KEY

awful	beef	canteen	department	eggs
former	garage	hardly	ICT	junk
knee	lunch	message	niece	oceans
post office	quite	relatives	socks	toes
underground	valley	welcome	X year	Zealand

LANGUAGE REVIEW 9–10

1 1 car   3 bike
     2 boat   4 foot

2 1 a nurse/ a doctor   4 an actor   7 a chef
     2 a builder   5 a mechanic   8 a shop assistant
     3 a hairdresser   6 an artist

3 2 I've cleaned my room.
     3 I've eaten my pasta.
     4 I've had a shower.
     5 I've bought a new phone.

4 2 My friend has just gone home.
     3 The rain has just stopped.
     4 I have just seen a terrible film.
     5 I have just heard a great joke.
     6 He has just booked a holiday.
     7 Our friends have just arrived.

5 2 The play hasn't started.
     3 You haven't finished your lunch.
     4 He hasn't gone for a walk.
     5 She hasn't cooked dinner for everybody.

6 2 Has Louise phoned her mum? No, she hasn't.
     3 Have Ronnie and Louise played tennis? No, they haven't.
     4 Has Ronnie done the housework? Yes, he has.
     5 Have Ronnie and Louise eaten all the bread? Yes, they have.

7 1 Are you going to be
     2 am going to stay
     3 are you going to do
     4 Are you going to miss
     5 am not going to revise

8 1 will have   3 will enjoy   5 won't be
     2 will arrive   4 won't get bored   6 will they cost

9 1 return   3 direct
     2 platform   4 change

10 1 How   4 so
     2 feel   5 shouldn't
     3 should

SKILLS ROUND-UP 1–10

1 1 C   2 B   3 D   4 A

2 1 T
     2 F Márton didn't know about Francesca's new job.
     3 T
     4 F July and August are the busiest months.
     5 F Dave thinks Márton should visit before July or August.
     6 F Francesca has said some nice things about Márton to Dave.

3 Yes, he does. She says yes.

Transcript 3.33

Anna   Hello?
Dave   Hi, is that Anna?
Anna   Yes, speaking.
Dave   Hello, it's Dave – Márton's friend from the Arcadia Hotel.
Anna   Yes, I remember. You've moved to the Lake District, haven't you?
Dave   Yes, I have.
Anna   Have you started your new job?
Dave   Yes. I started a week ago. It's great! Much better than my job at the Arcadia.

Anna   Good! I'm glad. Do you want to speak to Márton?
Dave   Yes, please.
Anna   OK. I'll just go and get him. He's in the kitchen.
Dave   Thanks.
...
Márton   Hi, Dave!
Dave   Hello. How are you?
Márton   Fine, thanks. And you?
Dave   I'm really well … Listen, did you get my last e-mail?
Márton   Yes, I did.
Dave   Well? Have you invited Francesca for a drink?
Márton   No, I haven't. Not yet!
Dave   Why not?
Márton   Well, I've tried to speak to her a few times … but she's always busy at reception.
Dave   You should go in a few minutes early one morning – it's always quieter in the mornings.
Márton   OK. Maybe tomorrow …
Dave   Definitely!
Márton   OK, OK. I'll ask her tomorrow!
...
Narrator   The next day, Márton arrives at the hotel a few minutes early. Francesca is working in reception.
Francesca Good morning, Márton.
Márton   Hi, Francesca. How are you?
Francesca Fine, thanks! And you?
Márton   I'm very well.
Francesca Good.
Márton   Erm … Are you working this evening?
Francesca No, I'm not. I finish at 6.00 today.
Márton   Me too! Hey, why don't we go for a drink after work?
Francesca OK, that's a good idea.
Márton   Great! Well, I'll see you at 6 o'clock.
Francesca OK. Oh, by the way …
Márton   Yes?
Francesca Have you spoken to Dave?
Márton   Yes, I have. In fact, I spoke to him last night!
Francesca I thought so.
Márton   Pardon?
Francesca Oh, nothing. It doesn't matter.
Márton   So, I'll see you at 6 o'clock.
Francesca Great! I'm looking forward to it.

4 1 b   2 c   3 c   4 a   5 a

5–6 Open answers

EXAM For further exam tasks and practice, go to Workbook page 96. Procedural notes, transcripts and keys for the Workbook can be found on the *Solutions* Teacher's Website at www.oup.com/elt/teacher/solutions

DYSLEXIA: A GUIDE FOR TEACHERS

A short introduction to dyslexia

What is dyslexia?[1]
- Dyslexia is one of several distinct learning disabilities.
- It is a specific language-based disorder.
- It's of biological origin (usually genetic).
- Characteristic symptoms are difficulties in single word decoding (reading) usually reflecting insufficient phonological skills. Dyslexia is manifested by varying difficulty with different forms of language. These often include, in addition to problems with reading, a conspicuous problem with acquiring proficiency in writing and spelling.
- These difficulties are often unexpected in relation to age and other intellectual and academic abilities (in some school subjects).
- These difficulties are not the result of a generalised developmental disability (these students have a normal IQ) or sensory impairment (they don't have seeing or hearing problems). Some dyslexic people have very good spatial orientation, visual or auditory memory and technical skills.

What dyslexia isn't (myths about dyslexia)
- Dyslexia is not an illness. However, it appears in two basic medical classifications of diseases: ICD-10 (European) and DSM-IV (American).
- Dyslexia is not a myth. It is a learning difficulty which makes all aspects of dealing with language (especially written language) harder. Most experts today agree that learning to write requires a lot of effort and takes time. It's crucial for dyslexic students to learn how to learn, find out what works for them and consciously develop their own learning strategies. Normally, with time, dyslexic students learn to use their talents and intelligence to cope with their problems.
- Dyslexia is not a lack of intelligence. Students who have been diagnosed as being dyslexic have at least a normal IQ and many of them are highly intelligent.
- Dyslexia is not laziness. However, some dyslexic students may try to use their dyslexia as an excuse for not working. It is important to understand that helping means demanding and motivating, not releasing or absolving from responsibility.
- Dyslexia is not 'no big deal'. People don't grow out of dyslexia. The dyslexic person learns to cope with his/her problems and to use favourable compensation strategies. The earlier help is given, the more effective it is. Constant failure leads to a lack of motivation and/or other negative strategies. These secondary effects are often more difficult to deal with later on. Early encouragement and learner training can therefore make all the difference to a dyslexic student's experience of school and learning.
- Dyslexia is not something rare. The problems associated with dyslexia are roughly similar in some 10 % of the population, which means that in an average classroom there are usually a few students with dyslexia.
- Dyslexic students are not all the same. Some of them, having experienced some difficulties in learning their mother tongue, don't have any problems with foreign languages. Some – suffering from severe dyslexia – can hardly learn a foreign language.

[1] definition taken from ODS Research Committee and National Institute of Health (1994)

- People don't normally grow out of dyslexia. However the symptoms change with time and they are different at different life stages. Their form depends on different educational methods, work input and individual characteristics (intelligence or the nature of deficits). The problems tend to come back after a break in training (e.g. after holidays) and in stressful situations (e.g. an exam).
- Dyslexia is not a reason for failing in life. This is proved by a long list of famous dyslexics (e.g. Hans Chrystian Andersen, Auguste Rodin, Thomas Alva Edison, Sir Winston Churchill, Albert Einstein, Jacek Kuroń). Dyslexic students can succeed at school – they just need the right kind of teaching.

Forms of dyslexia
Many researchers distinguish between Developmental Dyslexia in its general meaning as a syndrome of Specific Reading and Writing Difficulties and its forms:
Dyslexia (in its narrow meaning with reference to reading problems only)
Dysortography (spelling problems)
Dysgraphia (handwriting problems)

What is the cause of dyslexia?
Different factors (genetic and environmental) cause biological changes in the central nervous system which leads to certain dysfunctions. As a result the child's psycho-motor development is discordant.

Dyslexic symptoms in school
In most cases weaknesses can be identified in the following areas:

Visual and auditory perception and processing
This can result in difficulties with mastering written and sometimes also oral language:
- learning words/letters/sounds
- spelling: phonic writing (e.g. football/futbol), letters may be reversed, mirrored, replaced by similar ones (p-b-d-g, w-m-n), written in the wrong order (e.g. hlep/help), omitted or added.
- reading (accurate and/or fluent word recognition)
- pronunciation (because this requires good auditory perception and processing)
- expressive writing
- recognising and producing rhymes
- fluency in speech (less common)

Automaticity
- For example, applying even well-known spelling rules or retrieving common words from memory.

Memory
Dyslexic students may encounter problems with:
- short-term memory
- learning sequences such as days of the week and months of the year
- acquiring the knowledge of sounds and words

The technique of writing
- In the case of students with dysgraphia their handwriting can be illegible and the pace of writing slow (because writing requires good fine motor skills).

Spatial orientation
- Students may have trouble differentiating between left and right.
- They may find prepositions difficult (e.g. *under, on, above, below*).

Concentration
- Dyslexic students may get easily distracted and become mentally tired sooner than their peers.

Organisational skills
Dyslexic students may encounter problems with:
- time management (e.g. often coming late for a lesson, planning their work)
- problems with organisation of materials (e.g. problems with using their Student's Book as a source of useful information, designing the layout of their copybook).

Secondary consequences of dyslexia can be:
- low self-esteem
- low motivation for learning
- being passive (withdrawn)
- becoming aggressive as a form of protest
- becoming a classroom clown
- not enjoying learning/school or even refusing to go to school
- frustration

Dyslexia in the English classroom
Most of the general dyslexia symptoms (listed above) affect students' performance in English lessons. Typical problem areas in English are:

The alphabet
- which results in difficulties with spelling aloud and using dictionaries.

Vocabulary
- because of poor memory and problems with sequences, e.g. learning the 12 months. Dyslexics often experience difficulties with retrieving well-known words from memory.

Grammar
- even applying well-known rules.

All four skills:
- listening: because it requires good concentration span and memory, auditory perception and processing
- reading: because it requires good visual and auditory perception and processing, accurate and/or fluent word recognition
- speaking: (less often) because of problems with automaticity, memory and constructing complex sentences
- expressive writing: because of the semantic, morphological and syntactic aspect of the language. Dyslexics usually have problems with planning their essays. They also tend to write short, simple sentences and over-use high-frequency words.

Spelling
- because it requires good phonological skills, auditory and visual perception and processing, memory and automaticity. Dyslexic students may confuse, leave out, add letters and syllables as well as change their order.

Pronunciation
- For example pronouncing long words (because this requires good short-term memory, auditory perception and processing).

Interference
- The student may mix up all the foreign languages that he/she is learning, especially German and English.

General rules on how to deal with dyslexia

'In my experience, it is the continual sense of failure that makes the whole experience of dyslexia so negative. Obviously, when learning a foreign language in a regular classroom, dyslexic learners experience more problems than their non-dyslexic counterparts, but if you give them sufficient structure, time and practice to acquire the basics on all levels (reading, writing, speaking, comprehension) they can make progress. Mixed with non-dyslexics who learn easily in an intuitive, global way, the dyslexic learner will only experience failure through not receiving enough positive feedback: under this pressure he will start mixing and confusing his words in an effort to keep up.'

(Language Shock – Dyslexia across cultures, 1999).

Psychological aspects
Since students with dyslexia often have low motivation you should:
- Be positive and optimistic. Remember that motivation is the key to self-esteem and to success.
- Encourage the dyslexic student to have a positive attitude towards English. It's important for your dyslexic students to access the culture of English-speaking countries (e.g. listening to English music, getting in touch with native speakers, taking part in a student exchange).

Since students with dyslexia usually have a low self-esteem:
- Remember that learners with dyslexia need a lot of positive feedback and praise.
- Help to overcome your dyslexic students' difficulties but not forget about their strengths. It's not a good idea to spend all the time working on their problems!
- Ensure your students with dyslexia achieve some form of success and that they are aware of the fact that they have been successful. Remember it is better to go back a step and give the student a sense of success than to stay on a higher level without success.
- Realise that it's important to reduce the student's stress.

Dyslexic students don't usually believe in themselves, therefore, you should:
- Not be over-protective. Dyslexic students need help but only 'help that leads to self-help'. Your job is to encourage the student to be independent.
- Have high expectations but set reasonable goals.
- Have a positive attitude towards the dyslexic student.

Students with dyslexia may have problems with their classmates. Therefore a teacher should:
- Promote mutual help between students. The dyslexic student takes up a lot of the teacher's time and so it is important that the other students don't miss out.
- Protect dyslexic students from bullying by their classmates. Explain the situation of the dyslexic person, if necessary, in order to increase their peers' understanding.

Organisational matters

- Remember that most parents are experts concerning their children. It is important to get/keep in touch with dyslexic students' parents. Show your willingness to help in co-operation with the parents.
- Study your students' written assessments. They can be an important source of information about your students' strong and weak points. From such documents you can also find out how to work with your dyslexic student.
- Find out about your student's way of learning (especially his/her learning style) and respect it. Every student has individual preferences for visual, auditory, tactile or kinaesthetic processing. In addition some students prefer to work alone and some with others in groups.

General rules on how to teach dyslexic students[4]

> 'If the dyslexic child does not learn the way you teach, Can you teach him the way he learns?'
>
> *(H. T. Chasty – consultant in learning abilities and difficulties)*

Remember that dyslexic students can be especially demanding. Therefore:

- Apply an individual approach: what works well for one student may not necessarily work for another.
- Use a variety of activities to revise a topic or structure to keep students' interest.
- Find ways to help your students concentrate. Change the activity regularly and plan lessons including short breaks.
- Don't teach things that are similar one after the other.
- Learn to be well-organised. Dyslexic students need a regular routine to help them stay organised.
- Accentuate the student's abilities and teach through his/her strengths. Difficulties in reading and writing might be compensated by abilities such as a high IQ or visual/technical skills.
- Give exact instructions or explanations of tasks (short and concise).
- Let your students learn by doing. Ask them to prepare vocabulary charts, flashcards, posters, etc.

Use friendly material

- Use large fonts (12–14 point, for example Comic Sans MS).
- A clear layout. The page should be well laid out and not too full.
- Pictograms and graphics to help locate information.
- Picture dictionaries.
- Consistent colour coding.
- Listening material (tape or CD) for use at home.
- A 'window marker' for reading. (See figure 1 below.) It helps dyslexic students with reading. A student should hold it in such a position that the word that is being read appears in the opening (window). This way a student won't get lost while reading.

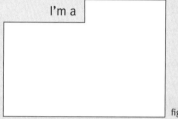

figure 1

---

[4] *'General rules on how to teach dyslexic students' is based on material prepared by D. Sapiejewska (2002)*

1.1 WHO'S WHO?

STUDENT A

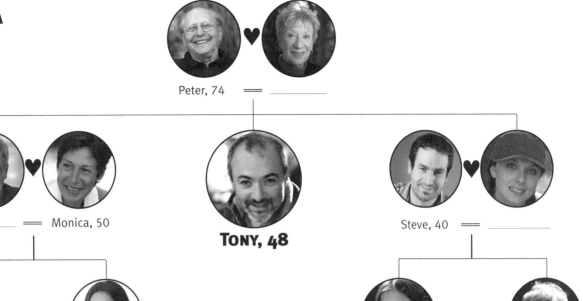

Peter, 74 ═══ _____

Monica, 50

TONY, 48

Steve, 40 ═══ _____

Joe, 23 _____

Emily, 12 _____

1 Look at Tony's family tree. Ask Student B questions to fill in the gaps.

Who's Tony's mother?
How old is she?

2 Draw your own family tree. Show it to Student B and give more information about who is who.

My brother's Adam. He's 19. He's a student.

✂ -

STUDENT B

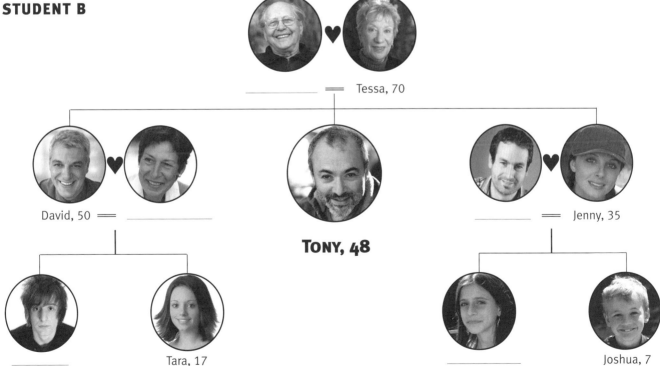

_____ ═══ Tessa, 70

David, 50 ═══ _____

TONY, 48

_____ ═══ Jenny, 35

_____ Tara, 17

_____ Joshua, 7

1 Look at Tony's family tree. Ask Student A questions to fill in the gaps.

Who's Tony's father?
How old is he?

2 Draw your own family tree. Show it to Student A and give more information about who is who.

My brother's Adam. He's 19. He's a student.

1.2 TWO COUSINS: SONIA AND SUZY

STUDENT A

1 Look at the pictures and tell Student B about Sonia.

Sonia goes to Springtown School in Oxford.

2 What do Sonia and Suzy have in common?

Sonia

STUDENT B

1 Look at the pictures and tell Student A about Suzy.

Suzy goes to Manchester High School.

2 What do Sonia and Suzy have in common?

Suzy

2.1 WAYNE ROONEY FACT FILE

STUDENT A

1 Read the facts about Wayne Rooney. Complete questions 1–5 to find the missing information.

Wayne Rooney comes from [1] _____.
He lives with his wife, Colleen.
Some people call him [2] '_____'.
He often eats salad for dinner.
He has got a tattoo of a cross on [3] _____.
He gets his clothes from Nike.
He has got a [4] _____ in his house.
His wife's mother cuts his hair.
He likes reading [5] _____.
He loves listening to Eminem.

1 _____ from?
2 _____ him?
3 _____ a tattoo of a cross?
4 _____ in his house?
5 _____ reading?

2 Ask Student B the questions and write the answers in the spaces.

✂ --

STUDENT B

1 Read the facts about Wayne Rooney. Complete questions 1–5 to find the missing information.

Wayne Rooney comes from Liverpool.
He lives with [1] _____.
Some people call him 'Roonaldo.'
He often eats [2] _____ for dinner.
He has got a tattoo of a cross on his arm.
He gets his clothes from [3] _____.
He has got a cinema in his house.
[4] _____ cuts his hair.
He likes reading *Harry Potter* books.
He loves listening to [5] _____.

1 _____ with?
2 _____ for dinner?
3 _____ clothes?
4 _____ his hair?
5 _____ listening to?

2 Ask Student A the questions and write the answers in the spaces.

2.2 YOUR LIKES AND DISLIKES

1 For each picture write the name of something or someone you really love or hate.

2 Find out what your partner thinks of the things you chose.

3 Now tell the class about your partner's likes and dislikes.

Mary loves *Sim City*.

		Your Partner		
		really likes	quite likes	doesn't like / hates
1 a film _____		☐	☐	☐
2 a school subject _____		☐	☐	☐
3 a music group _____		☐	☐	☐
4 a book _____		☐	☐	☐
5 a clothes shop _____		☐	☐	☐
6 a sportsperson _____		☐	☐	☐
7 a computer game _____		☐	☐	☐
8 a TV programme _____		☐	☐	☐

3.1 SPOT THE DIFFERENCE

STUDENT A

Describe your picture to Student B. Find six differences. Put a cross (x) next to each difference.
'My picture is of a classroom. There is a teacher in the room. The teacher is in front of the board ...'

STUDENT B

Describe your picture to Student A. Find six differences. Put a cross (x) next to each difference.
'My picture is of a classroom. There is a teacher in the room. The teacher is next to a student's desk ...'

(3.2) FIND SOMEONE WHO ...

Find someone who ...

	Student's name	More information
1 has to work at the weekend.	_____	Where ...? _____
2 has to baby-sit for their little sister or brother.	_____	How old ...? _____
3 has to go to bed before 12 p.m.	_____	What time ...? _____
4 has to make their own lunch.	_____	What ...? _____
5 has to get up before 7 a.m.	_____	Why ...? _____
6 has to walk more than 1km to get to school.	_____	Where ...? _____
7 has to do jobs in the house.	_____	What ...? _____

✄ -

Find someone who ...

	Student's name	More information
1 has to work at the weekend.	_____	Where ...? _____
2 has to baby-sit for their little sister or brother.	_____	How old ...? _____
3 has to go to bed before 12 p.m.	_____	What time ...? _____
4 has to make their own lunch.	_____	What ...? _____
5 has to get up before 7 a.m.	_____	Why ...? _____
6 has to walk more than 1km to get to school.	_____	Where ...? _____
7 has to do jobs in the house.	_____	What ...? _____

(4.1) PRONUNCIATION PELMANISM

brown	blouse	or<u>an</u>ge	pink
white	tie	<u>swea</u>tshirt	dress
<u>co</u>lour	<u>ju</u>mper	boots	track<u>sui</u>t
<u>ja</u>cket	black	jeans	green
shirt	<u>pur</u>ple	<u>trai</u>ners	grey
hair	wear	socks	top

Solutions Teacher's Book • Elementary **129**

4.2 LET'S MEET NEXT WEEK!

Monday	
Morning	
Afternoon	Evening

Tuesday	
Morning	
Afternoon	Evening

Wednesday	
Morning	
Afternoon	Evening

Thursday	
Morning	
Afternoon	Evening

Friday	
Morning	
Afternoon	Evening

Saturday	
Morning	
Afternoon	Evening

Sunday	
Morning	
Afternoon	Evening

5.1 HOW MUCH DO YOU WANT TO BET?

You can bet between 10 and 100 points for each sentence.

		CORRECT	INCORRECT	BET	WIN	LOSE
1	Nile is the longest river in the world.	O	O			
2	You are funniest student in the class.	O	O			
3	A desert is drier than a rainforest.	O	O			
4	The Mount Everest is the highest mountain in the world.	O	O			
5	New York is more colder than Florida.	O	O			
6	Your camera is better than mine.	O	O			
7	Emily is the most popular girls' name in the USA.	O	O			
8	Geography is easer than maths.	O	O			
9	A dolphin is more intelligent than an elephant.	O	O			
10	My English is worse than yours.	O	O			
11	Football is the more popular sport in the UK.	O	O			
12	July is hotter then April.	O	O			
13	Australia is smaller than Brazil.	O	O			
14	Russia is the bigest country in the world.	O	O			
15	His house is further from the school than mine.	O	O			

TOTAL

5.2 WILD!

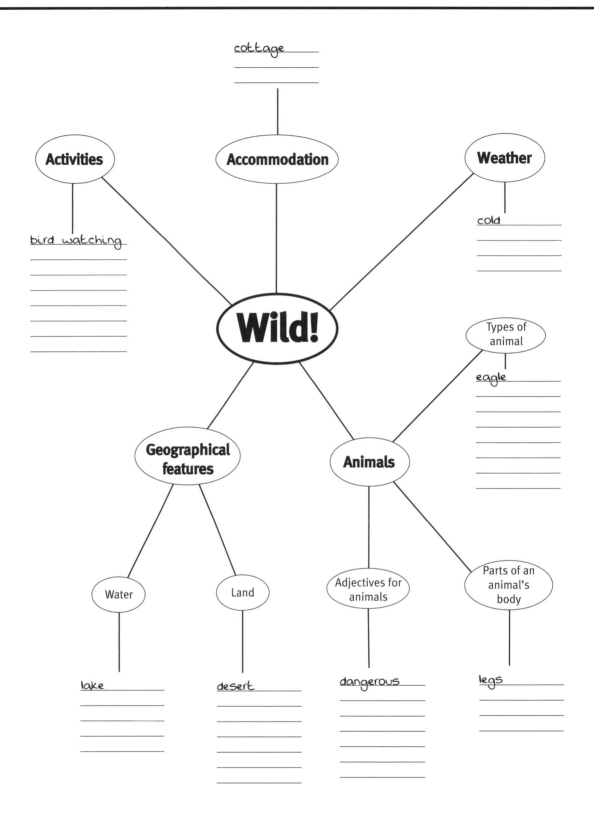

cottage
_____
_____
_____

Activities

bird watching
_____
_____
_____
_____

Accommodation

Weather

cold
_____
_____
_____
_____

Wild!

Types of animal

eagle
_____
_____
_____
_____
_____
_____

Geographical features

Animals

Water

Land

Adjectives for animals

Parts of an animal's body

lake
_____
_____
_____
_____

desert
_____
_____
_____
_____
_____
_____

dangerous
_____
_____
_____
_____
_____

legs
_____
_____
_____

---

aggressive beach bear ~~bird watching~~ campsite canoeing climbing ~~cold~~ ~~cottage~~ cycling
~~dangerous~~ ~~desert~~ diving dry ~~eagle~~ fast hippo hill horse riding hot intelligent island
jellyfish ~~lake~~ large ~~legs~~ mountains mountain biking ocean rainforest rare river sailing
sea shark snake tail tentacles tiger valley waterfall wet whale wing youth hostel

6.1 THE GOLDILOCKS BURGLAR

A burglar entered a house last night in Milwaukee, USA. He decided to take a television and a mobile phone.

Then he decided he was hungry and wanted something to eat so he cooked some steak and chips.

Then he wanted to check his e-mails. So he logged onto the computer and checked his e-mails.

After that the burglar was finally ready to leave the house.

Two hours later, the owners of the house, Mr and Mrs Spencer, arrived home.

When they entered the house they were shocked when they noticed the dirty plates on the table.

Then Mr Spencer noticed that the computer was still on.

He looked at the website. The burglar's name was there so he called the police.

Later that evening the police arrested the burglar.

(6.2) TELEPHONE ROLE PLAYS

Student A (Role card 1)

Your name is Ben / Anna. You have got a sister called Katharine. She is at her boyfriend's house at the moment. You don't know what time she's coming home. She wants you to take a message if anybody calls.

Student B (Role card 1)

Your name is Mark / Lisa. Call your friend Katharine. She is your best friend and you are just ringing for a chat. You don't need to leave a message. You're calling from your new mobile phone. She hasn't got your new phone number. It's 07992 376914.

Student A (Role card 2)

Your name is Andy / Angela Jones. You want to go to Glastonbury music festival with two friends. You reserved the tickets three weeks ago from a company called *TicketMaster*. You are very worried because the festival is on Saturday and you haven't got the tickets. Call *TicketMaster* and ask what's happening. The person you spoke to last time was Sam Smith.

Student B (Role card 2)

Your name is Sam Smith. You work for a company called *TicketMaster*. Your company sells tickets for concerts and festivals. Three weeks ago A. Jones reserved tickets for Glastonbury festival. The tickets are now ready. He/She has to come to the *TicketMaster* office to get them. The office is open from 9 – 5, Monday to Friday.

Student A (Role card 3)

You work as a secretary at a shop called *JJ Electronics*. The shop sells TVs, CD players, computers, etc. The manager of the shop is not in today. If any customers call, take a message.

Student B (Role card 3)

Last month you bought a CD player from a shop called *JJ Electronics*. Two weeks ago it stopped working. You returned it to the shop. They replaced it with a new one. Now the new one doesn't work! You are very angry. Call the shop and speak to the manager.

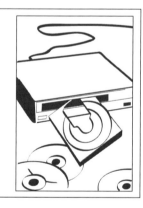

Student A (Role card 4)

Today is Monday. You are doing exams at the moment. Your last exam is tomorrow. After the exam you really want to see a film at the cinema. (Which film? ... you decide.) Call Kate / Kevin and ask if he / she can go to the cinema with you tomorrow evening. Think of a time and place to meet.

Student B (Role card 4)

Your name is Kate / Kevin. Today is Monday. You have a very important exam on Friday. (Which exam? ... you decide.) Your parents say you have to study every evening this week. But you can go out after the exam.

7.1 KEEP TALKING!

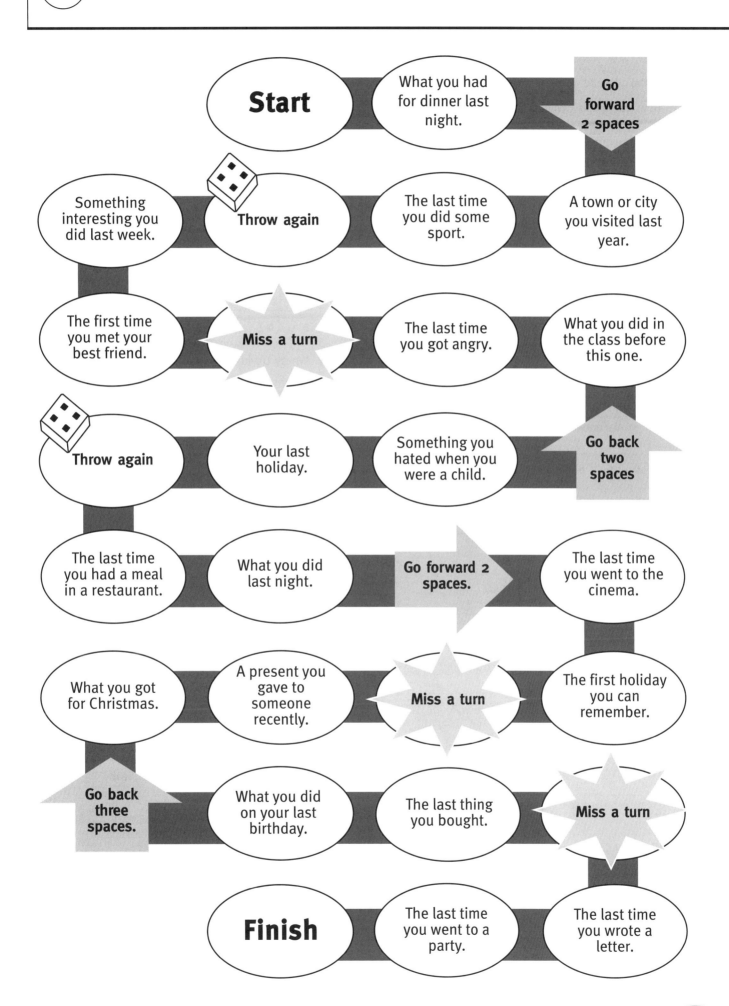

Start

What you had for dinner last night.

Go forward 2 spaces

Something interesting you did last week.

Throw again

The last time you did some sport.

A town or city you visited last year.

The first time you met your best friend.

Miss a turn

The last time you got angry.

What you did in the class before this one.

Throw again

Your last holiday.

Something you hated when you were a child.

Go back two spaces

The last time you had a meal in a restaurant.

What you did last night.

Go forward 2 spaces.

The last time you went to the cinema.

What you got for Christmas.

A present you gave to someone recently.

Miss a turn

The first holiday you can remember.

Go back three spaces.

What you did on your last birthday.

The last thing you bought.

Miss a turn

Finish

The last time you went to a party.

The last time you wrote a letter.

7.2 WORLD FAMOUS PEOPLE QUIZ

STUDENT A

1 Look at the quiz and write the questions.

1 How many plays / William Shakespeare / write /?

_____

a 27   **b 37**   **c** 55

2 Where / Mother Teresa / live / ?

_____

a Calcutta   **b** Delhi   **c** Madras

3 Where / Elvis Presley / live / ?

_____

a Memphis   **b** Miami   **c** Minnesota

4 How many / wives / King Henry VIII / have / ?

_____

a 6   **b** 7   **c** 8

5 What / Alexander Graham Bell / invent / ?

_____

a electricity   **b the telephone**   **c** the light bulb

6 When / John Lennon / die / ?

_____

a 1974   **b** 1978   **c 1980**

7 What / instrument / Einstein / play / ?

_____

a the violin   **b** the flute   **c** the piano

8 Which / of these pictures / Picasso / paint / ?

_____

a *Sunflowers*   **b *Guernica***   **c** *Moulin Rouge*

9 When / Neil Armstrong / become / the first man on the moon / ?

_____

a 1963   **b** 1965   **c 1969**

10 Where / J K Rowling / write/ the first *Harry Potter* books / ?

_____

a In a library   **b** At her sister's house   **c In a café**

2 Ask Student B the questions. Give him / her one point for each correct answer. Then answer Student B's questions.

STUDENT B

1 Look at the quiz and write the questions.

1 What / Cassius Clay / change / his name to / ?

_____

a Muhammad Ali   **b** Elton John   **c** Julius Caesar

2 Which / actress / Chris Martin / marry / in 2003 / ?

_____

a Kate Blanchett   **b** Nicole Kidman   **c Gwyneth Paltrow**

3 How many times / Lance Armstrong / win / the Tour de France / ?

_____

a 6   **b 7**   **c** 8

4 What / David and Victoria Beckham / call / their second son / ?

_____

a David   **b** Brooklyn   **c Romeo**

5 When / Nelson Mandela / come / out of prison / ?

_____

a 1988   **b 1990**   **c** 1991

6 Which / of these books / J R R Tolkein / write / ?

_____

a *Lord of the Rings*   **b** *Northern Lights*
c *Lord of the Flies*

7 For which / film / Roman Polanski / win / an Oscar in 2003?

_____

a *Frantic*   **b** *Oliver Twist*   **c *The Pianist***

8 What / Christopher Columbus / discover / in 1492?

_____

a Mexico   **b** India   **c The Caribbean**

9 When / Leonardo DaVinci / paint / *The Mona Lisa* / ?

_____

a 1503–6   **b** 1553–6   **c** 1603–6

10 What / Alfred Nobel / invent / in 1867 / ?

_____

a the balloon   **b dynamite**   **c** the calculator

2 Answer Student A's questions. Ask your questions. Give Student A one point for each correct answer.

8.1 SCHOOL LUNCHES AROUND THE WORLD

1 Do you usually buy lunch at school, bring a packed lunch to school, or have lunch at home?

2 Can you buy lunch in a canteen at your school? What's it like? Is it healthy?

3 Read the comments from pupils around the world writing about their school lunches and then answer the questions below. Write F for Finland, S for Switzerland, N for Netherlands, J for Japan and SK for South Korea.

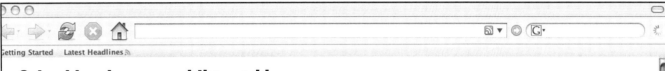

School lunches around the world.

Here in Finland, school lunch is free to all students. The food is usually quite healthy. In most places, the week's menu for each school appears in the local newspaper so our parents can check what we are eating. My school shows the menu on its Internet site as well. For example, I can see that tomorrow I'm having 'fish in lemon sauce'.
Thomas, *Helsinki, Finland*

In Switzerland, students in most schools go home at lunch time. This is good for three reasons. First, they have to walk home and back to school which is good exercise. Second, they get a home cooked meal (traditionally salad, potatoes or rice or pasta with a piece of meat and some fruit). And last, the family has a meal together which is good for family social life.
Nicole, *Zurich, Switzerland*

In most Dutch primary schools, there is no canteen and the students bring in a packed lunch. Teachers often reprimand students and their parents if their packed lunch is not healthy, e.g. if they have white bread rather than brown bread in their sandwiches.
Petra, *Amsterdam, the Netherlands*

In our schools everyone in the school, including students, teachers, secretaries, and even the head teacher eats the same lunch every day and most people love it. It consists of a bottle of milk, a bowl of rice, usually some kind of fish, a salad, some kind of soup usually with vegetables, and a piece of fruit. The menu changes every day.
Daisuke, *Kobe, Japan*

In Korea, schools don't offer any meals. Students always bring packed lunches and eat them in their classrooms. The students arrange the desks so they can sit in groups of 4-8. We always share our lunches. We don't think of lunch as our own. Our mums think of it as making a meal for the class and not just for their own child. For our packed lunch we usually have rice, a meat dish, eggs and some vegetables.
Jin Park, *Seoul, South Korea*

In which country or countries ...

1 do students get free meals at schools?

2 does everyone at school eat the same food at lunch-time?

3 do the students usually eat with their parents?

4 do the teachers try to make the students eat healthier food?

5 do the students get some exercise at lunch time?

6 do the students usually eat cooked meals at home?

7 do schools put their menu on the Internet?

8 do the students usually eat rice for lunch?

9 do the students' mothers prepare food for other children?

10 do the students have a different menu every day?

8.2 A MEAL AT THE WHITE HORSE PUB

1 Complete the menu with words from the box. Work with a partner.

| apple | beef | chips | curry | hot | peas | sauce | soup | water |

The White Horse Pub
Menu
Snacks and sandwiches

Vegetable [1]_____	£2.95
Ham and egg sandwich	£3.20
Beef and tomato sandwich	£3.30

Pizzas

Cheese, ham and tomato	£3.50
Ham and mushroom	£4.00
Sausage and chilli	£4.00

Meals

Roast [2]_____ with potatoes and vegetables	£6.50
Sausages with chips and [3]_____	£4.95
Chicken or lamb [4]_____	£5.50
Fish and [5]_____	£4.95
Pasta with ham and mushroom [6]_____	£4.95

Drinks

Tea	£1.20
Coffee	£1.50
[7]_____ chocolate	£1.50
Orange or [8]_____ juice	£1.20
Bottle of [9]_____	£1.00

Customer 1	Customer 2	Customer 3	Waiter / Waitress
Order your food and drink. Your food is cold. Complain to the waiter / waitress.	Order your food and drink. Your food is burned. Complain to the waiter / waitress.	Order your food and drink. The waiter/waitress brings the wrong drink. Tell him / her.	Take the customers' orders. But, there aren't any pizzas, beef or vegetable soup today.

9.1 MY DAY SO FAR ...

1 Read the prompts and write short notes for each one. Write your answers in any of the boxes but don't write them in the same order as the questions.

something you've learned at school today

something you've bought today

the number of drinks you've had today

a person you've sent a text message to today

something nice you've done today

something you've read today

the number of people you've said hello to today (in your own language)

something you've eaten today

a person you haven't seen today (who you usually see)

some transport you've taken today

a place you haven't been to today

something boring you've done today

2 Now swap worksheets with your partner. Ask your partner why he/she has written the words in the boxes.

Why have you written 'Anita'?

I haven't seen Anita today.

(9.2) TRAVEL INTERVIEW

1 Jack Carter is a singer in a band. He often travels around the world to do tours with his band. Read the interview with Jack. Match the questions with their answers.

2 Now ask your partner the questions from the interview.

b My friend Alex. I met him when I was two. We travelled around Spain and Morocco this summer. He's a very relaxed person and he tells funny stories. That's important when you're travelling.

c I had a really good time in Egypt last year. I went to the Red Sea. I travel a lot with work so it was really fun to do different things like scuba-diving and camel-riding.

i I'd like to go around Australia in a van for two or three months.

e It was in a restaurant in Sydney. I love trying new food, so I had crocodile and shark steak on a barbecue. It was superb.

1 What's your first holiday memory?
2 What was your best holiday?
3 Who is your ideal travelling companion?
4 What do you always take with you on a journey?
5 What was your worst travel experience?
6 What's the best meal you have had on holiday?
7 What's the first thing you do when you arrive at a new place?
8 What's your dream trip?
9 Where are you going for your next holiday?

h Five years ago I was on a plane to New York. Suddenly the pressure dropped in the cabin. It was so scary. All the cans of drink and packets of crisps exploded. We had to make an emergency landing in Chicago.

d The Lake District, when I was really small. My parents love going there. When you have been there about twenty times it gets a bit boring, but I have good memories of it when I was younger.

f I have a shower, then go out and walk around the places close to the hotel. If there's a beach I go into the water immediately.

a My MP3 player. It comes everywhere with me.

g I'm going to Japan next week. The band's doing a tour there.

10.1 REVIEW

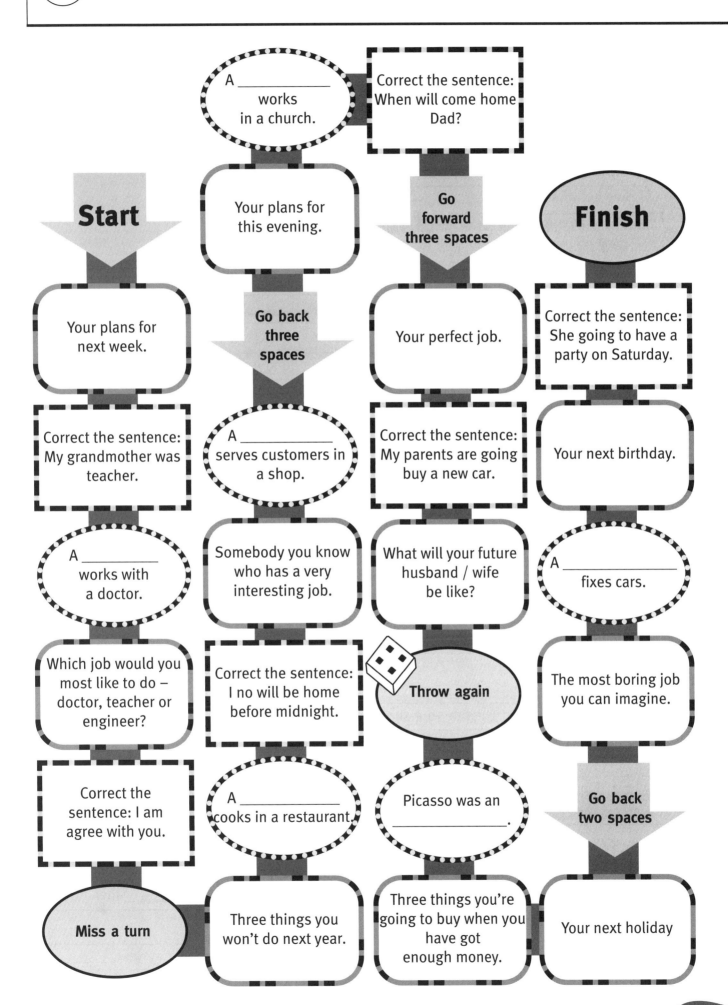

A _____ works in a church.

Correct the sentence: When will come home Dad?

Start

Your plans for this evening.

Go forward three spaces

Finish

Your plans for next week.

Go back three spaces

Your perfect job.

Correct the sentence: She going to have a party on Saturday.

Correct the sentence: My grandmother was teacher.

A _____ serves customers in a shop.

Correct the sentence: My parents are going buy a new car.

Your next birthday.

A _____ works with a doctor.

Somebody you know who has a very interesting job.

What will your future husband / wife be like?

A _____ fixes cars.

Which job would you most like to do – doctor, teacher or engineer?

Correct the sentence: I no will be home before midnight.

Throw again

The most boring job you can imagine.

Correct the sentence: I am agree with you.

A _____ cooks in a restaurant.

Picasso was an _____.

Go back two spaces

Miss a turn

Three things you won't do next year.

Three things you're going to buy when you have got enough money.

Your next holiday

(10.2) ALPHABET RACE

A My mum hates Eminem. She thinks he's _____.

B I like roast _____ with potatoes and peas.

C The _____ is the place where you have lunch at school.

D Harrods is a world famous _____ store.

E Would you like some bacon and _____ ?

F Many immigrants came to Britain from its _____ colonies.

G You keep your car in a _____.

H We _____ ever go to the cinema.

I My favourite subject is _____. I love computers.

J _____ food is very unhealthy.

K The middle part of your leg is your _____.

L _____ is a meal you have in the middle of the day.

M Sorry, Anna's not in. Can I take a _____ ?

N My sister's daughter is my _____.

O The Pacific and the Atlantic are _____.

P You can buy stamps and send letters in a _____ _____.

Q Robbie Williams is OK. I _____ like him.

R My aunt, grandfather, cousin, etc. are my _____.

S You wear _____ inside your shoes.

T You have five _____ at the end of your foot

U A train that goes under the city is the _____.

V A low area of land between two mountains is a _____.

W 'Thank you very much.' 'You're _____.'

X I saw a great film last night called _____-men III

Y I think in the _____ 2050 people will live on the moon.

Z Russell Crowe comes from New _____.